AMERICAN VIKINGS

AMERICAN VIKINGS

HOW THE NORSE SAILED INTO THE LANDS AND IMAGINATIONS OF AMERICA

MARTYN WHITTOCK

PEGASUS BOOKS

NEW YORK LONDON

AMERICAN VIKINGS

Pegasus Books, Ltd.
148 West 37th Street, 13th Floor
New York, NY 10018

First Pegasus Books cloth edition November 2023

Interior design by Maria Fernandez

Library of Congress Cataloging-in-Publication Data is available.

ISBN: 978-1-63936-535-7

10 9 8 7 6 5 4 3 2 1

Printed in the United States of America
Distributed by Simon & Schuster
www.pegasusbooks.com

To Jim and Donna Lindsay and their family,
with thanks for their friendship and hospitality over many years.
Recalling the Swedish Lundberg and Adolfsdotter ancestors,
who took part in the Scandinavian settlement of Wisconsin in the
1880s, contributing to the modern development of the story of
"American Vikings."

CONTENTS

Introduction ix

1 Who and What Were "Vikings"? 1

2 Inside the Heads of the Vikings 12

3 The Viking World 27

4 *Vinland* . . . the Edge of the World 35

5 Viking North Americans 54

6 Sharing the Stage with Vikings? 75

7 Competing Ethnic Origin Myths of "Discovery,"
in the Early USA 92

8 Vikings in the Midwest? 107

9 New England Vikings? 123

10 A Norse Home from Home? 144

11 A Darker Side to the Story 159

12 Vikings Reading Comic Books 173

13 The Vikings Go to the Movies . . . and Watch TV 186

14 American Vikings Meet QAnon 197

15 Merchandising Vikings 207

Afterword: Where Next for the American Vikings? 215

Acknowledgments 221

Endnotes 223

Index 249

INTRODUCTION

D id Vikings reach North America? The answer lies in medieval Norse sagas and in modern archaeology. Both are open to much debate and interpretation and this book explores and evaluates the evidence for these voyages and settlements. And it examines the ongoing impact of this on later contested identities.

I use the modern term "America" in both its geographical sense of the "North American continent"[1] (looking at evidence and claims from the Canadian arctic to the US Midwest), and also in its frequently used political sense, referring to "the USA" in particular[2] (where the "*Vinland* Vikings," both real and imagined, have had a huge impact on US origin-myths, comic books, films, TV, merchandising, and even twenty-first-century US politics). Hence the book's subtitle: *How the Norse Sailed into the Lands and Imaginations of America*.

It is a contested area. When I posted information regarding the forthcoming book on an online history forum, one response asserted: "Canadian Vikings. Americans have fantasy Vikings, no archaeological evidence for their settlement." This book addresses that issue, by evaluating the many claims for a Viking presence beyond the attested archaeological evidence from Newfoundland and the Canadian Arctic. In doing so, we embark on a fascinating journey that starts with the medieval sagas and archaeological assessments of many purported Viking sites, runestones, and one very significant coin, but ends with modern media presentations, merchandising images, and the polarized politics of the 2020s. What starts on Newfoundland in 1021, ends at the Capitol on January 6, 2021. And the "American Viking journey" continues.

Along the way, we will meet characters as varied as Thorstein Eriksson, Leif Eriksson, the intrepid female explorer Gudrid Thorbjornsdottir, and Erik the Red's murderous daughter Freydis. There will be unnamed Native Americans or Inuit (there is debate over this) who—at various times—battled with, traded with, were kidnapped by, these Viking immigrants and settlers. We will meet Saint Brendan, Madoc ap Owain Gwynedd, John Cabot, Christopher Columbus, and the Mayflower Pilgrims, all engaged in an unfinished "battle" with Vikings over a place in the origin-myths of the USA. The dramatis personae include a walk-on part by Benjamin Franklin, and a cast of nineteenth-century Scandinavian pioneers in the Midwest. The latter made a huge contribution to the ongoing dramatic story. The unlikely association of the Norse god Odin with the Second Amendment accompanies a Viking aspect to the conspiracy world of QAnon and contemporary white supremacist movements. Comic-book culture, film, and TV, combine with craft beers, questionable fancy-dress costumes, and the Minnesota Vikings football team (among other modern references to Vikings), to complete the story. When all is said and done, the original *Vinland* Vikings have sailed far into America, via both the turbulent seas of the North Atlantic and the yet more stormy seas of the human imagination. It is quite a journey—and it is far from over.

CHAPTER ONE

WHO AND WHAT WERE "VIKINGS"?

Vikings stir the imagination! They have a wild image and a perennial fascination, in the USA and globally. The combination of epic drama, adventure, travel, mythology, violence, and ancient culture grips the imagination. As a result, we find the Vikings appearing in a wide range of historical, archaeological, and popular and academic cultural studies. Viking-related themes also influence comic-book culture, a US football team name, craft beer, "factional" drama series on TV and worldwide streaming platforms, Hollywood movies, jewelry, and modern cultural identity. For more than a millennium the Vikings have traveled far and wide, not least across the turbulent seas of our minds and imaginations.

Their geographical reach was extraordinary. For a thousand years, legends claimed that Vikings settled in North America. It was, and is, a claim that stimulates the imagination and controversy, for it insists that Vikings influenced lands very far from Scandinavia.

This book separates fact from fiction, evidence from "fake news," myth from mischief. It involves claims regarding the furthest and most controversial of the Viking adventures, to North America itself and, after that, into the North American imagination. In exploring this epic story and the evidence for it, the North Atlantic world must be explored, since, today as in the year 1000, the claims regarding these Norse adventurers connect two worlds, the "New World" and the "Old" (both "New" and "Old" being terms rooted in a European perspective, since Native Americans had known their world for millennia). Furthermore, the search for the Vikings and their enduring legacy connects a wide range of different areas of human life, from archaeology to mythology; from travel and warfare to homemaking in a new world; from ancient history to modern public relations and even to radicalized ideology.

This search will also trace the trajectory from the realm of historical enquiry to the modern—and, at times, highly controversial—areas of contemporary culture and identity. It is a journey from the high seas of a millennia ago to the swirling waters and dark undercurrents of the online world of the twenty-first century.

The search for "American Vikings" will involve examination of thousand-year-old archaeological remains on the eastern seaboard of North America—that were dated as recently as the fall of 2021—and events at the Capitol, in Washington, DC, on January 6, that same year. Such is the nature of this exploration, for it connects the past with the present in the most astonishing ways.

No doubt, the warlike Vikings would have understood how their image could be "weaponized." In the same way, they would probably have grasped how their dramatic, violent, passionate, and discordant mythologies could appeal to some within a later time and cultural setting. They might, though, have been more surprised at how their image has been commercialized and commodified. But all these things have occurred.

In short, *American Vikings* explores how the Norse sailed into the lands *and* the imaginations of America.

But first, we need to establish something of the dramatis personae and the scenery that lies at the start of this epic drama . . .

Viking:
What's in a Name?

From the eighth century of the Christian era, raiders exploded out of Scandinavia in a way that shocked their contemporaries in Western Europe.

Their victims used various names for their attackers from the north. In Anglo-Saxon (Old English) writings the terms "Danes," "Northmen," and "pagans" or "heathens" were the ones most often used. What is surprising is that the term "Danes" did not carry much geographical accuracy in these mentions. As a result, when we find "Danes" appearing in the accounts of a particular Viking raid we cannot be sure that those responsible came from Denmark. This sounds bizarre but an example will illustrate the point. In 789, after reporting a raid on Portland, Dorset, in southwest England, the same entry in a chronicle says that those responsible were Danes—and that they came from Norway! Clearly a "label" could get detached from the "geography."[1]

Many other "labels" were also used to describe these ferocious northern raiders. The Franks, in what is now France and western Germany, called them the *Nordmanni* (northmen).[2] As a result, an area ceded to them in the tenth century would become Normandy, "land of the northmen."

Some have suggested that Slavs in eastern Europe knew them from their ruddy complexions as the *Rus* (red).[3] Or this name may have been derived from an Old Norse word for "rowers" or seamen, or perhaps from a coastal area of Sweden called Roslagen.[4] We will come across "Old Norse" again but, basically, it is an umbrella-term to describe languages spoken in Scandinavia in the early medieval period.

A related word, *Rhos*, was used in the Byzantine Empire (ruled from Constantinople),[5] whose rulers employed them as mercenaries and met Scandinavians who had traveled down the rivers leading from the Baltic and, eventually, had sailed into the Black Sea; and from there had traveled into the eastern Mediterranean and the Byzantine Empire. In the form *Rus* the word eventually gave rise to the national names of Russia and Belarus. This is because the roots of the historic Russian nation started as a mixed Viking-Slav state centered on Kyiv/Kiev, in Ukraine.[6] In recent times, these tangled roots of nationhood lie behind Russian nationalist claims that Ukraine is not an independent nation. It is not the only time the Viking legacy has been seized on by modern nationalists and those seeking to carve out cultural identity. We will meet this later in the USA. The Byzantines also called them "Varangians" (those who swear loyalty), and the mercenaries of the Varangian Guard served the Byzantine emperor in Constantinople (now Istanbul, Turkey). In Constantinople's church of Hagia Sophia, one of them carved a runic inscription that reads "Halfdan carved these runes," or "Halfdan was here," into the white marble parapet surrounding the balcony of the upper gallery of the church.[7]

In Ireland they were the "northmen" again (*Lochlannach* in Irish),[8] a designation similar to the one used by the Franks. For reasons that are obscure, the Irish went on to differentiate the Norwegians as *Finn-gaill* (white foreigners) and the Danes as *Dubb-gaill* (black foreigners).[9]

Far from Scandinavia, Islamic writers called them *al-madjus* (heathens),[10] in a religiously derived label similar to that used by

Anglo-Saxons, adding "May Allah curse them."[11] And, yes, they reached the Islamic lands which stretched from the Iberian Peninsula to the Middle East, and beyond to the Caspian Sea.[12]

Viking: More a Thing You *Did* than a Person You *Were* . . .

What is surprising to the modern reader is the fact that we hardly ever hear them called *Vikings* outside of Scandinavia at the time. Although several possible origins have been proposed, we have no definite answer to the question of where the familiar term *"Viking"* comes from.[13]

In Old Icelandic (a variant of Old Norse) the word *vik* (bay, creek) may have been used to describe seamen hiding in, or sailing from, these coastal inlets. This would have been an understandable label, whether it was meant as the neutral *sailor* or the more rakish *pirate*. In this way, a geographical term may have become a group-name. An area of southern Norway was called Vik, so another label rooted in geography may have become attached to those sailing from this area. On the other hand, the Old Icelandic verb *vikja* (moving, turning aside) may have come to describe seafarers who were always "on the move."[14]

These possibilities are rooted in geographical origins, but occupation may also have been in the mix when it came to the definition as it developed. Later Old Norse Scandinavian written sources call a raider a *vikingr* and a raiding expedition of such people a *viking*. This reminds us that "the word 'Viking' is something you *did* rather than what you *were*."[15]

For many who were described in this way, this would have been a part-time occupation. At other times of the year or during other phases of their lives, they would not have gone out "viking" or been considered "Vikings." Then they would have been farming and trading. Viking as a part-time activity—a kind of medieval job-share—is not how we have come to understand it.

For many who used it, "going viking" did not carry a negative connotation. In Old Norse sources, going out "viking" was an adventure, taking part in a spot of muscular free enterprise. However, those on the receiving end of one of these muscular free-enterprise activities viewed things very differently. It is not surprising that the victims of the Vikings coined their own terms—and these were often not positive or complimentary. Even the red-faced foreigners of the Slavic and Byzantine accounts suggest a sense of an alien "other." Although, as we have seen, more neutral geographical terms were also used (*Danes, Northmen*), even when these were usually deployed in the context of a generally negative account. There was definitely no "romance of the Vikings" for those who were the focus of Viking attentions.

Viking names, such as Thorfinn Skull-splitter, a tenth-century Earl of Orkney, reveal that the Vikings themselves reveled in their own violent reputations and warrior prowess. As one historian wryly put it, regarding a tenth-century Viking king of York: "He wasn't called Eric Bloodaxe because he was good with the children."[16]

So, given all these alternatives, when did the term "Viking" come into English usage? Old English had a similar word for such raiders. Old English—the name used for the language spoken by the Anglo-Saxons in England before the country was conquered by the Normans (from France) in 1066—is the root language of modern English (by way of Middle English). The Old English form *wicing* or *wicingas* was derived from the Old Norse word—but does not appear as a label for Scandinavian pirates until the tenth century. And it was only used rarely—but, when used, it had a negative connotation.

Yet, some English east-coast place names contain the word. In these cases, it may have been derived from a Scandinavian personal name. If so, we are back to a more positive spin on the label, since the person in question almost certainly carried the name with pride. As in: "I am an adventurer," rather than "My employment is smash-and-grab . . . and worse." However, that positivity is not surprising, given that the person in question in these cases was almost certainly a Scandinavian settler who had come to England to take land. Examples include: Wickenby (Lincolnshire) which means "*Viking's by*" (village); Wiganthorpe (Yorkshire) which means "*Viking's thorp*" (dependent farm); Wigston (Leicestershire) which means "*Viking's tun*" (village).[17] The last example couples a Scandinavian personal name with an Old English place name term.

After this, far from common, use in Old English, the word did not surface again until almost a millennium later when, during the nineteenth century, it finally became the standard term for ancient Scandinavian invaders. That is a long time out of use, given that today it is so frequently deployed. Such is the strange history of language.

In fact, its modern spelling, *Viking*, is not recorded before 1840. Since then, it has come to describe those involved in raiding expeditions, as Scandinavians originally used the term, and Scandinavians generally during the "Viking Age" (as it was never used in the past). However, it is now so popular that it is the label-of-choice for most people, and it would confuse many if we insisted on using something else. Nevertheless, we need to remember that few of those meeting the original Vikings would have recognized the term; and, most strikingly, Scandinavian merchants and settlers would not have thought that it applied to them, since it was not what they did. However, "Vikings" is now the go-to label. So, that is the one we will use.

"Vikings" or "Norse"?

What is less contentious is the conclusion that (for all their differences) they shared many common cultural characteristics, and this included their mutually understood dialects of what we now call the language of "Old Norse."

The term *Norse* is used to describe the various peoples of Scandinavia who spoke the Old Norse language between the eighth and thirteenth centuries C.E. While it had eastern and western dialects, it would have been generally mutually understood across the range of areas within which it was spoken. A third recognizable form was spoken on the island of Gotland in the Baltic.

The Old Norse language later developed into modern Danish, Faroese, Icelandic, Norwegian and Swedish. In addition, there once existed the so-called Norn languages of Orkney and Shetland that are now extinct. Old Norse was, originally, the language of the Vikings.[18]

Some modern experts prefer the term "Norse" to that of "Vikings" as a group term, but we will use "Norse" when describing the language or culture (as in "Norse mythology," the beliefs of Vikings), but we will generally use "Viking" for the people and the period (as in the "Viking Age").

Voyages into the Mind . . .

Vikings have planted themselves firmly in history and mythology.

In England, the Viking Wars gave rise to some of the greatest myths of English national history. Consequently, we have mental images of slaughtered monks at the monastery of Lindisfarne; King Alfred burning the cakes when he was hiding from Viking marauders; Erik Bloodaxe, ruling at York when it was a

Viking kingdom; Ethelred the Unready vainly battling invaders and earning his unfortunate moniker; the Massacre of St. Brice's Day, when it was later alleged that the skins of slaughtered Danes were nailed to church doors (most have turned out to be cowskin); King Cnut ordering the waves on the seashore to halt—and getting his feet wet (this story grossly misrepresents the original tradition, which stressed his Christian piety, not his pride).

In Denmark, King Harald Bluetooth united the nation, converted to Christianity, and centuries later his nickname was borrowed by Bluetooth technology to describe devices united in function. St. Olaf in Norway died in a battle between Christians and pagans and became the national patron saint.

In France, the Vikings are still remembered as the founders of the Duchy of Normandy. From there their descendants would conquer lands as far removed as the British Isles, after the Norman Conquest of 1066, and southern Italy.

In Ukraine, Volodymyr/Vladimir the Great married a Byzantine princess, beginning the Orthodox history of Russia; his cultural importance has been contested most recently in the wake of Russian invasions of Ukraine in 2014 and 2022.[19]

In Iceland, the formative heroic days of the Viking Commonwealth republic are part of Icelanders' sense of national identity and, in that land of fire and ice, modern Icelandic is the closest surviving language to Old Norse—the language of the Vikings.

Such core national myths are reflected across the areas affected by Viking raiding and settlement. Across Scandinavia and Iceland, it is the rugged independence and voyaging that is celebrated as part of the national character. In the modern US Midwest, we find attempts to connect Scandinavian-derived settler communities with heroic ancestors from the Viking past.[20] Even Marvel comics and their film adaptations make connections with mythical ideas about

Thor and the Norse gods, even if in highly inventive and imaginative ways. There is still a thread that runs back to the distant past.

Some of these images and associations are negative; others positive. What is undeniable is that they remain vibrant and widespread. An interesting case in point occurs if one enters "Viking" as an internet Images search. Such is the nature of the internet, it is recommended that this is done on a "Safe Search" setting! The largest number of images are of warriors. They appear clad in mail shirts (the correct term, rather than *chain mail*) and with swords and axes. Some are half-naked. A lot of them wear the familiar horned helmets, despite the total absence of such items from archaeological excavations of Viking-Age sites. The occasional helmet is winged. Also unknown from archaeology. There are, as one would expect, quite a lot of longships. The occasional woman appears dressed in "Viking costume" and armed with an axe, sword, helmet, shield; one assumes that these are representing Valkyries but may, instead, be based on the fragmentary evidence for Viking female warriors. Some of these costumed women look like they might have been very cold if they went out wearing these particular costumes on a real longship! There is the occasional logo for an American football team, a brand of beer or a computer game (most of these involve *horned* helmets of course).[21]

These are the Vikings as many like to imagine them. Here there is romance, drama, ruggedness, courage, and battle. There is also a threat of violence but, on this safe setting, the emphasis is generally on adventure, manliness, or romance. All the images seem in keeping with the phase of raiding from the Viking Wars. It is probably safe to assume that all those depicted are pagan.

This popular image ignores the fact that Viking settlers converted to Christianity within a couple of generations after the phase of raiding, wherever they settled. Consequently, none of the Vikings—as popularly depicted—are seen in church and one would not imagine that they ever would have been there, unless it was in the act of striking down a monk or lifting a silver reliquary as stolen booty.[22] The reality was more complex, as we shall shortly see.

The Vikings have sailed far into the world of imagination and, at times, of fantasy. Where they sailed geographically also needs a little exploration, if we are to fully understand how their adventures eventually became intertwined with the history of North America. We will shortly address the geographical extent of that "Viking world," but first we will embark on a short excursion into the "Viking mind."

CHAPTER TWO

INSIDE THE HEADS
OF THE VIKINGS

So far, we have defined something of "who" and "what" a
Viking was. This has given us a brief look into the mindset
of these ancient adventurer-pirates because *Viking* was a term of
self-identification and presentation, even though we will continue
to use it in its more generalized form of a useful label for a wide-
ranging group of Scandinavians and their society. But this matter of
mindset and cultural identity is an important one because it helps
to explain something of the enduring fascination with these people
in later periods. As with so much of the past, people engage with it
because it resonates with some aspect of the present, even if that is
due to the "present" imposing its own construction on the "past,"
to validate or justify some aspect of itself.

As part of this laying down of foundations for our later explorations, a quick examination of something of Norse (Viking)
mythology is essential if we are to understand one of the reasons
why Vikings continue to grip the popular imagination today.
While the factors driving that interest are complex, the role of the

dramatic Norse mythology needs to be borne in mind. For a significant number of people, over the centuries that bridge the Viking Age with the present, an interest in this mythology (or selected and reworked parts of it) has been an important ingredient in the process of engagement.

This is noticeably so in the twenty-first century when some people have attempted to construct a form of neo-paganism, but this interest was also recognizable in the nineteenth and twentieth centuries.

Sometimes it is associated with an active attempt to reconstruct something of Viking Age religion, even though the fragmentary and unsystematized form of the original makes this highly difficult to recreate.

At times it has been associated with some forms of radicalized nationalism (think Nazi use of runes or the SS Panzer Division named "Wiking," or modern white supremacist tattoos); and all based on a reimagined white, warrior, Germanic past, that serves the needs of extremist groups in the present.

More often the Viking myths appeal to a harmless interest in mythological warriors, dramatic adversaries, and magical weaponry, that is nothing more than the stock-in-trade of fantasy fiction which incorporates dragons, mighty hammers, dwarfs, and dangerous quests. From *The Lord of the Rings* to Marvel comics and films, these themes and tropes of the past have given rise to many imagined worlds and fantasy adventures.

In all these areas—from the innocent fictional adventure to the far-from-innocent manipulation of the past to support extreme ideologies—Norse mythology has offered a quarry from which much can be hewn, sorted, selected, chiseled, and reworked.

What is intriguing is that this process is nothing new. Thirteenth-century Icelanders indulged in a similar exploration of their pagan and mythological pasts, even though every one of them who took part in this collating, recording, and reordering, was a Christian—a fact often missed or ignored by modern readers of the documents that originated in Iceland and elsewhere in the Middle Ages.[1] By that time, conversion to Christianity had—it seems—sufficiently defused the potency of these ancient myths, or at least a major part of them. They could be explored and reimagined safely because they were no longer believed.

It was a continuation of this antiquarian interest—but within a Christian context—that made it acceptable for nineteenth-century Midwestern Scandinavian pioneers and settlers to celebrate runic scripts and ancient warrior activities as part of their cultural identity. It was acceptable because these things had become religiously inert and could be used as cultural identifiers in a very different age, without risk of evoking actual pagan beliefs. More to the point, such things (runes and warrior ideology) had continued to be used by Scandinavian cultures long after these societies had converted to Christianity. In this sense, they had already long been adapted, reimagined, and repurposed. The reimagination of the past—an essential feature of the route to American Vikings—was a well-trodden way.

However, recent history has shown that, when a modern "detonator" is inserted, such things can be weaponized. But that belongs to a later chapter. For now, a quick excursion through Norse mythology is all that is required to give us an overview of its character.

What Did the Vikings Believe before Their Conversion to Christianity?

Before their conversion to Christianity, the Vikings believed in a pantheon of northern gods, goddesses, and mythical semidivine heroes and supernatural beings. Most were clearly gendered in some way, although fluidity in how this was expressed meant that exceptions existed alongside the apparent norms.

Male Norse divinities included: Odin, Thor, Freyr, Loki, Baldr, Hod, Niord, and many more. Female divinities included: Freyia, Frigg, Sif, and Hel. Of the male divinities, Odin was often described as "All Father" and was regarded as the chief of the Norse gods. In the mythology he ruled from his hall, which was called *Valhalla*.

It is clear that the Norse mythology envisaged two families or races of gods. These were known as the *Aesir* and the *Vanir*. These had, it seems from the sources, once fought each other but then made peace and intermarried. It is likely that this narrative was developed in order to explain how disparate beliefs, from different periods of time, had been combined. The narrative attempted to make all the divinities part of the same "story."

In this "story" the gods and goddesses lived in a place known as *Asgard*, which was connected to other worlds of being by the bridge called *Bifrost*. In a complex (and not always consistent) cosmology, it was envisaged that different worlds of being were united by the ash-tree known as *Yggdrasil*. This included *Midgard* or Middle Earth, the realm of people. This last feature is now well known through its incorporation into the cosmography of J. R. R. Tolkien's *The Lord of the Rings*. In the original construct, the idea of a tree—with its roots, trunk, and branches—provided a vivid image of how different levels of time, being, and awareness, could be connected, while still having individual identities and features. It also emphasized the connectedness of these different worlds.

As well as the gods and goddesses, major players in the Norse mythology were the *jotunn*, often translated into English as "giants." These were usually portrayed as the enemies of the gods, with Thor frequently described as the crusher of giants' skulls using his great hammer, which was called *Mjolnir*. It is this weapon that features in his portrayal in Marvel comics and the related films. Conflicts with giants could occur for many reasons. The giants were often portrayed as desiring beautiful goddesses, and many of the conflicts occurred as the gods sought to deny the giants possession of one goddess or another. Other conflicts were sparked by personal feuds or competition over weaponry or prestige. It should be noted that "giants" in Norse mythology were not necessarily exceptionally large, although often were.

On the other hand, some of the gods were portrayed as being married to giantesses. These included the giantess Gerd, the daughter of the mountain giant Gymir, who was the wife of Freyr of the *Vanir*. Another was the giantess Angrboda, with whom the trickster-god Loki had children. These monstrous offspring were Fenrir the giant ravenous wolf, *Jormungand* the huge *Midgard* Serpent, and Hel the ruler of the Norse underworld. The English word *Hell* is derived from her name. Fenrir appears, as the werewolf "Fenrir Greyback," in the Harry Potter series by J. K. Rowling; and as an antagonist in the 2020 videogame *Assassin's Creed Valhalla*. Norse mythology has traveled far and wide over time.

Norse mythology was very complex and was never formalized or subject to a unifying religious organization to order and systematize it. As a result, it was "dynamic and fluid rather than static."[2]

It should also be noted that, alongside the beings already described, were elves, dragons, dwarfs, and female Valkyries who chose dead warriors to go to serve Odin in his hall in *Valhalla*. As an aside, the usual plural of "dwarf" is "dwarfs," rather than "dwarves." However, the latter form was popularized by Tolkien, who once confessed: "I am afraid it is just a piece of private bad grammar, rather shocking in a philologist; but I shall have to go with it."[3] More in line with the traditional spelling was Disney's *Snow White and The Seven Dwarfs*. This is a small insight—as earlier noted regarding Thor and Fenrir-wolf—into how far characters from Norse mythology have entered popular culture and imagination, albeit in highly reworked modern forms and on the basis of centuries of reworking of the original material.

In Norse mythology, it was also believed that this series of worlds would eventually come to a cataclysmic end. This would occur on the Day of *Ragnarok*. Then it would be that the forces of chaos would break loose. Key actors in this destruction would include the giants, Fenrir the wolf, and *Jormungand* the *Midgard* Serpent. As a result, *Asgard* would be stormed, and the gods consumed and killed.[4]

How Do We Know All This?

Most of what we know about these Norse myths comes from two medieval sources. These are the thirteenth-century *Prose Edda* and the *Poetic Edda*.[5] These two sources combined tell us most of what we now know about Norse mythology. The term *Edda* may be derived either from the Old Norse word *othr* (poetry) or the name of a character found in one of the poems in the *Poetic Edda*, or from the Latin *edo*, (I compose). The myths were not originally known by these names, and *Edda* in the titles of these two collections was assigned by later scholars. Together, these two sources tell us most of what we now know about Norse mythology and the key actors within it.[6]

There are, though, also clues about the mythology in *skaldic* poetry (a form of Norse poetry),[7] in the sagas, and in place names. Norse legends, which often include rather more human-focused plots, are found mostly in the sagas. Most of these sagas were written in thirteenth-century Iceland.

The *Prose Edda* is also known as the *Snorra Edda* or the *Younger Edda* and it is believed to have been written by Snorri Sturluson. He was an Icelandic chieftain, in the early thirteenth century. Snorri was also the author of a work called *Circle of the World* (*Heimskringla* in Old Norse), which was a collection of sagas about the early Norwegian kings. Snorri lived a life almost as dramatic as some of the characters in the stories he recounted. He was eventually assassinated in his house at Reykholt, Iceland, in the fall of 1241, having been attacked by a rival Icelandic chieftain who was acting as an agent of the king of Norway. It is still possible to stand on the spot where this famous Icelander met his death.

This dramatic story is relevant to the history of American Vikings because it is thought to be conflicts with the king of Norway which drove many Scandinavian settlers to sail, first to Iceland, and then to Greenland. It was from there that voyagers eventually reached the lands of North America that had previously been unknown to them.

The *Poetic Edda* is a collection of anonymous Old Norse poems. It is found mainly in a manuscript now called the *Codex Regius*.[8] These poems focus on Norse mythology and the ancient Germanic heroic world generally. These are all written as *eddic* poems, a popular form of Old Norse poetry. This form of poetry is generally looser and less complex than the more well-evidenced *skaldic* verse. Although the surviving manuscript of this source of mythological information was not written until the 1270s (again, in Iceland), it is generally accepted that the poems in it date from before Iceland's conversion to Christianity in the year 1000. However, it is difficult to identify where these poems were originally composed.[9]

Finally, a rich source of Old Norse literature can be found in the *sagas*.[10] These were written mostly in Iceland. These Norse sagas are generally classified using titles which indicate their thematic content: "The Kings' Sagas," "Sagas of Icelanders," "Short Tales of Icelanders," "Contemporary Sagas," "Legendary Sagas," "Chivalric Sagas," "Saints' Sagas," and "Bishops' Sagas." Composed predominantly in Iceland, they are mainly in prose, although some of them contain both *skaldic* and *eddic* poetry embedded in the text. Apart from the "Legendary Sagas," such as the *Saga of the Volsungs*, these are often realistic and at least loosely based on real individuals living in Iceland in the past. These dramatic and engaging tales feature stories about the migration to Iceland; other early Viking voyages; and raids and the bloody feuds and disputes which occurred in Iceland. The characters in these stories are often very human in their portrayal and, despite the extreme situations they often find themselves in, relatable to modern readers.[11]

The Icelandic context of North Atlantic exploration and settlement was the original "Viking Wild West," although other pioneers would soon discover lands (and conflicts) which took them and their families even further to the west.

Some sagas also refer to the wider Viking diaspora. Those that particularly interest us are the sagas that chart the way in which the settlement of Greenland eventually led to the Viking discovery of North America. More on that shortly.

The sagas appear historical, but they must be read with some caution. This is because they are primarily works of literature which also contain traditional material. Nevertheless, as we shall soon see, we can use them to get a view of how later generations (in the thirteenth century) remembered and presented traditions concerning expeditions to North America, which we now know did occur around the year 1000.

Norse Mythology Was
Recorded by Christians

It is important to remember that all these manuscripts were written by practicing Christians, usually in Iceland, which had been officially Christian for more than two hundred years by the time these accounts were written: none of the evidence for Norse mythology and religion was assembled by believers in it who lived during the Viking Age.[12]

This is a striking thought, as it reminds us that we are always viewing Norse mythology through a medieval Christian lens. This is not unique, as the Vikings are not alone in having their beliefs later recorded by Christians who did not subscribe to the earlier pagan beliefs. The same is true of the evidence for Irish (Celtic) and Anglo-Saxon paganism. Consequently, this may mean that some handling of the original material has changed it, to make it more understandable and acceptable to Christian readers and listeners. For example, this may have affected the way Odin is described as "All Father." It may also have impacted on the characterization of Loki. In the mythology the writers portrayed him as a complex and ambiguous troublemaking character. This may have been influenced by Christian beliefs about the devil. It is now hard to be sure about this, but it is a real possibility.

Another written source for pagan Viking practices comes from a man named Adam of Bremen. He was a German chronicler and monk who wrote in the second half of the eleventh century. His writings record gods named Thor, Wotan (Odin) and Frikko (Freyr), and describe how they were worshipped in a temple at Uppsala in Sweden.[13]

Interestingly, it is Thor rather than Odin who is recorded as the chief god by Adam. Similarly, Odin is also depicted mainly as a god of war—rather than as the god of poetry that we see in the later sources from Iceland. One of our saga sources for North America will refer to one of the original explorers of America as being a follower of "Old Red Beard" (Thor) and being in conflict with his Christian fellow explorers.[14] This reminds us both of the popularity of the cult of Thor in the Viking Age and the fact that it was a mixed group of Christian and pagan Vikings who first sailed to North America and began the exploration of the continent.

This is also an important reminder that Viking pagan beliefs may have changed over time and varied somewhat from place to place. We should beware of assuming that the surviving written sources represent how these beliefs were held, always and everywhere, among Scandinavian communities in the Viking Age. Variety and complexity would have been the norm, rather than uniformity.

Despite this, what is consistent across all of these written sources, are the names of the gods and goddesses. As a result, we can be fairly certain that these were the divinities that the people of early medieval Scandinavia worshipped; beliefs that some of them took to North America. This seems clear, even if we cannot be completely certain about the exact belief system that prevailed in the Viking Age.

Other Evidence for Norse Mythology

The evidence from archaeology can also be used to test the picture that we get of Norse beliefs from the later written evidence. So-called "Thor's hammers" were clearly worn as pendants across Scandinavia and also in Britain.[15] Birds accompanying a mounted warrior on decorated helmets found in Sweden probably represent

Odin with his two ravens named *Hugin* and *Munin* (thought and memory).[16] An amulet from Öland, Sweden, in the shape of a woman carrying a drinking horn probably represented a Valkyrie.[17] A carving of Odin's eight-legged magical horse *Sleipnir* was found on the Baltic island of Gotland.[18] In addition, there are ship-burials which have been excavated in Norway, Sweden, and the British Isles, as well as sacrifices of animals and occasionally of people.

Runestones from Denmark, Sweden, and Norway illustrate the importance of an angular twiglike alphabet used by the Norse in the Viking Age. These are usually found on memorial stones but the images, as well as the words carved on these stones, give an insight into the belief system of some of those who produced them. Runes were used for practical everyday communications and also for religious or magical purposes. The use of runes in magic is found in a story that forms part of *Egil's Saga*. There the poet, Egil, used runes to cure a young girl, who had previously been cursed by the use of false runes. This echoes a mythological tradition in the *Edda* that Odin sacrificed himself to gain the knowledge of rune-magic. It should also be noted that runes continued to be used for communication after the conversion to Christianity and were not just a feature of pagan belief and practice. Hence, we will come across their (alleged) use in North America from later in the Middle Ages.

All of these pieces of archaeological evidence corroborate themes and practices found in the later written myths. As a result, fairly widespread acceptance of the Norse beliefs (as known from literature) clearly occurred across a wide area during the Viking Age. On the other hand, while there is evidence for common beliefs across what we might call a wide "Norse culture area," we should not expect uniformity. This is because the beliefs were not codified or policed by a common religious authority at the time. There was no centralized priestly caste or organization.

Other clues fossilize Viking Age beliefs in some surprising contexts. The modern English *Thursday* (containing the Old English form of the Old Norse name Thor) and *Wednesday* (Woden/Odin's day) show that there was once belief in these deities across a wide area. It should be noted that the Old Norse names *Odin* and *Thor* were also known by their Old English forms *Woden* and *Thunor* before the Christian conversion of Anglo-Saxon England in the seventh century.

Place names, too, record the worship of these Scandinavian deities in England. These include the name of the Wansdyke (Woden/Odin's dyke) earthwork in England's West Country and extending into central southern England. Along with this are the many Grim's Ditches (formed from the word *grima*, "the masked one," another name for Woden/Odin) in several places in England. Further afield and less surprisingly, given the later conversion date (c. 1000), we find the names of Viking gods in the Icelandic landscape, such as at Thórsmörk (Thor's valley) and many other places.

Across the lands settled by the Vikings—from Sweden to Iceland—the names of Norse gods and goddesses, dwarfs, dragons, and elves still appear on the modern map and are linked to woods, rivers, and other natural features.

During the ninth and tenth centuries—at about the time the sagas say Vikings first reached North America in the late tenth century—other Vikings reintroduced their forms of these gods to Christian Anglo-Saxon England, before the pagan newcomers converted to Christianity. As a result, in the United Kingdom today, there still survive scenes that illustrate Odin's fight with the ferocious wolf Fenrir at *Ragnarok,* carved on a cross from Kirk Andreas on the Isle of Man. We can see Thor fishing for the gigantic *Midgard* Serpent, *Jormungand,* on a standing cross from Gosforth (Cumbria); and this cross also has a female Valkyrie carved on it. The number of depictions of Thor's conflict with the *Midgard* Serpent, in Scandinavia and the British Isles, indicates the considerable geographical reach of this myth across different Norse communities.[19] The legendary swordsmith, *Regin*, can be seen forging the hero Sigurd's sword on a stone cross from Halton in Lancashire, and this same cross has a carving which also shows Sigurd roasting a dragon's heart. All of these are scenes from Norse myth and legend.[20] As well as this, the *Anglo-Saxon Chronicle* refers to Viking armies carrying raven banners—which represented the companions of Odin—and which also appear in the Viking myths as recorded in the *Eddas*.[21]

No doubt some of those Vikings who traveled to North America carried these ideas in their heads; these would have been "Old World" northern beliefs taken to the "New World" in the far west. This Norse pagan mythology has continued to influence many modern portrayals and characterizations of Vikings in the USA and elsewhere.

However, others who took part in that perilous westward adventure traveled there as Christians (as we shall see in a later chapter looking at the voyages to *Vinland*). And this is an important reminder that the Viking Age was Christian as well as pagan. The latter gave way to the former; the hammer of Thor succumbed to the cross of Christ.

Christianity and the Vikings

Scandinavia and its far-flung settlements were some of the last Western European communities to convert to Christianity. Iceland did not convert until the year 1000 and Norway and Sweden contained significant numbers of pagans for even longer. In northern Norway and Sweden, as well as along the Baltic and in Russia, pagan

Vikings interacted with other non-Christian religious beliefs, from Sami shamanism to the gods of the Balts and Slavs. The eventual kingdoms of Denmark, Norway, and Sweden did not establish their own independent church archdioceses—like those in kingdoms further south in Europe—until 1104, 1154, and 1164, respectively. This was well into the Middle Ages.

Pagan resistance to this conversion occurred in some areas of Scandinavia. King Sigurd the Crusader, of Norway, led a crusade against Småland, in the southeast of the Swedish kingdom, in the early twelfth century, to forcibly convert the locals from paganism to Christianity.

Even after these dates, many Scandinavian communities took centuries to become as fully Christian in their culture and practice as communities in more established Christian kingdoms, such as in the British Isles, France, or among the Germans.

This mixed-economy of faith reveals itself in several ways. Runic inscriptions from Bergen, in Norway, show lingering pagan beliefs as late as the thirteenth century. In Iceland, the thirteenth-century sagas reveal that farming communities with mixed Christian and pagan beliefs continued for many generations after the "official conversion" in the year 1000. Furthermore, even that "official conversion" only stopped the open and officially sanctioned practice of pagan beliefs and sacrifices. This was accompanied by something of a "don't ask, don't tell" policy being adopted there. On the isolated farmsteads many families continued pagan activities much as before, but they did it in a lower-key way, with a less visible profile.

However, many other Viking communities had a history of being "Christian Vikings" that was several centuries old by the early twelfth century. This was a marked characteristic of the Viking diaspora. In these areas, Vikings converted to Christianity within a couple of generations in almost every place they settled. By the year 1150, many communities in England that had developed from earlier Viking settlement had been Christian for almost three hundred years. Some in Denmark had been Christian for over 150 years. In Normandy, for about two hundred years. Even in Iceland, a century and a half of Christian faith marked out many farming families by the year 1150. And that is before one considers the Scandinavians who had settled in what became southern Russia, or the Byzantine Empire of the eastern Mediterranean, and had converted in the late tenth century.

One would be forgiven for not knowing this, given the emphasis in popular culture on the Odin-worshipping warriors of film and fiction. But reality was more complex, and most of the Vikings we will come across as we explore the Norse voyaging to North America will be Christian. This brings us to the geographical extent of the "Viking world."

CHAPTER THREE

THE VIKING WORLD

There was a great variety of experiences in, what we might call, the "Viking world." Vikings' raiding, trading, and settlement took them huge distances. They devastated the kingdoms of Anglo-Saxon England; settled in Ireland and Normandy; raided Spain and settlements on the Mediterranean, and sold North African slaves in the Viking kingdom of Dublin; explored the eastern Baltic and sailed down the river systems of what is now Russia and Ukraine to reach the Black Sea and the Caspian Sea; appeared in Baghdad on camels (they really did!); founded the first Russian state of *Kyiv/Kiev Rus* in Ukraine, central to the "deep story" of the war there that broke out in 2022; and they colonized the northern isles of the Faroe Islands, Iceland, and Greenland. From the latter they sailed to North America. The Viking world stretched from western Central Asia to the North Atlantic.[1]

A Quick Tour of the "Viking World"

Modern historians tend to use the term the "Viking Age" to describe a period which ran from the late eighth century until about 1100.

During this time Scandinavians raided and at times settled across a wide geographical area from North Africa, in the south, to the North Cape, in the north, from Russia and the Caspian Sea, in the east, to Greenland and the coast of North America, in the west.

Writing, probably in the late 840s, the director of posts and intelligence in the Baghdad Caliphate, Ibn Khurdadhbih, recorded that traders he called *ar-Rus*, brought merchandise to Baghdad on camels. They claimed to be Christians. However, this may have been because this reduced their tax burden (being "people of the book" rather than pagans). It may not amount to evidence for genuine early conversion, as he links their religious claim to them paying lower taxes because of their professed beliefs. What is equally striking is that these Viking traders had got as far as Baghdad in modern Iraq.[2]

Far to the west of these camel-riding Vikings, the settlements in Iceland and Greenland were critical to the movement to North America. It was not until the 860s that Iceland caught the attention of Scandinavian adventurers, but from the 870s, they migrated and settled there. Dateable volcanic ash, which seals the oldest farmstead, unearthed in what is now Reykjavik, broadly supports this chronology.

The settlement of Iceland then progressed very quickly. By the 930s, the foundations of Icelandic society had been established. The oldest written sources claim that the reason for the migration there was to escape the domineering rule of King Harald Finehair of Norway. The Icelandic commonwealth-state that developed is presented in these sources as very different from the increasingly hierarchical system in Norway.

Later sagas mention the desirable resources of Iceland including whales, walruses, and great auk.[3] As in Norway, Icelandic life was overwhelmingly rural and the focus was mainly pastoral. The new lands on Iceland offered the first settlers immense opportunities that could be easily exploited with minimum effort.

One version of the later *Book of Settlements* (*Landnamabok*) says that the initial discovery was made by a Norwegian Viking named Naddoddr, while another sources credits it to a Swede called Gartharr Svavarsson who lost his way in a storm. Yet another tradition claimed that the first Viking to reach Iceland was Floki Vilgertharsson, who used a raven to guide him there.

The settlement of Iceland coincided with a reversal of Viking fortunes in mainland Europe. In particular, the Irish conquest of Viking Dublin led to a considerable Norse movement from there to Iceland.[4] Once started, this emigration to the northwest would eventually encompass Greenland and would, in time, stretch as far as North America.[5]

Modern DNA testing shows that a large proportion of the female genetic heritage on modern-day Iceland is Irish-derived; from women brought there as wives, slaves, or both combined. These genetic studies in modern Iceland reveal that about 19 percent of men and 62 percent of women there have Irish or British Isles DNA.[6] The Norse settlers who migrated to Iceland from Ireland, Scotland, and the Hebrides, brought with them these Gaelic-speaking wives, followers, and slaves. As a result of this, Celtic names of Icelanders can be found in the sagas, such as *Njall* from the Old Irish Niall and *Kormakr* from Cormac.

And so, to Greenland. The famous Viking explorer, known as Erik the Red, first visited Greenland from Iceland in 983. There had been rumors of the place since about 930 when it was sighted by a storm-driven Viking sea captain. Greenland is not "green," and Erik gave the island its name to make it sound more attractive to other settlers. He had many enemies and was looking for a place he could settle after having been exiled from Iceland. At its height the

Viking colony in Greenland numbered about four thousand and lasted until the fifteenth century; by which time the colony there was in terminal decline.

According to the chronicler Ari Thorgilsson, the first Icelandic explorers of Greenland discovered deserted huts, parts of boats, and stone implements.[7] These indicated that others had visited the area before. We now know these were the indigenous people of the pre-Inuit or paleo-Inuit "Dorset Culture." The Vikings contemptuously dismissed them as *skraelings* (screechers, wretches), a term they would later employ regarding Native Americans. Desperately trying to maintain their Scandinavian farming economy to the end, the Greenland Vikings failed to learn from the more successful lifestyles of the people of the proto-Inuit "Thule culture" who had replaced those of the earlier "Dorset culture." The Norse survivors were probably assimilated by these pagan indigenous peoples, although conflict with them may have physically eliminated the last Norse of Greenland.

Erik named his settlement Brattahlid. It was located in what became known as the Eastern Settlement. In time, three areas of settlement developed in Greenland. These were predictably termed the Eastern Settlement, the Western Settlement, and the Middle Settlement. All were sited on fjords located in southwestern Greenland.

Erik's son, Leif the Lucky, later visited Norway where he was converted to Christianity. He was then sent back to Greenland, with some missionaries, to convert the settlers there. This seems to have resulted in a quick, if at times nominal, conversion to the new faith. There is evidence that a range of religious practices were found in the Greenland colony in the first couple of generations. The surviving literature records pagan rituals carried out by the seeress, Thorbjorg; Christian belief and practice associated with Erik's wife,

Thjodhild; and the remarkable exploits of a woman named Gudrid who, in addition to journeying to *Vinland* (North America), later went on pilgrimage to Rome and eventually died as an anchorite (a form of nun) in Iceland. We will hear more of Gudrid, and her adventures in North America, shortly.

Greenland was home to many who later struck out further west and eventually reached the shores of North America.

How Do the Danes, Norwegians, and Swedes Fit into This?

In the early part of the Viking Age there were no recognizable nations in Scandinavia, so we use the names *Denmark, Norway,* or *Sweden* to describe geographical areas. A little later they constituted loose political units, but not distinct nation states. However, from the tenth century onward we see the gradual emergence of kingdoms in Denmark, Norway, and, finally, in Sweden. The borders of these early kingdoms were fluid for many generations; and there were political rivalries for dominance: Kings of Denmark ruled at times in Norway, but at other times kings of Norway ruled an independent kingdom. Kings of Denmark also ruled large parts of southern Sweden; and a Christian king of Norway could later feel able to launch a crusade against pagans in Sweden because it was a much weaker kingdom.

Norwegians raided and then settled Shetland, Orkney, northern Scotland, the Western Isles of Britain, and Ireland. They eventually set up a Viking kingdom in Dublin. There were times when kings of Dublin were also kings of York, in England. Back home, it was well into the tenth century before Norway's future as an independent kingdom free of Denmark seemed possible. Even then it was often dominated by or directly ruled by Danish kings at various times until the early eleventh century.

In contrast, the Danes raided the coasts of eastern and southern England and the coast of France. All the Viking raiders were described as "Danes" in some Anglo-Saxon sources. Denmark dominated the trade routes from the North Sea into the Baltic. The Danes controlled regions in southern Sweden and often acted as overlords of Norway. Denmark became increasingly centralized by the eighth century. By the ninth century, it was strong enough to threaten the coast of the Frankish empire in the Low Countries and along the Channel coast of France. After this, it fragmented in the late ninth and early tenth centuries but was reunited in the late tenth century.

Swedish Vikings mostly sailed eastward into the Baltic. From there they explored down the river-systems of what would later become Russia. It was these Vikings who married into Slavic elite families, created the first Russian state centered on Kyiv/Kiev, and eventually converted to Orthodox Christianity in the late tenth century. For much of this time, Denmark ruled large areas of the south of what we now call Sweden; and the rest of the country lacked political unity. There seem to have been two main political units in Sweden: the *Svear* (centered on Uppsala) and the *Gotar* (centered on the plains of Östergötland and Västergötland, near Lake Vättern).[8]

This was the "Viking World," from which the movement to North America sprang.

Why Did the Viking Expansion Occur?

There is a lot of debate over what triggered the explosion of movement out of Scandinavia in the later eighth century. Changes occurring *within* Scandinavia combined with events *outside* of the region to trigger the start of raids and later of settlement.

In the eighth century an increased population in Norway sparked competition for scarce resources. Internal power struggles, in a gradually more unified state, meant that warriors on the losing side looked elsewhere for a means of gaining wealth and prestige. This led to raids on foreign territories.

For Denmark, their southern frontier was threatened by the expansion of the Christian Frankish Empire. This was an external factor that encouraged greater Danish political unity as a defense against the Franks. Danes who had been left out of this process of internal unification looked outside Denmark for a future. Raiding beckoned. At the same time, those Danish nobles who did well in the power struggle financed their newly gained powerbase by launching raiding expeditions abroad. Only now they could do so from a stronger base at home.

Increased international trade from the seventh century onward meant that Scandinavians were very familiar with the wealth of their neighbors to the south and south-west. They knew there were rich targets to raid. And they mixed trading with raiding as they went "viking." This was assisted by a seafaring tradition, from which improved oceangoing vessels developed that were suitable for long-range activities.[9] In time these ships would reach America.

There was also another—and unexpected—factor which prompted the start of Viking raids. Changes taking place in the distant Islamic Caliphate, in the Middle East, from the 740s onward led to the center of political power shifting from Damascus to Baghdad. This turbulence disrupted the flow of Islamic silver to Scandinavia. For years Islamic merchants and their middlemen had carried silver to northern Europe. There they traded it for slaves, furs, and amber. Political conflict and changes in the Caliphate disrupted this trade. In the late ninth century the Caliphate lost control of the silver mines in what is now Tajikistan. The flow of silver northward dried up. Scandinavian economies were destabilized. Silver, which had allowed Scandinavian elites to engage in traditional gift-giving to cement social relationships, became scarce. Facing this change, raiding (going "viking") offered an alternative way to get their hands on precious metals and slaves.[10]

So it was that changes, emanating from as far from Scandinavia as Baghdad, rippled out like a stone thrown into a pond. These changes would trigger the expansion now known as the "Viking Age." In time, this would lead to Europeans reaching North America for the first time. It was an extraordinary example of the law of unintended consequences.

CHAPTER FOUR

VINLAND . . .
THE EDGE OF THE WORLD

The earliest evidence for American Vikings is inextricably linked to the stories of a land known as *Vinland*. It is here that the Norse raiders and traders—who are well known from the chronicles and archaeology of the Old World—attempted their first settlements in the New World. Any exploration of American Vikings has to start with the stories of *Vinland*.

Viking sagas, recorded in Iceland in the thirteenth century, tell of voyages to a land that lay to the west of Greenland. Beginning with these Norse sagas, we will explore the intriguing, dramatic, and violent basis of the claim; and the geographical North American clues which are revealed in these ancient sources. For it is becoming increasingly clear that what were once considered fanciful tales are rooted in realities. While some of the details and dialogue may owe more to the skill of later saga-writers than to historical reporting, overall, the topography and events these stories reveal offer persuasive evidence that they communicate real activities which connected the Norse world to North America around the year 1000.

The Icelandic Road
to North America

We know that Viking explorers settled Iceland in the later years of the ninth century. This began in the 870s, according to Icelandic sources such as the *Book of Settlements* (*Landnamabok*) and the *Book of Icelanders* (*Islendingabok*).

From Iceland, they pushed further west to Greenland in the 980s. As we have seen, there had been rumors of that place since its sighting by a storm-driven Viking sea captain in about 930. It should be noted that the climate was milder in the North Atlantic compared with today and it was even possible to grow some crops on Greenland. The eventual Norse settlement there lacked a centralized authority or organization and was a mixture of Christians and pagans who continued to follow old Norse beliefs.[1] Only when the Christian church succeeded in establishing formal institutional controls and organization (in the twelfth century) was it possible to insist on Christian norms of behavior across Greenland, but this was later than the period in which Greenland settlers first pushed further west to North America. As a result, we will find both Christian Vikings and pagan Vikings taking part in the earliest explorations of North America.

Accounts of these western pioneers are found in two sagas from Iceland: *Erik the Red's Saga* (*Eiriks saga rautha*)[2] and *The Saga of the Greenlanders* (*Graenlendinga saga*).[3] The earliest surviving manuscripts date from shortly after 1264, in the case of *Erik the Red's Saga*, and 1387, in the case of *The Saga of the Greenlanders* (when it was copied into a larger compendium).[4] However, both clearly drew on much earlier material and almost certainly existed as accounts prior to the date of the earliest surviving manuscript. It is difficult to know which of the two is the oldest tradition. Nevertheless, it is reasonable to conclude that both probably constitute early thirteenth-century accounts of much earlier events, likely composed c. 1200, as they were remembered and understood at the point of composition.[5]

Together, they tell an extraordinary story of adventure, courage, violence, betrayal, and settlement. While both sources pose problems of how some aspects of their accounts should be interpreted and their historicity assessed, a number of experts consider *The Saga of the Greenlanders* to be more reliable in some respects. While opinions differ, it can be argued that it provides a rather more detailed account, with more identifiable topographical descriptions.[6] It also differs in some areas regarding encounters with Native Americans compared with what we find in *Erik the Red's Saga*.[7]

Many of the original settlers who ended up in Greenland originated in Norway and were attracted by new pastures and exasperated with the growing power of the Norwegian rulers.[8] Others came from Ireland, including Vikings who had settled there but had decided to move on, and native Irish who had either been enslaved or had thrown in their lot with the Norse.[9] Both ethnicities will appear in the later settlement of North America. What is also clear is that the Vikings who pushed on to Greenland and further west—many of whom originated in the commonwealth of Iceland—were independent-minded, distrustful of authority, quick to violence, and prone to feud. This was a culture which distinguished Iceland from many other Norse colonies.[10] Organized around *gothar* (chieftains), these groups of relatives, allied adventurers, dependents, servants, and slaves were pioneers with attitude. This would soon become apparent in North America.

We can get a picture of what the later Icelanders thought had earlier occurred around the year 1000, by combining information from both the sagas. This is because one source often adds detail to something that is only recorded in outline in the other; or it may have its own information which does not contradict what is in the other saga. Sometimes they offer distinctly different versions of the same traditions, but never such as to discredit the overall account. For example, *Erik the Red's Saga* says that it was Erik's son, Thorstein Eriksson, who purchased a ship from the father of a woman named Gudrid Thorbjornsdottir (we will hear more about her in due course) in which to sail west to *Vinland*. In contrast, *The Saga of the Greenlanders* says that the ship was purchased from a Viking called Bjarni Herjolfsson, by Erik's son, Leif. And we have noted differences when it comes to recording encounters with Native Americans.

Clearly, the later traditions drew on varied earlier oral material that was not always harmonized. And they are works of literature, in which material was filtered through the work of unknown editors and the stories were separated from the events they describe by at least four generations.[11] Consequently, we must assume a measure of imagination and artistry in their composition. However, while they differ over details, the role of individuals, and the ordering of events, they never disagree about the central claim: Viking settlers moved from Iceland to Greenland; and from there to "*Vinland*." In short, the Vikings made it to North America, and, together, these sagas tell the story.

Greenland, the Start of the Adventure

In the same way that St. Louis, Missouri, has been described as the "Gateway to the West" in the nineteenth-century territorial expansion of the United States, so Greenland was for the Viking explorers of North America in the tenth and eleventh centuries. It was the jumping off point for adventures further west.

These westward movements were assisted by a three-hundred-year period known as the "Medieval Warming," during which storms in the North Atlantic lessened both in intensity and frequency, and pack ice was significantly reduced. This assisted the Viking explorers in navigating their northerly route to North America via Greenland.[12]

One of those explorers who would later achieve fame in the story of the settlement of *Vinland* was a woman named Gudrid Thorbjornsdottir. With her father, in a group of thirty settlers, she traveled to Greenland from Iceland in the late tenth century. The saga evidence indicates that she and her father were Christian.

Other settlers of Greenland, who would feature in the later North American adventures, were Bjarni Herjolfsson, Erik the Red, and Erik's children, Leif, Thorvald, Thorstein, and his illegitimate daughter Freydis. All would play a part in the next movement west; Freydis murderously so.

The Discovery of the North American Continent

The later Icelandic sagas give two accounts of how land to the west of Greenland was first discovered.

The Saga of the Greenlanders tells how a traveler named Bjarni Herjolfsson was blown off course on a sea voyage to Greenland and saw a strange land which was far to the west of known territories. It was forested, with low hills. Since it was strange territory, he did not anchor or explore it. Instead, he resolved to try to get back to Greenland. After two days sailing, he chanced on more land which was wooded and flat. However, it had no glaciers, so he knew it was not Greenland. Once again, he decided not to put ashore. Next, after three days sailing east, he reached yet another land, with mountains and glaciers. Sailing around it revealed that it was an island. Four more days of sailing eastward eventually brought him and his ship back home to Greenland.[13]

Despite the activities of Bjarni Herjolfsson, when it came to exploring America, it was Leif Eriksson who played the main part. According to *The Saga of the Greenlanders*, Leif bought Bjarni Herjolfsson's ship and then asked Erik the Red, his father, to accompany him on an exploration to the west. However, Erik decided that he was too old for such adventures. So Leif set off, but, according to the account in *Erik the Red's Saga*, he, like Bjarni Herjolfsson, was blown off course and he too came upon an unknown land far to the west of Greenland. *Erik the Red's Saga* emphasizes that, in the newly discovered land, Leif found wild wheat and vines, along with maple trees.

Variants of this story present him as getting lost on a journey from Norway to Greenland; this contrasts with the tradition which says he set off from Greenland. These are differences in detail between these accounts, but none detract from the main point of the story: Leif found a land where vines and wheat were growing. And this land lay to the west of Greenland.

On the way, Leif saw the same succession of shorelines that are associated with the journey of Bjarni Herjolfsson. These lands Leif named *Helluland* (Stone-slab Land), *Markland* (Forest Land), and eventually *Vinland* (Vine Land or Wine Land).[14]

By comparing the descriptions in the sagas with North American topography, we can be fairly certain that the places mentioned in the sagas correspond to real places. *Helluland*, as we have seen, is named from the Norse word for "flat stones." The most likely location of this is the east coast of Baffin Island in the Canadian territory of Nunavut. It may also have included the mountainous region of northern Labrador. Both are tundra ecozones. *Markland*, named from the Norse word for "forest," almost certainly refers to the southern coast of Labrador. *Vinland*, with its reference to winemaking fruits, probably refers to the area from Newfoundland to the Gulf of Saint Lawrence and, perhaps, as far south as New England. The latter is certainly a very real possibility.

Helluland was explored a little by Leif. Its rocky expanse, absence of grass, and its glaciers made it unsuitable for settlement. *Markland* was noteworthy for its white-sand beaches and woods. *Vinland* seemed the most attractive prospect. On an island north of it, he and his crew made camp. From there, they sailed into a sound that was between that island and the mainland. After sailing some distance from the sea, they beached their boat near where a river flowed from a lake into the sea. As the tide returned, their ship was lifted, and they sailed up the river and into the lake.

They decided to spend the winter there and built houses made from the plentiful timber. They noted the abundance of large salmon in the lake and in the river, and felt that the land offered a more attractive location for farming and livestock rearing than either Greenland or Iceland. It seemed to have a gentler winter climate than either and more hours of daylight through the winter months.

From there they began to explore the surrounding territory but were careful to always leave half their party at the basecamp, while the other half went exploring. And those exploring always kept together. During such an expedition, the land gained its name. Leif's foster-father was with the group and became separated from the others. When they were eventually reunited, he excitedly told them that he had discovered grapes growing. As a result, they called the place "*Vinland*" (Wine Land).[15] They also cut wood to carry back with them onto their ships. Their camp later became known as "Leif's Camp."

The next spring, Leif sailed home to Greenland. On the way he rescued a Norwegian named Thorir and his crew who had been shipwrecked and were surviving on a low rocky island. Thorir was traveling in the company of Gudrid Thorbjornsdottir, his wife. As this rescue was very lucky for the stranded travelers, people called him "Leif the Lucky" afterward.

Back on Greenland, Thorir and Gudrid, his wife, spent the winter at Leif's farm. There Thorir fell ill and died, as did Leif's father, Erik the Red. Gudrid survived and would later become one of the first settlers in *Vinland*.

Following the Way to a New "Wild West"

News of the discovery of *Vinland* soon spread. Leif the Lucky's brother, Thorvald Eriksson, also sailed to *Vinland* and reached "Leif's Camp." His adventure is recorded in *The Saga of the Greenlanders*.

Like his brother Leif before him, Thorvald spent the winter there and, in the spring, he explored westward and was impressed by the abundance of timber and the white-sand beaches.

After another winter there, he explored eastward. This ended badly and his ship was driven ashore in a storm and badly damaged. There the explorers met the indigenous peoples of this new land. And, in a dark foreshadowing of future conflicts, this meeting led to murder. Discovering nine of the natives hiding under three boats made from animal hide, Thorvald and his men killed all but one. This one escaped and sounded the alarm. Consequently, many more Native Americans appeared and attacked

the Viking killers with bows and arrows. The attackers were contemptuously dismissed as *"skraelings"* by the Viking settlers.[16]

It is difficult to tell which indigenous people were involved in
conflicts with the Norse in the sagas. They may have been ancestors of the later Native American *Beothuk* people, or may have been
members of the contemporary culture now sometimes referred to
as the *Thule* people (or proto-Inuit). Consequently, there is some
debate over whether the Vikings interacted with Native Americans,
or Inuit, in these western explorations. The answer is that they
probably met both groups of people. Consequently, when we refer
to "Native Americans," in these contexts, a more accurate term (at
times) might be the more all-encompassing "Indigenous Peoples."
However, it seems likely that most of those the Norse met in the
exploration of *Vinland* were ancestors of later Native American
tribes, so that is the term usually used in this book.

What is clear is that, while the Scandinavian explorers may
have used contemptuous racial slurs to describe these people, the
indigenous would prove more than a match for the newcomers.
With the advantage of numbers, they would determinedly defend
their lands against these Europeans in ways that would make the
Viking settlement unviable. Responding to the earlier Norse killings
of the men under the three boats, other indigenous warriors attack
the Vikings and an arrow mortally wounded Thorvald. It should
be noted that *Erik the Red's Saga* asserts that this death occurred
in a different expedition, and it is hard to choose between the two
versions of the event.

His men buried him at a place that they named *Krossanes* (Cross
Point). Thorvald specifically ordered his companions to "mark my
grave with crosses at the head and foot,"[17] because he was a Christian. With this telling detail we have the first record of any Christian
buried in North America. It is not now possible to securely identify

where this took place. The saga account indicates that it occurred in a sheltered cove on a forested cape, within "fjords," to the east of the place that the Vikings later called *Kjalarnes* (Keel Point). The exact location is unknown and the subject of much speculation. It may have been somewhere on the coast of Newfoundland or perhaps the coast of Labrador or Cape Breton Island. The saga tells us that the survivors then sailed back to Greenland.

Despite this setback, others were determined to try their luck in the new lands. We last met Gudrid Thorbjornsdottir in the winter that her husband died, while they both were staying on the farm of Leif the Lucky. Following this, she married Thorstein (son of Erik the Red) but he also died and she was once more widowed. Finally, she married a new settler on Greenland, named Thorfinn Karlsefni. Together with him, she set out for *Vinland*. It seems that she had planned such a voyage with her second husband but had been thwarted by bad weather.

So it was that yet another expedition set out. We get an abbreviated version of the adventure in *The Saga of the Greenlanders* and a more developed version, with some differences in events and those involved, in *Erik the Red's Saga*. However, they clearly record the same general series of events and, when combined, they tell a dramatic story. It is also possible that the prominence given to Thorfinn Karlsefni's activities in *Erik the Red's Saga* is due to it being composed at the time of a campaign to canonize a descendent of Karlsefni (named Bishop Bjorn Gilsson) and this may have encouraged an emphasis on the significance of his heroic ancestor.

Gudrid and Thorfinn Karlsefni set off in the company of Freydis, the illegitimate daughter of Erik the Red, and her husband. *Erik the Red's Saga* specifically mentions Freydis, whereas *The Saga of the Greenlanders* records her having her own murderous trip to *Vinland*. It seems likely that she went twice and that is what is assumed here. They were also joined, *Erik the Red's Saga* tells us, by Erik the Red's son, who was called Thorvald (who went on a separate expedition according to *The Saga of the Greenlanders*). Their intention was to create a pioneering settlement and so they took livestock with them. It is no exaggeration to say that this party constituted the first European pioneers on the North American continent.

After passing lands that seemed to correspond with *Helluland* and *Markland*, they discovered the keel of a ship (evidence that they were not the first to sail this far west) at a place they called *Kjalarnes*. This is referred to without comment in *Erik the Red's Saga*,[18] and it is clearly a record of a genuine tradition concerning this find. From it we may deduce that the Viking adventurers, who were later spoken of in the sagas, were not the only Viking explorers touching on the shores of North America in the late tenth and early eleventh century. This is an intriguing clue and a reminder of the interconnected nature of the North Atlantic world that long predated Columbus and Cabot in the fifteenth century; the Spanish colonists who followed this; the English, French and Basque fishermen and whalers in the sixteenth century; and the colonists at Jamestown and Plymouth in the seventeenth century. Five hundred years before the earliest of these, it seems clear that Vikings were already there. On the other hand, the discovery of the keel may be a nod in the direction of the account found in *The Saga of the Greenlanders* which says that Thorvald's ship was damaged there.

To return to Gudrid, Thorfinn Karlsefni, and their party. After the discovery at *Kjalarnes*, they eventually came to a shoreline that they named *Furdustrandir* (Wonder-beaches) due to the great expanse of sand. Speculation regarding the location of these has ranged from southern Labrador to Cape Cod. However, the most likely location of the beaches is in the vicinity of Cape Porcupine, on the southeastern coast of Labrador.[19]

There they put ashore Irish scouts (evidence of the ethnic mix of this "Viking" group), who eventually reported back with news of wild grapes and wheat. It seemed that it was an ideal place to homestead. They sailed into a sheltered anchorage that, according to *Erik the Red's Saga*, they named *Straumfjord*.[20] The name means "Current-fjord" in Old Norse. In *The Saga of the Greenlanders*, it seems that this same location is referred to as *Leifsbuthir* (Leif's Camp).[21] That the same place or general area is being referred to by different names in the two accounts seems clear, because both sagas say that, at this location, they discovered a beached whale. However, this shared identification is not accepted by all who have analyzed the text, and it may be imposing too much geographical accuracy on what are literary sources.

It has been suggested that Leif's Camp is the place now known as L'Anse aux Meadows, on Newfoundland, and archaeologically attested as having been a Viking-Age settlement (see chapter 5).[22] However, there may be a danger of assuming that the only place now known to archaeology must be the same as this named settlement site from the saga evidence. In contradiction of this identification, it has been asserted that the description of Leif's Camp is dissimilar to the situation at L'Anse aux Meadows,[23] and that Leif's Camp is more likely to have been located further south, perhaps on Passamaquoddy Bay, on the border of Maine and New Brunswick, at the mouth of the Bay of Fundy that separates Nova Scotia from New Brunswick.[24] Other suggestions for its location have included several in the vicinity of Cape Cod, but this seems too far south—although not impossible.

The extreme high tides in the Bay of Fundy *may* explain the name of *Straumfjord* (Current-fjord), although this has also been suggested as a reference to the Strait of Belle Isle between New-foundland and Labrador, due to the strong or broad currents in the vicinity. If the latter, its entrance was mistakenly thought to be a fjord when it was named.[25] Consequently, the matter of locating the sites in question is complex.

As a result, the exact location of *Straumfjord* and *Leifsbuthir* remain uncertain, but L'Anse aux Meadows has been the choice of a number of historians for the latter, although it would be contested by others who have studied both text and topography.

The fact that *The Saga of the Greenlanders* specifically names the place—wherever it was located—as Leif's Camp, makes it clear that the remembered topography of North America, from earlier expeditions, was influencing the decisions of subsequent explorers. The key thing for both sets of adventurers was that it provided a base at which they could rest and take stock of their situation.

However, that winter they hit trouble as they lacked sufficient provisions and fell ill from eating meat cut from a dead whale. There were also tensions within the group between Christians and pagans over what was causing their problems and how best to respond to the crisis. The writer(s) of *Erik the Red's Saga* explained that the explorers prayed to God but one of their number, Thorhall the Huntsman, rejected their reliance on Christian faith and claimed that a beached whale they had found was a reward for his composing a poem in honor of the pagan god Thor. Thorhall remarks: "Didn't Old Redbeard prove to be more help than your Christ?"[26] But the whale meat made them sick and so they threw it away, called on the mercy of God, and the weather improved so they could go fishing. The saga-writer(s) went on to say that Thorhall the Huntsman, who continued to compose pagan poetry, this time to Odin, was eventually driven ashore in Ireland by storms and was there enslaved. This was clearly stating a Christian verdict on his paganism. Eventually, the improved weather, abundant fish stocks, game to hunt, and eggs to gather, saved them from starvation.

From their initial point of settlement, Thorfinn Karlsefni explored further, reaching a place they called *Hop* (Tidal Pool), because there a river flowed out of a lake into the sea, but sandbars at the mouth of the river meant that they could only sail into it at high tide. There they discovered fields of wild wheat, vines growing on the hills, and rivers full of fish. That winter there was no snow and their livestock grazed outside. They also began to trade with the local Native Americans. The trade was organized around the Vikings providing milk, dairy products, and red cloth, in return for animal hides. The so-called *skraelings* also wanted to trade for weapons but Thorfinn Karlsefni would not allow this. It also became clear that the Native Americans were afraid of the bull that Thorfinn Karlsefni and Gudrid had brought with them. While they were there, Gudrid gave birth to a son, and she named him Snorri. He was the first of the Vikings to be born in *Vinland*; the first European North American. Both *Erik the Red's Saga* and *The Saga of the Greenlanders* concur regarding this historic event.[27]

In time, relationships with the local people broke down. One, it seems, tried to take a weapon and was killed. In response, the *skraelings* attacked the settlement and many of the attackers were killed. The battle was made famous by the actions of Freydis, the daughter of Erik the Red. As Viking men fell back in the face of the attack by the *skraelings*, Freydis, though pregnant, frightened the attackers off by baring her breast and slapping it with the flat of a sword-blade.

After this, Thorfinn Karlsefni decided that they could not remain there, for they would be under constant danger of attack. As a result, they sailed back up the coast and killed five of the *skraelings* that they discovered sleeping in animal-hide sleeping bags. However, Thorvald, the son of Erik the Red, was killed by an arrow.

This happened near *Kjalarnes*, where they had earlier discovered the abandoned keel of a ship. This is the death which *The Saga of the Greenlanders* claimed occurred in another and different expedition. It is hard to decide between the two conflicting claims.

What stands out in *Erik the Red's Saga* is it is stated that the one who fired this fatal arrow was a one-legged creature. In an otherwise prosaic account, this (apparently) mythological episode is hard to fathom and stands out from the rest of the retelling. Eventually, having buried Thorvald, they ended up back at *Straumfjord*, aka "Leif's Camp."

There the men fell out over women. Those men who had no wives tried to take those of the married men. By this time, as *Erik the Red's Saga* reminds us, they had been in *Vinland* for three years and the strain was beginning to tell. However, they continued to explore and, on returning to *Markland*, this saga tells us that they came upon five of the *skraelings*: a bearded man, two women and two children. They caught the children, taught them the Norse language, and baptized them.[28] One hesitates to call these "converts," since it is not clear that they had any choice in the matter. However, what one can say is that they were the first recorded Native Americans to be baptized as Christians.

What became of the Native American man and the two women is unclear. This raises the question of whether there were other cases of close associations between the Norse and Native Americans. There is some evidence which suggests that mtDNA (specifically a subclade of haplogroup C1), found among Icelanders, may have been derived from Native American women who were introduced to Iceland, probably in the medieval period. However, it should be noted that—as the research concludes—while C1e may be derived from a Native American origin, an Asian or a European origin cannot be ruled out.[29] Furthermore, if it was derived from

North America, the exact time and the mode of transmission cannot be categorically stated.[30] Nevertheless, it is an intriguing piece of evidence which may be rooted in the Norse voyages to, and from, *Vinland.*

On the return trip, the survivors traveled loaded with the produce of North America: wood, wild berries, and animal skins. On the way back to Greenland they lost one ship at sea. From Greenland they went to Iceland, and then on to Norway to sell the things they had brought back from *Vinland.*

Settlement in the New World had proved more demanding than expected. They were at the end of their supply lines and their numbers were too few to resist attacks by indigenous peoples. But it was not the end of attempts to settle *Vinland* in the eleventh century.

Murder on the Western Frontier

Freydis—the breast-slapping woman who had, we are told, terrified Native Americans with her display of female courage—had something of the *Valkyrie* about her (see chapter 2). She also had homicidal tendencies.

Sometime after the battle at *Hop*—and having returned to Greenland—she went back to *Vinland* with her husband. *The Saga of the Greenlanders* describes this as her one journey, but it is likely that she went twice, and that it was a previous sailing which was recorded in *Erik the Red's Saga.*

Once again, they returned to "Leif's Camp," but once there, the members of this expedition fell out. It was a disagreement that was to have lethal impact. It seems that Scandinavian-style longhouses had been constructed at this spot by earlier settlers.[31] However, Freydis refused to allow some of the expedition to use these. She insisted that Leif the Lucky—her brother—had given her exclusive use of them. It was an attitude which was short on pioneering spirit and comradeship. Consequently, the rejected members of the expedition set up camp further from the sea, beside a lake.

Over the winter, relations between the two groups of settlers frayed further. The later saga writers insist that Freydis encouraged this dissension. She told her husband that she had been badly treated by members of the other group and encouraged him to take revenge. The saga then tells how an attack was launched against the other party. This occurred while they slept. All the surprised men were tied up and then killed on the orders of Freydis herself. However, there were limits to this feud, as far as her male allies were concerned. None of the men in the group led by Freydis were willing to kill the five women who were members of the community that had been attacked. Finally, we are told, Freydis herself killed the other women with an axe. It was a vicious and bloody end to this North American adventure.

After this, the survivors returned to Greenland. On arriving there, Freydis told them to be silent about what had happened, or they, too, would be killed. The fiction was put about that the missing settlers had remained in *Vinland*.

However, news of the atrocity leaked out. She was condemned by Leif the Lucky, but the rules of kinship prevented him from visiting justice on his own sister.

So ended the earliest recorded Viking settlement in North America.

Where Does this Leave Us in Our Search for American Vikings?

Claims that Bishop Erik Gnupsson, of Greenland, took part in a failed expedition in 1121, intending to reach *Vinland*, make it clear that the way west remained on the mental map of Greenland Vikings. However, after this, *Vinland* drifted into a realm of myth and legend. The lands discovered in the *Vinland* sagas were, until fairly recently, regarded as being the products of medieval Norse imagination.

However, there is now solid archaeological evidence which identifies a Viking Age settlement as having been at L'Anse aux Meadows, on the northern tip of Newfoundland in Canada.[32] While the site at L'Anse aux Meadows has been identified as the camp known as *Straumfjord*, aka Leif's Camp, this is not absolutely certain and the settlement at L'Anse aux Meadows may not have been mentioned in the sagas at all. Grapes (the defining feature of *Vinland*) are unlikely to have ever grown on Newfoundland in the period in question.[33] So, *Vinland* itself clearly lay somewhere else, further south. We should not assume that the compilers of the sagas knew about every Norse expedition and its attendant settlements. Nevertheless, since October 2021 we can date the occupation there, whatever it was called in the eleventh century.

It is to that Viking archaeological evidence, from L'Anse aux Meadows, that we will now turn. We will see how clues excavated there can take our Viking journey even further south—perhaps as far as Connecticut. And from that point we will pick up possible Viking trails that may take us as far west as Minnesota and to coastal sites in Massachusetts and Rhode Island. Assessing the quality of this evidence will help us decide how far the American

Vikings penetrated both the land, and the minds of those who came afterward.

It is certain that what came later built on an earlier reality. The sagas are rooted in actual events. While some aspects may have been embellished, and some claims clash, it is reasonable to assume that, to a very large extent, the later Icelandic writers were drawing on genuine traditions. There were American Vikings.

CHAPTER FIVE

VIKING NORTH AMERICANS

The stories found in *Erik the Red's Saga*[1] and *The Saga of the Greenlanders*[2] left a lingering memory which insisted that settlers in the Viking Age had made it to North America. It was, as we have seen, the latest in the westward movements that had first taken them to the British Isles, then to Iceland, and on to Greenland. After this time, the idea of *Vinland* was very much on the mental map of Scandinavians.

While people in the generations after the writing of the sagas might hold different views regarding their authenticity, many believed that they contained, at the very least, a historic core. To this tradition was added other reports of movements to the mysterious lands of the far west.

The Relevance of Bishop Erik

We have briefly seen (in chapter 4) that later traditions claimed that Bishop Erik Gnupsson, of Greenland, took part in an expedition, in 1121, which was intending to reach *Vinland*. Erik Gnupsson was the first bishop of Greenland, with an episcopal see there at Gardar, although he only held this post for a fairly short period of time.

The sagas tell that a leading Greenlander named Sokki Thorisson—who was a wealthy farmer of the Brattahlid area in Erik the Red's Eastern Settlement—sponsored the idea of a separate bishop for the people of Greenland in the early twelfth century. He eventually gained the approval of the Norwegian king, Sigurd I Magnusson, "the Crusader" (1103–30), and Bishop Erik was appointed because of this ecclesiastical development. Most of the clergy who ministered in Greenland came from Norway.

However, the scant documentary evidence connecting Bishop Erik with *Vinland* leaves us with a conundrum. Was he engaged in yet another failed attempt to settle *Vinland*, or was he going to attend to the spiritual needs of a Norse community that was established there? The difference between the two options is profound. If it was the first, he was simply the latest in a series of westward adventurers; if the second, the tradition suggests a community of Norse people existed in North America until at least the early twelfth century. As a result, if there was a continuous settlement, Bishop Erik could be considered to be bishop of both Greenland and *Vinland*; although it should be noted that the sources do not actually mention that such a *joint* bishopric existed. Given the context of the accounts found in the sagas—which suggest movement to the far west around the year 1000—this could indicate the existence of a Norse colony in the New World which lasted for over a century. It is this latter possibility which caused some in the past to label Bishop Erik as "the first bishop that exercised jurisdiction over any part of America."[3] He was apparently appointed to his post in Greenland during the papacy of Pope Paschal II (1099–1118).

Other interpretations of the scanty evidence regarding Bishop Erik have focused on suggestions that he embarked on a missionary activity which aimed to convert Native Americans to Christianity. Later advocates of this interpretation believed (without any convincing evidence) that, in the sixteenth century, it was possible to detect "vestiges of the Christian faith . . . among the Indians of Quebec and the Atlantic Provinces."[4]

The problem is that the evidence regarding Bishop Erik is brief, to put it mildly. The *Annals of the Kings of Iceland* (*Annales Islandorum Regii* or *Konungsannall*) simply record: "1121 Bishop Erik from Greenland went to look for *Vinland*."[5] So, should we read that as meaning: He went in search of the *place* (a bit of exploring and adventuring)? Or was it: He went in search of the *community there* (providing pastoral support and spiritual leadership)? As Mark Twain put it, regarding a matter of choice at the end of chapter 28 of *Huckleberry Finn*: "You pays your money and you takes your choice!"

It should also be noted that the annal within which this—albeit brief—reference is found was not itself written in 1121. No Icelandic written sources survive from as early as this. In fact, the reference that is found in the *Annals of the Kings of Iceland* was part of a much later source which was compiled in 1300–28. It is known as *Manuscript GKS 2087 4°* It is, itself, likely based on earlier thirteenth-century histories, which may have drawn on yet earlier sources. This does not render it invalid; it simply reminds us that it is not a contemporary voice regarding events which occurred in 1121.

Several other late-medieval manuscripts also record this venture to *Vinland* but are not independent corroborative sources. They are clearly dependent on each other, and it is just a question of which manuscript predated the others and influenced them. Alternatively, they may draw on a common source, now lost to us. What is clear is that no record contemporary with Bishop Erik has survived. And none of the other sources adds anything substantial to our knowledge of him and his travels. The only additional material provided, in some, is the confirmation that he was "the *Greenlanders'* bishop" at the time he ventured to *Vinland* (for example in the *Annals of Gottskalk*, compiled in the sixteenth century but based on earlier annals). This confirms his base and his role, as outlined in the *Annals of the Kings of Iceland*. Some of the other sources simply record the voyage of the bishop, without any reference to Greenland—but that was, it seems, clearly the jumping-off point for a voyage to North America.

A much later (but not very reliable) source, the Danish poet and historian Claus C. Lyschander (1558–1624), also says that Bishop Erik went to Vinland and, while there, established both the Christian faith and a colony which still existed in Lyschander's time.[6] This would mean that the colony continued until the late sixteenth or early seventeenth century. Given that this would imply a community in existence since about the year 1000 (or at least from 1121) this would have allowed the settlers four to five centuries in which to conduct further exploration down the eastern seaboard and into the interior of the North American continent. This would have had huge implications for evidence left behind for modern investigators to discover. The possible implications of this will be explored in later chapters.

However, it should be added that this claim by Lyschander is questionable, to say the least! Despite this severe reservation about his claim, we will return to explore the *possibility* of Norse activities in North America, as far on as the late-medieval period, in chapters 8 and 9. Incidentally, Lyschander also records a tradition that Erik was buried at Gardar in Greenland in 1146. In a tangential piece of Viking-related information, Gardar, in Pembinar County, North Dakota, was established (chiefly) by later Icelander pioneers in modern times and echoes the name of Erik's seat in Greenland.

Back to Bishop Erik. The *Law Man's Annals* (*Logmannsannall*) mention him leaving Iceland in 1112 (given as 1113 in another source), with the enigmatic words: "Voyage of Bishop Erik."[7] The assumption is that the "voyage" in the annal was to Greenland. This attests to his existence and places him in the North Atlantic world at the right time but it tells us nothing more about *Vinland* or anything else for that matter—which is very frustrating. As with the *Annals of the Kings of Iceland*, this source was written much later than the event being described. In fact, it was almost certainly compiled sometime after 1412.[8]

While there is no record of Bishop Erik's consecration at Lund (Sweden)—as was the practice at the time—we do know that his successor as bishop of Greenland was consecrated there in 1124, and he reached Greenland in 1125.[9] So, whether Bishop Erik had died by 1124 or had never returned from *Vinland* is hard to tell. Either way, he exits history at this point.

His importance is that he points to the possibility of ongoing Scandinavian travel to North America after the events that are so colorfully retold by the sagas that we explored in the last chapter.

Other Clues Regarding the Links to *Vinland*

Other written accounts also mention journeys to North America after those that appear in the sagas and (apparently) in the annals that we just examined.

It seems that these voyages went as far as *Markland* (probably the coast of Labrador), very possibly to collect lumber that was lacking in Greenland, and which could be found on Labrador in the medieval period. Voyages also took place to *Helluland* (probably

Baffin Island). The connection here may have been to trade there with indigenous peoples.

The *Markland* reference is from the Icelandic *Elder Skalholt Annals*, compiled c. 1362. Under 1347 is an entry that reads: "There came also a ship from Greenland . . . It was without an anchor. There were seventeen men on board, and they had sailed to Markland, but had afterward been driven hither by storms at sea."[10] A similar, though abbreviated, account can be found in the *Annals of Gottskalk* and also in the largest surviving Icelandic medieval manuscript, called the *Book of Flatey* (*Flateyjarbok*) which dates from the late fourteenth century.

Helluland appears, in passing, in mythical sagas (such a saga is known as a *fornsaga*), which illustrate how the far west had entered a twilight world where history mixed with mythology. The *Saga of Halfdan Eysteinsson* (*Halfdanar saga Eysteinssonar*), dates from sometime after 1350. It contains an enigmatic statement that "[a ruler named] Raknar brought Helluland's deserts under his sway, and destroyed all the giants there . . ."[11] The mention of giants shows how far memories of *Helluland* had drifted into the realms of Norse mythology. Giants (as we saw in chapter 2) were regarded as beings which inhabited wild places and were thought of as enemies of civilization and order.

What is interesting is that the passage in the *Saga of Halfdan Eysteinsson* is not the only mention of *Helluland* in these mythical sagas. In the *Saga of Arrow-Odd* (*Orvar-Odds saga*), a later manuscript of the saga contains references to hunting a fugitive in "Helluland's deserts."[12] Other sagas refer to mythical rulers of the wilderness of *Helluland*. These stories are found within a genre of sagas known as *landvaettasogur* (stories of a country's guardian-spirits). In such stories, *Helluland* is a barren and mysterious place.[13]

Hints of fabulous lands to the west can be found in other (late-medieval) accounts too. In the *Saga of Halfdan Brana's-Fosterling* (*Halfdanar saga Bronufostra*) a ship is driven off course until it eventually arrives at a place of "smooth sands," "high cliffs," and "glaciers."[14] This has echoes of the kinds of landscapes described in the *Vinland* sagas that we examined in chapter 4; and the context suggests that the writer had the lands of North America in mind.

Finally, the Icelandic *Book of Settlements* (*Landnamabok*) refers to a mysterious place named "White Man's Land" or "Ireland the Great" and its discovery. The same place has a mention in *Erik the Red's Saga*. It was considered to have been located somewhere in the vicinity of *Vinland*. However, these sparse references provide little significant information regarding its relationship with North America.[15]

A little more relevant may be brief records in annals, from the late thirteenth century onward, of "New-land" to the west of Iceland. This probably refers to the eastern shores of Greenland, although some historians have suggested—based on little secure evidence—that it could refer to Newfoundland.[16]

What all this evidence reveals is that the connection of Viking adventurers with North America did not end with the abandonment of the settlement there, as recorded in the famous sagas which tell of its discovery and exploration around the year 1000. The place continued to provoke the Norse imagination. Subsequent journeys there may well have occurred. The idea of *Vinland* was kept alive.

Archaeological work in the twentieth and the twenty-first centuries has uncovered evidence directly connected with at least some of these journeys westward. We can now firmly date one of these sites. Since the fall of 2021 we can confidently talk of securely dateable proof that these Viking journeys took place. And, in examining that, we can begin to reconstruct a little of the lives of the Viking pioneers who reached North America many centuries before Columbus sailed to the New World.

The Evidence from
L'Anse aux Meadows

It is in Newfoundland that the securely dated evidence has been unearthed. The site in question—known as L'Anse aux Meadows—lies at the northern tip of Newfoundland's Great Northern Peninsula. Overlooking the Black Duck Brook, the site lies near the shallow waters of Epaves Bay. It faces the Strait of Belle Isle and the coast of Labrador, which is 28.5 miles (46 km) away. It is about 16 miles (26 km) due north of the town of St. Anthony.

The site today is on an open plain. However, in the early eleventh century, balsam fir, larch, birch, and poplar grew there. This continued until the twentieth century. Consequently, we should imagine it as a more wooded landscape than it is today. To the south, a high and rocky ridge extends out into the sea.

The Vikings—whose settlement will shortly be examined—were not the first people to occupy the site. Before the Vikings arrived, five different Native American groups lived there intermittently from 4000 B.C.E. onward. One Native American group lived there after the end of the short-lived Norse settlement.

However, it is the Scandinavian settlement which has attracted a lot of attention, and which has recently been dated using modern scientific methods.[17]

The Discovery of the Site

Newfoundlander William Munn was the first to suggest that, with its low, grass-covered mounds, the place might be the location of one of the main Viking sites of *Vinland*, mentioned in the Icelandic sagas. These sagas had become increasingly discussed in North America since the mid-nineteenth century and several explorers aimed to locate them.

Munn was the publisher of a major St. John's newspaper, called *The Evening Telegram*, and he wrote several articles in 1913–14 on the subject of Viking settlement. These later gave rise to a book titled: *Wineland Voyages: Location of Helluland, Markland and Vinland*.[18] Munn also suggested that the site known in the sagas as *Hop*, might have been in the vicinity of Little Harbor Deep or Great Cat Arm in White Bay (both on Newfoundland).[19] However, it was the location at L'Anse aux Meadows which was to prove the most fruitful.

A similar theory, regarding L'Anse aux Meadows, was presented by a Finnish geologist named Väinö Tanner in 1939. Following this, the Danish archaeologist Jørgen Meldgaard investigated the area in 1956. Meldgaard surveyed the area and dug a little on the site using test-pits. While he did not continue the work, the activities there generated a lot of local interest in the place.[20]

Enter the Norwegians Helge Ingstad and his daughter Benedicte, in 1960, who started work in the area which would eventually prove decisive. Helge's wife was the archaeologist Anne Stine Ingstad, and she led the first excavations at L'Anse aux Meadows which lasted from 1961 to 1968. It was this which proved that the site was from the Viking Age and dated to the time-setting of the sagas in the eleventh century.[21]

However, despite this important discovery it remained unclear how long the site was occupied. Nor was it clear how those who lived there related to local Native Americans who also lived in the area.

While the site was designated as a "National Historic Site of Canada" in 1968 and placed under the management of Parks Canada, an international advisory committee recommended further excavations. Since then, a number of leading archaeologists have carried out important excavations at the site. These include: Bengt Schönbäck (1973–75) and Birgitta Wallace (in 1976 and 2002). Alongside this, several natural-sciences investigations also occurred. As a result of these investigations, L'Anse aux Meadows was named as the first UNESCO World Heritage Site in 1978.[22] The UNESCO award described it as "a unique milestone in the history of human migration and discovery."[23]

Further excavations took place between 2007 and 2009. These were led by archaeologists Jenneth Curtis and Todd Kristensen. These explored the Native American settlements on the site and in the surrounding area and placed the Viking site in a wider cultural and historical context.

Studies of the site and its finds have continued. For example, in 2018 fieldwork was undertaken to sample the peat bog which lies about ninety-eight feet (30 m) east of the Norse ruins, for a paleoenvironmental assessment of the Norse settlement. These researchers also applied new analysis to existing radiocarbon data.[24] As we shall review at some length, the dating of wood from the site produced extraordinarily accurate results, published in late 2021.[25]

Today, L'Anse aux Meadows is the site of a popular interpretation center and ongoing archaeological research. As a result of the discoveries made there, we can now imagine the lives of these first American Vikings.

The Evidence Unearthed

What was found was, and is, remarkable. Eight wood-framed, sod-walled, buildings were excavated. These had left a footprint of low walls. These were organized into four complexes. Two of these consisted of a large hall with a small hut beside it. A third complex was made up of a large hall, a small hut, and a small house.

It is highly significant that the large halls were constructed in a distinctly Icelandic style dating from the late tenth and early eleventh centuries. This is consistent with the time usually considered to be represented in the sagas.

All the buildings were constructed with sod (turf) over a wooden frame. Consequently, these are often termed "sod houses." Regarding the smaller huts on the site, two were "pit houses," which were dug below ground level. This type of hut went out of style in the late eleventh century.[26] A round hut, of a type often interpreted as providing accommodation for slaves or others at the bottom of the social scale, was also excavated. This type of hut seems associated with this use in Scandinavia and suggests that some slaves accompanied the original movement from Greenland (one remembers the two Irish who appear in one saga account).

The settlement was located about 328 feet (100 m) from the shoreline and was constructed on a narrow terrace beside boggy ground. The Black Duck Brook runs through the terrace and would have provided local fresh water.

In addition to these huts assumed to accommodate people, a fourth complex included an iron-smelting hut, which was built into the bank of the brook and lay closer to the shoreline. This hut was open-ended and contained a small stone-and-clay furnace. In this, iron was smelted, using the small deposits of bog-ore found close by. Near this lay a pit which was used for making charcoal.

This would have been used as fuel in the iron-production in the furnace. From the small amount of slag discovered at the site, it seems that the furnace was only used once and produced a very limited amount of iron.

All the above is consistent with a small Viking Age settlement of a kind found in Iceland and across Scandinavia. This was corroborated by the small number of artifacts recovered from the site. These included: hundreds of wood chips; about fifty discarded wooden objects; smelting-slag from the iron production; slag from smithing; a plank from the bottom of a boat; and discarded nails from boat repairs; finally, eleven worn-out fire strikers of red jasper, used with an iron "fire steel" to create a spark, were found inside and outside all the halls. The latter are the equivalent of discovering modern discarded match boxes or barbeque firelighters. It seems that the occupation was contemporaneous in all the buildings, with different complexes having different functions.

The fire strikers may provide clues regarding the original homeland of some of the settlers. Those associated with two of the halls are made from jasper from Iceland. Four out of five from the largest hall are made from jasper from Greenland. This particular find-spot may indicate that the leader of the expedition came from Greenland. Two of the fire strikers are made of jasper from Notre Dame Bay, which lies on the northern coast of Newfoundland, and indicates an area explored by the settlers.[27]

A plank, discovered at the site, included pegs made from Scots pine. This tree did not grow in North America in the Viking Age but was common in Norway. It points to the origins of the boat from which the plank came.

Stones found in one of the huts may have been weights for fishing nets. Otherwise, there is no evidence for food production of any kind. This absence points to the site being a base and not a homestead.

A soapstone lamp probably reached the site as a result of trade with the more northerly indigenous group known as the *Dorset* people. This suggests that not all contacts were marked by violence.

Also found were several small personal objects: a ringed pin (to fasten a cloak), of a type dated to the tenth and early eleventh centuries in Scandinavian settlements; a small spindle whorl used in textile production; a whetstone that would have been used for sharpening needles and scissors; textile work tools; a broken bone pin found in the fireplace in the middle hall could have been either a hair or clothing pin (although it might have been a needle used for knitting socks, hats, and mittens); small fragments of a gilded ring; and a glass bead. The ringed pin, traditionally worn by men, and the textile equipment found there, traditionally associated with women, indicates the mixed-gender nature of the community.

Overall, the number of artifacts suggests that the site was only used for a short period of time, perhaps ten years. It was not a permanent home in the New World.

The Community at L'Anse aux Meadows

It seems it was not a settlement that reflected normal family life. There were women—but not many. There were apparently no children. Most of the activities focused on carpentry, boat repair, iron smelting, and smithing. It looks more like a male-dominated base for repairs,[28] and for further exploration.

It seems that there were sleeping places for between seventy and ninety people. It has been estimated that, from the amount of sod and lumber required for the construction of the structures, it would have taken sixty people two months to build, or ninety people a month and a half. Given that the entire Greenland colony comprised only about four hundred people in the early eleventh century, those explorers who went to L'Anse aux Meadows formed "a larger workforce than Greenland could spare for any other such enterprise."[29] In short, the North American adventure stretched the human resources of Greenland to their limits.

Although it was not a large community, there seems to have been some social complexity, as reflected in the varied buildings. This probably included some slaves. The size of the two largest halls suggests the presence of chieftains and their followers. Of these the largest probably housed the leader of the settlers. Intriguingly, even the smallest of the halls at L'Anse aux Meadows is twice the size of the building that is believed to have been Erik the Red's Hall at Haukadalur, in Iceland. Clearly, the New World offered scope for expansion.

It has been noted that the smallest hall (containing fewer rooms than the other two) may have been built by a successful middle-ranking farmer and his followers. The small house is the kind of accommodation lived in by a lower-class servant or retainer. And the smallest, the round hut, may have housed slaves. The sunken huts would have been used by workers for activities rather than as accommodation. Stones that may have been used as loom weights suggest weaving was taking place.

L'Anse aux Meadows was not a fully rounded homestead. It was a base-camp which made the most of the varied sea currents flowing in the Strait of Belle Isle. From it, explorers could search for things that were regarded as valuable in Greenland. This probably included fur, lumber, and luxury consumables such as walnuts and grapes. Lumber (cut and initially worked on site before transporting it) may have been a particular attraction. Of the five voyages to *Vinland* mentioned in *The Saga of the Greenlanders*, three mention lumber being taken back to Greenland. *Erik the Red's Saga* also refers to wood being taken back home from *Vinland*. In further support of this, chests discovered by archaeologists in Greenland were made from larch or tamarack, native to North America but unknown in Scandinavia. Boat parts made from spruce and larch (North American trees) have also been found in Greenland. While these may have come from driftwood, it is more likely that they were brought back from North America by explorers who were harvesting a resource from the New World.

What is noticeable, and significant, is what is missing. Excavations revealed no barns, nor did they find any other structures associated with keeping livestock. There is no evidence of grazing regimes employed at the site, nor storage of winter fodder. Along with the exposed nature of the site, it is clear that it was not a pioneering homestead. Had the Vikings wanted this, they could have selected more sheltered anchorages on the eastern coast of the Northern Peninsula.

What is definite is that it was a base for further exploration, both inland and down the coast. Finds of three butternuts and butternut wood—trees which do not grow further north than eastern New Brunswick—indicate that the Vikings at L'Anse aux Meadows must have explored the Gulf of St. Lawrence or even further south. This is corroborated by wood chips from American basswood or American linden trees, a tree native to eastern North America, and found (in areas relevant to L'Anse aux Meadows) from southeast Manitoba, east to New Brunswick; and southeast to South Carolina (although such a southerly exploration has not been corroborated by other evidence). Overall, this adds to the evidence for exploration of the Gulf of St. Lawrence, although voyages could have gone further south down the eastern seaboard of what is today the United States.

This possibility is supported by finds from other trees with a more southerly distribution, in particular: elm, beech, and eastern hemlock. In addition, the butternuts (or white walnuts), found at L'Anse aux Meadows, grow from New Brunswick and southern Quebec west to Minnesota, and south to northern Alabama. Once again, they offer the *possibility* that long-range voyages occurred to the south. However, the most northerly part of this growing-range is perhaps more likely to be relevant. In addition, butternuts and wild grapes grow in the same area and ripen at the same time. If *Vinland* was named from grapes—and, as we will see in chapter 8, this is not entirely clear—the reference would probably have been to the Fox Grape.[30] It can be found along the eastern seaboard of North America from Nova Scotia down to Georgia.[31] Again, it reinforces the possibility of southerly journeys, but these may have gone no further south than Nova Scotia. It should be noted that—apart from the enigmatic name of *Vinland* now being associated with the site by modern researchers—there is no evidence for grapes being consumed at L'Anse aux Meadows. Clearly, it was not *Vinland*. That lay further south.[32]

There is a similar lack of evidence there for direct contact and conflict with Native American peoples who would have been the ancestors of the later *Mi'kmaq*, the *Beothuk*, and the *Innu* peoples. However, given the evidence for explorations going far from the camp, such contacts and conflicts could have occurred elsewhere.

As we saw in chapter 4, there is some debate over whether the Vikings interacted with Native Americans or Inuit in these western explorations. On balance, it was probably primarily Native Americans that the Norse met once they reached *Vinland* and associated areas.

Dating the Site to 1021

In the fall of 2021, dramatic news broke that threw fresh light on the settlement at L'Anse aux Meadows and confirmed its identification as a site from the Viking Age. Tree-ring analysis of three pieces of worked-wood from the site were dated to the year 1021.[33] These were from discarded sections of branches and tree stumps.[34]

As the abstract to the report puts it: "Our new date lays down a marker for European cognizance of the Americas, and represents the first known point at which humans encircled the globe."[35] That the discovery of this dating evidence was published exactly one thousand years after the historic event had occurred in the Viking Age is extraordinary.

The results are ground-breaking because most of the previous suggestions regarding the dating of the site were based on an analysis of the type and style of the architectural remains and the limited number of artifacts discovered; and interpretations of the Icelandic sagas (see chapter 4), which were written centuries after the events they describe. These new results underpin dating with solid scientific evidence. Previous work based on carbon-14 dates had failed to provide precise-enough dating information; and this previous broad spread of the date-envelope was not consistent with the archaeological evidence which indicated a brief period of occupation at the site.

This is why the most recent dating evidence is so exciting and so revealing. To cut a long and technically complex story short, the new technique used knowledge of cosmic radiation events which synchronize with dendrochronological tree-ring evidence, particularly a phenomenon known as "the AD 993 anomaly." Each of the three wooden objects, examined to provide the new dating evidence, revealed this signal (from the year 992 or 993) located twenty-nine growth rings (years) before the bark edge.[36]

The selection of the wood for this new analysis was guided by detailed research by Parks Canada and rested on the wood in question coming from the Norse archaeological deposit and also having clearly been modified by metal tools. This was evident from characteristically clean, low angle-in cuts, employing cutting tools of a type not used by contemporary Native Americans. The wood analyzed came from at least two different species. These were fir, possibly wood from balsam fir, and wood from juniper/thuja.

The result of this analysis was extraordinary. It established beyond doubt that the "cutting year" of the trees involved was 1021. This is the only secure calendar date for the presence of Europeans in the Americas before the voyages of Columbus. And those first Europeans were Vikings!

What is as remarkable is that the same date was found on all three of the trees examined. That this indicated Viking activity *at the site* that year is clear because the wood on all these trees included the, so-called, "waney edge" (the natural edge, which may include the bark) of the lumber used. Such a layer would almost definitely have been lost in water if the wood used came from driftwood. And, unlike in Greenland, the settlers had no need to forage for driftwood because at L'Anse aux Meadows, at the time in question, there was plenty of local woodland growing close to the site and available for use. In addition, if the wood had been washed up on the shoreline, the likelihood of all pieces exhibiting the same dendrochronological dating evidence is statistically highly unlikely. In short, the trees were cut down by Viking settlers, as part of one episode in 1021.[37] And they cut the trees down at L'Anse aux Meadows.

However, just to complicate things, research carried out in 2018 suggests that Viking activity at the site could have lasted for a century. As well as carrying out sampling from the peat bog, this work also applied what is called Bayesian statistical modeling to the legacy radiocarbon data from the site.

This conclusion does not imply a *continuous* Viking occupation there for a century. That, "given the shallow cultural deposits [that is, the sparse evidence left behind], seems unlikely." What it indicates is "the possibility of sporadic Norse activity beyond the early eleventh century."[38] Even when the dating evidence is read in this limited way, the result is still extraordinary. We can imagine the final Viking ships putting in at L'Anse aux Meadows as late as the first quarter of the twelfth century, having originally established the settlement c. 1021. This possible twelfth-century date is, of course, in exactly the time-period associated with Bishop Erik that we examined a little earlier.

L'Anse aux Meadows and the Sagas

So, was L'Anse aux Meadows one of the sites referred to in the sagas? As we touched on in chapter 4, we cannot be absolutely sure. However, there is one saga-settlement-site that may fit the location at, and use of, L'Anse aux Meadows and that is the one called *Straumfjord*, which features as a core site in *Erik the Red's Saga*. This appears to be the place that *The Saga of the Greenlanders*, refers to as Leif's Camp, where Thorfinn Karlsefni set up a settlement.[39] However, as we have seen, speculation that Leif's Camp may have been at L'Anse aux Meadows has been challenged and certainty is not possible.

Nevertheless, if L'Anse aux Meadows was that place, then the new dating evidence would be consistent with this since Leif

Eriksson (a *Vinland* explorer in both sagas) is thought to have died c. 1019–25. And others who followed him to *Vinland* were probably younger. This ties in with the dating evidence for the establishment of the settlement there. The name *Straumfjord* (Current-fjord, Stream-fjord, or Tide-fjord in Old Norse) could fit the coastal geography, and character of the sea, in the vicinity of L'Anse aux Meadows.

In addition, *Straumfjord* is described as a base for explorations in a number of directions. This included the exploitation of various resources, including lumber and grapes, which occurred from a more southerly summer camp which was called *Hop*. If L'Anse aux Meadows, on Newfoundland, was *Straumfjord*, then *Hop* was probably located in what is now eastern New Brunswick.[40] Or perhaps in Maine. But *Hop* could have been even further south, and this has encouraged the search for Norse sites far down the eastern coast of what is now the USA. To that we will return in chapter 9, when we search for New England Vikings.

However, it should be noted that other suggestions regarding the location of *Straumfjord* range from Northern Canada's Ungava Bay, to as far south as the entrance to the Hudson River. Despite this, L'Anse aux Meadows is a strong contender for being this named historic Viking settlement in North America or was at least related to it in some way.

This possibility is supported by the late-sixteenth-century Icelandic *Skalholt Map*. This includes a peninsula labeled *Promontorium Windlandiae*.[41] Its shape, relation to Greenland, and comparable latitude to the British Isles, all point to it being Newfoundland's Great Northern Peninsula. On the northern tip of which lies L'Anse aux Meadows. The *Skalholt Map* exists today in a copy made in 1668, which claims to be a copy of an original from 1570, although it was probably not drawn earlier than 1590.[42] Even though vines did not grow at L'Anse aux Meadows, it seems clear that its general location was still associated with *Vinland,* although that lay further south.

On another early map—the *Resen Map,* from 1605—the *Promontorium Windlandiae* is also described as *bonae forte Vinlandiae pulchrae* (the promontory of *Vinland* the good).[43] Hans Poulson Resen, a Danish bishop and scholar, claimed that this map was partly based on an earlier Icelandic map, which was several hundred years old.[44] This ancient map may itself have been rooted in traditions which stretched back to the eleventh century. If so, it seems to echo the location of the first dateable Viking settlement in North America, at what we now call L'Anse aux Meadows.

The *Vinland Map*—which came to light in 1957 as a purported fifteenth-century map and was acquired by Yale University—is now considered to be a twentieth-century forgery.[45] Its reference to land southwest of Greenland, labeled *Vinlanda Insula* (Island of *Vinland*), has no historic validity.

Even if it is concluded that L'Anse aux Meadows cannot be categorically connected to one of the sites named in the sagas, its corroboration of the saga claims is remarkable and of huge significance. At last, we can securely date the activities of Vikings in North America. Prior to this, these claims had languished in a misty world of myths and legends. And in that misty world, the Vikings were not alone. Indeed, there were a number of others who vied with them for the accolade of being the first European discoverers of North America. And that rather crowded stage meant that, for centuries, the more reliable Norse claims were regarded with suspicion. It is to those other claims that we now briefly turn and, in examining them, we will consider how they caused problems for the Viking contention, and it is possible that one rival claimant may have preceded the Norse.

CHAPTER SIX

SHARING THE STAGE
WITH VIKINGS?

We have explored the evidence for Norse settlers reaching North America around the year 1000. There were, we now know, American Vikings. It was not just a literary invention of the compilers of Icelandic sagas.

However, these Scandinavians are not the only Old World medieval travelers claimed to have reached North America. Other claims abound. To some extent this has rather muddied the waters, as the saying goes. This is because, for some time, the association with these other alleged New World travelers somewhat obscured the evidence that Vikings *did* get to North America. All became part of a fantastic pre-Columbian circus of supposed North Atlantic explorers.

One claim involved an Irish account which centered on Saint Brendan, who it alleged sailed to America in the sixth century. This was in the Celtic tradition known as "White Martyrdom," whereby Christians sacrificed their lives by renouncing the world in the service of God. Then there was the Welsh claimant, Madoc ap

Owain Gwynedd, who is said to have landed in Mobile, Alabama in 1170. The Scots' claim was lodged on behalf of Henry Sinclair, Earl of Orkney, who is said to have reached Westford, Massachusetts, in 1398. Examining these competing claims helps explain why, encouraged by the hunt for pre-Columbian European settlers, Viking claims abound, and also why the validity of the Viking claim was often overshadowed by these other assertions. But there may be a connection between one of these traditions and the voyages of Vikings.

The Voyage of Saint Brendan

Saint Brendan is, undoubtedly, the most famous of those for whom claims are advanced regarding a trans-Atlantic journey. Brendan of Clonfert (c. 484–c. 577) has been described as one of the "Twelve Apostles of Ireland." He is also known as "Brendan the Navigator," "Brendan the Voyager," and "Brendan the Anchorite." According to legend, he discovered somewhere called the "Isle of the Blessed."

The approximate dates of his birth and death and some details of his life are found in Irish annals and genealogies. It seems that the earliest mention of Brendan can be found in the *Life of Saint Columba* (*Vita Sancti Columbae*), written between 679 and 704. However, the earliest mention of him as an ocean-going explorer appears in a document called *The Martyrology of Tallaght*, the oldest Irish list of martyrs, which dates from the ninth century.[1]

While *The Martyrology of Tallaght* is the earliest reference, the most detailed description of his journeying can be found in a medieval document known as the *Voyage of Saint Brendan the Abbot* (*Navigatio Sancti Brendani Abbatis*).[2] It was certainly a popular story. The earliest surviving version of the *Voyage* dates from around the year 900, but there are over one hundred surviving manuscripts of the account found across Europe and translated into many languages. The *Voyage* was clearly written with a Christian purpose, to present the life of its saintly protagonist, but it also refers to natural phenomena, intermixed with fantastic activities and persons. There are similarities between it and other—mythical—Irish accounts of voyaging heroes. It made such an impression on contemporaries, and others in the later medieval period, that cartographers included references to "Paradise" or "St. Brendan's Island" on their maps.[3] Also, an Anglo-Norman version exists which packaged the story for a new medieval audience in England and western France.[4]

Which brings us to the voyage, as outlined in these accounts. The claim is that Brendan and his monk-companions "prepared a light vessel, with wicker sides and ribs, such as is usually made in that country [Ireland], and covered it with cow-hide." This hide was "tanned in oak-bark," and the joints were treated with tar to waterproof it. They "put on board provisions for forty days, with butter enough to dress hides for covering the boat and all utensils needed for the use of the crew." The rather surprising reference to butter refers to a substance used to keep the hide flexible. Brendan "then ordered the monks to embark, in the name of the Father, and of the Son, and of the Holy Ghost."[5]

What follows is an account which drew heavily on established medieval Christian traditions, but which includes clues that some aspects of real geography may have been utilized too. Consequently, the mention of demons hurling fiery slag from an island where rivers of fire flowed, and great "crystal pillars," may refer to volcanic Iceland and to icebergs.

Inspired by a report he had heard of "The Promised Land for Saints" (*Terra Repromissionis Sanctorum*) Brendan set off to find this place. For seven years, Brendan and his companions sailed the seas and had various adventures involving several places visited. They stopped off for a short time on "The Island of Sheep"; made camp on the back of a whale (thinking it an island, until they lit a fire and discovered otherwise); visited "The Island of Birds"; and other places—some marvelous, others terrifying.

A number of these places remind us of the real topography of the North Atlantic. The islands characterized by their sheep and birds may refer to the Faroes; an isolated rock may be Rockall; the fire and ice are reminiscent of Iceland.[6]

After seven years of sailing—visiting some of the same places repeatedly—they finally reached "The Promised Land for Saints." This land was "extensive and thickly set with trees, laden with fruits, as in the autumn season." On reaching a huge river their exploration of the hinterland was ended.[7]

However, this is a geography that is both spiritual and topographical. They discovered "no night was there, but a light always shone, like the light of the sun in the meridian," and they met a "young man of resplendent features, and very handsome aspect," who assured them that he was a Christian and that they had reached the land of blessing sought by Brendan and his companions.[8]

From it they returned home having been instructed to take "as much of those fruits and of those precious stones, as your boat can carry; for the days of your earthly pilgrimage must draw to a close, when you may rest in peace among your saintly brethren." Furthermore, they were told that the land will remain hidden until sometime in the future when "days of tribulation may come upon the people of Christ." This apocalyptic claim enhances the otherworldly nature of the place, which must await the preaching of the Gospel to all nations before it is once again revealed. After this, the travelers loaded their boat and "embarked once more and sailed back through the darkness again."[9] Finally, they reached their home once more.

Saint Brendan and North America?

A great deal of time and effort has been spent trying to prove that Brendan was the first European to reach North America. The difficulty faced in linking the written evidence to geography explains why pre-Columbian sea charts placed the land Brendan discovered in areas as far apart as southern Ireland and what we now know to be the equator.[10] This is particularly striking, since such charts ignored the evidence that Brendan voyaged in northern latitudes.

Despite the enthusiasm of a dedicated group of supporters, there is no reliable evidence that Brendan reached Greenland, least of all America.[11] However, this does not prove that he did not get there. The British explorer, historian, and writer, Tim Severin, proved that it is possible that a leather-clad boat could have reached America. In 1976, Severin built a replica of Brendan's currach and, with a three-person crew, sailed it from Tralee in County Kerry (Irish Republic) to the vicinity of Peckford Island, Newfoundland, where in June 1977 the voyagers were stopped from reaching land by adverse winds. This proved that a vessel, such as the one described in the *Voyage of Saint Brendan the Abbot*, could reach North America.[12] Severin's film of the voyage, entitled *The Brendan Voyage* (1978), inspired the Irish composer Shaun Davey to write an orchestral suite also entitled *The Brendan Voyage*.[13]

Severin's experiment found that leather quickly deteriorates in sea water. However, the medieval text indicates that the leather was "tanned in oak bark" and then coated in "butter" or "grease" to make it waterproof and that extra "butter/grease" was carried on the voyage. Severin found that this worked. While translations sometime render this "grease" as "butter," it was very likely that it was lanolin or wool grease, a wax secreted by sheep and giving off a terrible smell when used in large amounts.

Severin's journey attempted to replicate the original route. This assumed that Brendan followed, what we might call a "stepping-stone" strategy. This, it has been suggested, had taken him along the western coast of Ireland, and then to the Outer Hebrides of Scotland. This would have kept the original voyage close to shore. However, this was followed by a longer leg on the open sea from Stornoway to the Faroe Islands. There is justification in this since the Faroes are a fairly convincing match for two of the islands mentioned in the medieval account. These are "The Island of Sheep" and "The Paradise of Birds." From there the twentieth-century voyagers sailed to Iceland. This could plausibly be the place which Saint Brendan called the "Island of Smiths." Such a description would have been very apt for such a volcanic island. From there, Severin and his team sailed west to reach Newfoundland.

We have no proof that Brendan followed this route, with his companions, in the early medieval period, but the technology at Brendan's disposal *could* have underpinned such a voyage.[14] When pondering the possible implications of this, it is worth recalling that some historians in the early part of the twentieth century similarly dismissed the possibility of Vikings sailing to North America.[15] They were wrong.

It has even been suggested that in the 1490s Christopher Columbus learned, from the text of the earlier voyage, that currents and winds favored westbound travel by a southerly route from the Canary Islands. However, an eastbound trip would be assisted by following a more northerly route. As a result of Brendan's earlier experience, it has been suggested, Columbus followed this sailing pattern on all his voyages.[16]

So, given this, how should we assess the nature of the Brendan evidence? The conclusions tend to fall into three main camps:

(a) The voyage is a totally fictional Christianized version of a well-established tale of a voyage to a "Land of the Blessed" in the western ocean but imagined from a Christian rather than a pagan perspective.[17] According to this: "It constitutes an inner journey rather than an actual one." This interpretation would reject any geographical use of the text to identify the route and places visited by Brendan and his companions.[18]

(b) The voyage is based on a real traveler's adventures, albeit far more localized (perhaps Brendan reached as far as the Hebrides) than the gigantic extension found in the *Voyage of Saint Brendan the Abbot*.[19] This would explain some of the geographical features, without taking the voyagers to North America.

(c) The voyage is a mythologized version of a real adventure which encompassed the Faroes, Iceland, and North America. Suggestions as to his landing place, in such an adventure, have varied from Newfoundland to as specific a location as the northern end of Long Island Sound, in the vicinity of Groton, Connecticut.[20] *Chi-Rho* symbols, a monogram of the first two letters of *Christ* in Greek, are said to have been found carved at the Gungywamp complex and to date from c. 500–700, evidence, it has been claimed, of the influence of Brendan and his followers who landed there.[21] Gungywamp is an archaeological site located in Groton, Connecticut, and has produced artifacts dating from c. 2000 B.C.E.–770 C.E., a stone circle, and the remains of structures which are both Native American and colonial.

If Brendan did succeed in reaching North America, it is possible that a memory of such a voyage prompted later Norse adventurers (c. 1000) to make a similar voyage. If so, there was less accident and more design in the westward voyages of the Vikings. We know that there were Irish members on at least one of the *Vinland* voyages and, given the Viking settlements in Ireland and the Irish DNA among Icelanders, an Irish influence on the later voyages is not beyond the bounds of possibility.

The Western Adventures of Madoc ap Owain Gwynedd

Brendan is not the only Celt credited with a North American voyage. Madoc (or Madog) ap Owain Gwynedd was, legend claims, a Welsh prince who sailed to America in the year 1170.

The legend describes him as a son of Owain Gwynedd (or Owain Gruffudd), who left North Wales to escape violent civil strife there. The story, as it survives, is rooted in the tradition of a sea voyage conducted by a Welsh hero, in the style of figures from Welsh mythology. Although it may have drawn on early medieval beliefs that were themselves rooted in pre-Christian mythology, the story became popular during the sixteenth century. This was largely because English and Welsh writers, in this Elizabethan period, claimed that the voyage meant that Britain had a prior claim to

North America which predated that of the Spanish.[22] Tudor geopolitics were as much in the mix as medieval Welsh legends.

It should be noted that Wales had been conquered by England in the late thirteenth century. As a result, English writers annexed and co-opted Welsh history if it suited them, as earlier generations had seized Welsh land.

The Origins of the Claim

In 1559, the *Chronicle of Wales* (*Cronica Walliae*) was written by Humphrey Llwyd but never published. It was the first attempt to create a history in English of the lives and deeds of the kings and princes of Wales, from Cadwaladr to Llywelyn ap Gruffudd, who was the last native ruler of Wales. The *Llanstephan manuscript* of the work is kept in the National Library of Wales.

In compiling his work, Llwyd translated versions of the twelfth-century Welsh medieval text called the *Chronicle of the Princes* (in Welsh, the *Brut y Tywysogion*)—itself compiled by Caradoc of Llancarfan—from Welsh and medieval Latin into English. Llwyd explicitly stated that his main source was "the Welsh Cronicle." However, he expanded this by adding some historical information he found in the work of the chroniclers Matthew Paris (died 1259) and Nicholas Trivet (died 1328), alongside several other earlier historians.[23]

Within Llwyd's composite work lies the claim that Madoc sailed to America; and later returned to Wales to recruit additional settlers. After gathering eleven ships and 120 men, women, and children, he sailed west a second time to "that Westerne countrie."[24]

The next stage in the development of the claim occurred in 1573, when the Welsh cleric and historian David Powel took over the task of preparing Llwyd's manuscript for publication. Powel expanded Llwyd's work and published the *Historie of Cambria, Now Called Wales* in 1584. It was a very significant book as it influenced ideas concerning Welsh medieval history for several centuries. It was responsible for bringing the legend that Prince Madoc had discovered America in about 1170 to a wide readership. This was politically potent at the time, as the legend was used to justify English encroachments on Spanish territory in the Americas.

The story, as outlined by Powel, claimed that Madoc sailed from Llandrillo (Rhos-on-Sea) in Wales. Tired of internecine warfare at home, he and his companions set out to explore the western ocean. They allegedly discovered a far-off and rich land in 1170. There they founded a colony.[25] The idea resonated with the ambitions of those who heard the claim. For example, the famous John Smith, an early English explorer of Virginia, confidently wrote, in 1624, that Madoc had reached the New World in 1170.[26] This was centuries before the voyages and claims of the Spanish.

The "Geography" of the Madoc Claim

Where was "that Westerne countrie"? Powel's *Historie of Cambria* claimed that Madoc sailed west "to a land unknown," where there were "pleasant and fruitfull countries" which were "without inhabitants."[27] In short, there is little specific geography in his account. If that associated with Brendan is imprecise, the claim associated with Madoc is even more unclear. Madoc's landing place has been suggested to be in areas as varied as:

> *Mobile, Alabama; Florida; Newfoundland; Newport, Rhode Island; Yarmouth, Nova Scotia; Virginia; points in the Gulf*

of Mexico and the Caribbean including the mouth of the
Mississippi River; the Yucatan; the isthmus of Tehuantepec,
Panama; the Caribbean coast of South America; various
islands in the West Indies and the Bahamas along with
Bermuda; and the mouth of the Amazon River.[28]

The *Historie of Cambria* claims that, when later Europeans explored the eastern seaboard of North America, reports filtered back of Native Americans who "honored the crosse," which was taken as evidence that "Christians had beene there before the comming of the Spaniards."[29] However, it was surmised that these early Christian explorers had been few in number and had assimilated, including giving up Welsh and adopting the Native American language of the area within which they settled.[30] Powel stated that he thought the area explored was in Mexico, as he claimed that Welsh words could still be distinguished there within Native American speech.[31] This is a highly fanciful assertion. He also claimed that, at the time of the Spanish conquest, the native people believed that their rulers were descended from "a strange nation, that came thither from a farre countrie."[32]

While we may be skeptical, others have run with the claim. This idea of "Welsh Indians" clearly appealed to several seventeenth-century explorers in the New World. In 1608, Peter Wynne was part of a British exploratory party to the villages of the Monacan people, above the falls of the James River in Virginia. Following this, he wrote a letter claiming that some in the party of explorers thought that the way the Monacans pronounced some words resembled "Welch." Wynne himself was a Welsh-speaker.

Wynne was not alone in making such claims. Later that century, the Reverend Morgan Jones told Thomas Lloyd (William Penn's deputy), that he had been captured in 1669 in North Carolina by a tribe he identified as the Doeg. Jones recounted that the chief spared his life when he heard him speak Welsh. This was because he understood it! Jones's report went on to say that he lived with the Doeg for several months. During that time, he preached the gospel in Welsh. The claim was recorded in 1686.[33]

In 1953, the Daughters of the American Revolution even erected a plaque at Fort Morgan on the shores of Mobile Bay, Alabama, which read: "In memory of Prince Madoc a Welsh explorer who landed on the shores of Mobile Bay in 1170 and left behind with the Indians the Welsh language."[34] This plaque was removed by the Alabama Parks Service in 2008 and put in storage. One may surmise that they were not persuaded of its veracity when it came to charting European settlement in the area.

The matter is made even more complex by the fact that the account in the *Historie of Cambria, Now Called Wales* insists that nobody returned from the second voyage. In short, even the legend gives no clues as to the consequences of Madoc's journeys. It is therefore even more remarkable that later traditions then asserted that the Welsh pioneers explored far up the river systems of North America and are credited with raising impressive structures as they went. These included stone forts along the Alabama River, said by the local Cherokee (we are told) to have been built by "White people."[35] Other later claims have the Welsh ultimately ending up in the Midwest or the Great Plains.

These are clearly attempts to attribute Native American achievements—such as the mounds of the Mound Builder culture and other structures—to Europeans. It is a piece of ethnic appropriation based on dismissal of the complexities of Native American cultures. Other versions credited the Welsh with the architectural achievements of the Aztecs, the Maya, and the Inca.[36] The same approach—as we shall see—has characterized some of the claims about American Vikings and their alleged architectural achievements.

In the nineteenth century, fanciful accounts referred to "Welsh Indians," and the favorite claim was to identify them as the Plains tribe of the Mandan.[37] No less a famous explorer than the painter George Catlin asserted (in *North American Indians*, 1841) that he had found descendants from the voyage of Prince Madoc. Catlin had lived for eight years among various Plains peoples, including the Mandan. Others, too, made fanciful claims—and these still appear on credulous websites today—that nineteenth-century explorers found close similarities between Mandan and Welsh. The story had legs. Earlier, President Thomas Jefferson had heard of Welsh-speaking Indians. Writing to explorer Meriweather Lewis, in 1804, Jefferson referred to Welsh Indians "said to be up the Missouri."[38]

Other accounts named the Zunis, Hopis, and Navajo as perhaps being descendants of the Welsh explorers. Brigham Young dispatched a Welshman to the Hopi to search for Welsh-speakers. Unsurprisingly, none were discovered. But interest in the project did not diminish. In 1863 three Hopi men were brought to Salt Lake City to be "besieged by Welshmen wanting them to utter Celtic words." Once again hopes were disappointed.[39] One wonders what the Hopi thought of the bizarre obsession of these white men. Despite this, the Welsh-American Mormon missionary, Llewellyn Harris, after visiting the Zuni in 1878, wrote that they used many Welsh words in their language. There is no evidence to substantiate this extraordinary claim.

No persuasive archaeological proof has been found to support the claims regarding Madoc in North America. Despite this, several sites are still cited as evidence of the presence of the Welsh explorer and his colonist supporters.

One of these is a rock formation and peninsula known today as the Devil's Backbone. It is located at Fourteen Mile Creek, on the Ohio River. Situated in Charlestown State Park near Charlestown, Indiana, it lies across the Ohio River from Louisville, Kentucky. Local legend claims this as the location of a stone fortress built by the Welsh settlers.

Another site, in northwest Georgia, involves a legend connected to a mysterious rock formation on Fort Mountain. It has been suggested that Cherokee traditions regarding the ruin may have been influenced by the legends of the "Welsh Indians."[40] If so, it would be an example of a claim that crossed cultural boundaries, in a way that went well beyond Madoc's crossing of the ocean in real life.

In 1799, John Sevier, the first governor of Tennessee, wrote an account which referred to an alleged "discovery" of six skeletons wearing brass armor which was inscribed with the Welsh coat-of-arms.[41] The claim was related to the idea that Madoc and the Welsh were the first European settlers in Alabama.[42]

Is There Any Reason to Think Madoc Made It to America?

The short answer is: No. There is no credible support for it. It is clear that the whole Madoc account originated in medieval romance, which was indebted to voyages found in Celtic mythology. This was probably also influenced by the very popular stories connected to Saint Brendan.

It seems that the earliest dateable reference to Madoc can be found in a short ode in rhyming couplets, or *cywydd* in Welsh, composed by the Welsh poet Maredudd ap Rhys ferch Powys. He was alive c. 1450–83 and lived in the Welsh region of Powys. His poem mentioned "Splendid Madog," an adventurer "who desired not land but only the worldly wealth of the sea."[43]

However, when it comes to an actual trip to North America, the evidence is not at all persuasive. Which brings us to another unconvincing claim.

Henry Sinclair, Earl of Orkney

Henry I Sinclair, Earl of Orkney, Lord of Roslin (c. 1345–c. 1400), a Scottish and a Norwegian nobleman, has been credited with a voyage to North America in the late fourteenth century, c. 1380.

The claim has no basis in fact. It rests on an assertion, made in 1784, by the German-Scots naturalist Johann Reinhold Forster that "Prince Zichmni"—who appears in letters allegedly written around the year 1400 by the Zeno brothers of Venice—led a voyage across the North Atlantic and was actually Sinclair. The claim involves the brothers Nicolo and Antonio Zeno, who allegedly entered the service of "Prince Zichmni" and explored north and west into the Atlantic.

These letters and an accompanying map were allegedly redis-covered and published in the early sixteenth century. This book was published by a member of the Zeno family in Venice in 1558, and is catchily titled *Of the unveiling of the islands of Frislanda, Eslanda, Engrouelanda, Estotilanda and Icaria made under the Arctic pole by two Zeni brothers, M. Nicolo il K. and M. Antonio* (*Dello scoprimento dell' isole Frislanda, Eslanda, Engrouelanda, Estotilanda e Icaria fatto sotto il Polo artico da' due fratelli Zeni, M. Nicolo il K. e M. Antonio*). According to various interpretations of the *Dello scoprimento*, the voyages reached several islands in the North Atlantic, and even reached Nova Scotia.[44]

However, the claim is clearly a hoax by the Zenos or their publishers.[45] Nicolo hardly left Venice and this includes the years when he is supposed to have been with Prince Zichmni. He died in Venice c. 1402. Antonio died c. 1403. There is nothing to link Sinclair to the supposed Zichmni and absolutely no reason to think that Sinclair sailed to North America.

The map, which accompanied the claim, was accepted as genuine for over a century after its publication in 1558 and confused several later cartographers and explorers. Neither it, nor the story of the voyage, adds anything to the history of the exploration of North America. Even the original hoax makes no such claim. It clearly states that Zichmni landed in Greenland (or "*Engrouelanda*").[46] It was later (including modern) writers who tried to make a connection with the New World. Even though supporters of the idea continue to make this claim, there is nothing in the material to substantiate the belief.

The Significance of These Claims in the Search for American Vikings

The tenacity of these claims over many centuries—despite the lack of convincing corroborative evidence—made it difficult for many to accept the claims made on behalf of Viking voyagers to the New World. In short, these other claims considerably muddied the waters and made people reluctant to believe the stories of the Norse.

However, while the voyages of Madoc and Henry Sinclair should be consigned to the category of unconvincing legend, that of Brendan may have rather more going for it. Details in the story, and what we have learned from the voyage of Tim Severin, mean that there is the faint possibility that some kind of reality might—just might—lie behind this strange account of seafaring monks.

Perhaps a brave set of Irish monks, determined on "White Martyrdom," did in fact cross the North Atlantic even earlier than the Norse. After all, there is good reason to think that Irish monks reached Iceland before Scandinavians did. The Irish chronicler, Dicuil, who wrote in 825, recorded that some Irish monks, seeking distant spiritual solitude, had discovered the island of Iceland sometime around the year 800. The later *Book of Icelanders* (*Islendingabok*), compiled by the Icelandic priest Ari Thorgilsson in the early twelfth century, claimed that "the Irish seekers after solitude remained in Iceland and only left when the pagan Vikings arrived."[47] Furthermore, "Icelandic traditions claimed that the Scandinavians discovered croziers (a bishop's staff, usually with a crook made from metal) and books left behind by the monks."[48]

This makes the story of Brendan a little more plausible. From Iceland, he could have made the same perilous journey that was later traced by Norse sailors. And it is possible, as we have noted, that a lingering memory of an earlier voyage may have encouraged the later Viking explorations westward, even if the Norse sources share none of the credit with the earlier Irish monks.

However, even if this was so, Brendan still cannot oust the Vikings from their position of being the first to have their voyages *archaeologically attested*. While a memory of an earlier voyage may have fed into the Norse understanding of lands lying far to the west, only the Vikings can categorically be stated to have made it to those distant western shores. While the other adventurers may, indeed, share the stage with Vikings, they only have walk-on parts when compared to the main Viking events.

CHAPTER SEVEN

COMPETING ETHNIC ORIGIN MYTHS OF "DISCOVERY," IN THE EARLY USA

Before we look at other possible evidence for Viking settlement in North America—beyond that at L'Anse aux Meadows, which can be fairly closely connected to the medieval sagas—it is necessary to pause for a moment and consider how these Viking saga-claims played a part in eighteenth-century and nineteenth-century debates over origin myths in the USA. This is because this was a formative period in the cultural history of the early United States, as writers with a European heritage sought to establish who were the first "discoverers" of North America. We should add, at this point, that for these writers and thinkers this meant which Old World *non–Native American* explorers were the first to find and then settle in what Europeans called the "New World." In this cocktail of competing origin myths, the Vikings became an important ingredient. And, in time, their importance in this debate helps explain

much of what came next in the search for any evidence that had
survived in the newly minted USA.

Competing Origin Stories: The Rise and (Relative) Decline of Columbus

In the English-speaking colonies that were founded, in what would
one day become the United States of America, origin myths started
fairly early on. Everyone knew that the first European to reach
North America was John Cabot (Giovanni Caboto), whose 1497
voyage, commissioned by the English king, Henry VII, sailed from
Bristol, England, and made landfall probably either on Newfoundland or on the nearby Cape Breton Island. No one at the time in
England knew about the Viking expeditions of the late tenth or
early eleventh century, but it is one of the intriguing coincidences
of history that Cabot landed in the same general area as these Norse
explorers had, centuries earlier.

Despite the historic role of Cabot, there was myth woven into
the narrative of "discovery" from early on. We have seen how as
early as 1559, Humphrey Llwyd's unpublished *Chronicle of Wales*
(*Cronica Walliae*) was promoting the mythical voyage to America
of Madoc ap Owain Gwynedd. It was a claim which gained more
attention in 1584, following the publication of David Powel's *Historie of Cambria, Now Called Wales*. It served to challenge Spanish
claims of preeminence in the Americas.

After the American Revolution of the eighteenth century, John
Cabot was displaced in the popular imagination by Christopher
Columbus. This raises the intriguing question of why Columbus
was considered to be a suitable person as a founding figure within
the newly minted United States, given that he had never set foot

on the land that would later become the USA. During his lifetime Columbus thought he had landed in some hitherto unexplored part of Asia in 1492. The answers are complex.

In many ways, Christopher Columbus was a useful figure when eighteenth-century Americans sought to celebrate their origins in a way that downplayed their recent position as colonial subjects of the British Crown.[1] It is surely significant that it was in the last decades of the eighteenth century—as Americans created a post-British identity—that the North American myth of Columbus developed and was adapted and promoted in the new nation. William Robertson's book, *History of America* (1778), proved to be highly influential in this formative process. It devoted hundreds of pages to the story of Columbus,[2] and was "available to more American colonists than was any earlier source."[3] In October 1792, Jeremy Belknap (1744–98), of the recently established Massachusetts Historical Society, delivered an important "Columbus Day" address, in Boston. In it, he suggested that America should have been named "Columbia." Many others agreed with this point of view and argued that the Americas and the nation of America itself had been misnamed by celebrating Amerigo Vespucci, since his role (they argued) was minor when compared with the achievements of Columbus.[4] As the American Revolution approached, there had been those who favored Columbia as the name of the soon-to-be new nation.[5]

Following the break from Britain, the names of Columbus and Washington were frequently linked when the virtues of the new nation were extolled.[6] This idea of a duumvirate of foundational figures is revealed in some early naming practices. While the US capital was named "Washington," the government district within which it was located—ceded by Virginia and Maryland in 1791—was named the District of Columbia. As if this is not emphatic enough, Washington's farewell address was published in 1796 as "Columbia's Legacy."[7]

Overall, there were several things working in Columbus's favor as he was reimagined in the new republic. He started well as a useful figure because he was not British. He was, therefore, free from any association with the old colonial rulers. On top of that, the revolutionary Americans thought that they had identified someone else who had been dependent on monarchs who had not recognized his true worth. In this convenient construction, he reminded them of their own problems in dealing with King George III. In such ways are national myths born. Columbus's westward adventures also seemed to point the way to their own further western expansion at the expense of the Native American nations; albeit with a long way further westward for the new nation yet to travel. They also liked his gritty determination which appeared to prefigure the kind of rugged individualism that they so valued in their own emerging self-image. And, finally, while Columbus's achievements were those of a Catholic (a bit of a problem for American Protestants), they could side-step this by latching onto the providential tone in which the Christian discovery of the New World was couched.[8]

However, the Columbus myth soon ran into some problems. During the second half of the nineteenth century the mythical status of Columbus began to be questioned in the USA. As we will shortly see, that occurred at an opportune moment for the Viking contenders for the role of "American Discoverers."

The threat first came in the form of the Mayflower Pilgrims. Their impeccable English Protestant character (never mind they were religious radicals on the run) stood out in an age when "From 1880 to 1924, some four million [Catholic] immigrants from southern Italy came to America, joining an earlier group of Italian

immigrants, mainly from the northern peninsula."[9] In response
to this large number of new Catholic immigrants, the established
American-born population frequently reacted with both anxiety and
hostility.[10] Poor Columbus, so useful when replacing the British,
was now falling victim to emerging American "nativism." On the
other hand, the Italian newcomers worked hard to keep the focus on
Columbus as a response to this ethnic antagonism.[11] Mythmaking
is complex.

Despite this, Columbus did not vanish as an origin myth but
the water was getting muddied. The World's *Columbian* Exposition
of 1893 in Chicago was originally scheduled to celebrate the four-
hundredth anniversary of Columbus's voyage in 1892—but he was
no longer in the pole position that he had once held. And the way
he was presented was getting rather complex and contradictory. The
confidence was going out of the movement, even as 1492 was being
celebrated.[12] Other myths had formed to challenge him. He never
quite went away, but things would never again be as they had been
in the Halcyon Days of Columbian fame in the late eighteenth and
early nineteenth centuries.

Today, even the celebration of Columbus Day—first celebrated
in New York in 1792—is on the wane, and several states have
replaced it with celebrations of Indigenous Peoples' Day. Berkeley,
California was the first of a growing number of US cities to replace
Columbus Day with a celebration of Indigenous Peoples' Day, in
1992. Now, Columbus Day is not even a city holiday in Columbus,
Ohio. How times—and national myths—change.

As Columbus waned, two other origin myths emerged. The
first continues to hold center stage. The second has always played
second fiddle to it, but—even in that secondary role—Vikings
could finally have some of the limelight. But first, the legendary
role of 1620.

Enter the Mayflower Pilgrims . . .

From the eighteenth century onward, the significance of the Mayflower Pilgrims of 1620 increased as a counterpoint to Catholic
Columbus. As mythical founders, they were attractive in a number
of ways. In sharp contrast to the Jamestown, Virginia settlement
founded in 1607, the little colony which was established at Plymouth, Massachusetts in 1620 was based on families and—while it
also included economic migrants—was overwhelmingly considered
to be a "godly enterprise." With its aim of building a "New Jeru-
salem" of holiness in the American "wilderness," it could easily be
presented as brave families of pioneers marked out by their religious
faith. This offered a more attractive origin myth than the testos-
terone fueled—mostly male—colony of Jamestown, to the south.

Along with the much larger body of immigrants who arrived
in Massachusetts Bay from 1630 to 1645, the Mayflower Pilgrims
had a profound sense of being on the right side of history. Or, as
they would have said it, being in line with God's providence. In
this, they were more distinctive, ordered, and unified than the
other seventeenth-century European colonies in North America.[13]
The "godly venture" in Massachusetts was a fine public relations
opportunity for later mythmakers because it went hand in hand
with a sense of supreme confidence as later Americans continued to
stamp their ownership on the new land. This became a key ingredient in the idea of an "American Israel," which was exceptional and
blessed by God. Ongoing ideas of American exceptionalism owe a
great deal to this. And, while Church and state were separate, it was
clear which was meant to influence which. This was to be another
enduring legacy in the USA.

This characteristic was accompanied by an emphasis on
"choice" and "contract," whereby people chose freely to be part of

a community and had rights and obligations as members. Rooted in the Mayflower Compact, signed onboard ship in November 1620—which drew together all the male signatories in a joint enterprise—it was an attractive source of later US identity as a community of empowered citizens.

This fed into the idea of Thanksgiving. In 1817, New York State was the first to announce an annual Thanksgiving holiday. Other states followed, although there was no unanimity regarding the day(s) chosen for it. It was devised through focusing on the famous Harvest Home celebrated by the Pilgrims at Plymouth in the autumn of 1621 (which they never called a "Thanksgiving"). But Thanksgiving was here to stay.

In 1863, President Abraham Lincoln proclaimed Thanksgiving on the final Thursday in November. After the Civil War ended in 1865, traditions of how to mark Thanksgivings varied from region to region but continued the trend of community festivities seen before the Civil War and harking back to 1621. Consequently, Thanksgivings became marked by community events, sports, and feasts, as well as family meals. People in fancy dress spilled onto the streets of New York in the 1890s. The Mayflower Pilgrims were firmly on the calendar. Columbus had nothing to offer which could compete with this.

Nevertheless, although they added very important religious and cultural ingredients to the US origin myth, no one could claim that the Pilgrims were the *first* Europeans to "discover" North America. So, it was back to Columbus or Cabot, although, as we have seen, Cabot's connection to English imperialism always rather dogged him in the competition for primacy in the search for the most satisfying origin myth, and Columbus was too Catholic and Italian. So, maybe, there was someone else?

Which brings us to the rise of the Vikings in the competition for European mythical discoverers of America. For, even while the

Pilgrims were rising to prominence, the foundations of the Norse challenge were being laid. And, even as Columbus was being celebrated in a rather conflicted way in 1893, Vikings were once again on the move. And they were starting their campaign in some unusual places, geographically speaking. But then, mythmaking is a complex and a malleable process, as we shall see.

The Emergence of the Vikings as North American Discoverers

As we have seen, during the nineteenth century the primacy of Columbus was challenged as that of Cabot had been before him. And the Mayflower Pilgrims were not the only contenders for the new role of prime origin myth. Enter the Vikings. While they would never displace the Mayflower Pilgrims, with their sacred mission and the popularity of their reimagined Thanksgiving, Vikings would make a pitch for a place in the mythmaking sphere.

As early as 1773, Benjamin Franklin wrote to the Boston minister, Reverend Samuel Mather, that "about 25 years since," a learned Swede had persuaded him that "America was discovered by their Northern People long before the time of Columbus."[14] That would place Franklin's conversion to the Viking theory in about 1748. That is very early in the history of the rediscovery of the Norse option. Mather was prepared to imagine all kinds of ancient peoples who might have traveled to America in the distant past and this included "the Norwegians and Icelanders."[15]

In 1816, the *New York Weekly Museum* printed a recent lecture by Dr. Mitchill, in the College of Physicians, concerning "the migration [in the distant past] of Malays, Tartars and Scandinavians, to America."[16] These included those "from Lapland, Norway, and Finland who, before the tenth century . . . settled themselves in a country which they called Vinland."[17] Dating this to "before the tenth century" was a century too early but was in the right general time frame and he was clearly basing this suggestion on some knowledge of the Icelandic sagas. In a twist, which vividly illustrated the racist attitudes of his time, he declared that these Scandinavians settled in the eastern region of what became the USA and were responsible for any impressive earthworks located in western New York State, because these could not possibly have been built by Native Americans and were clearly "of Danish character." However, after long and bloody warfare, they were defeated by the Iroquois and the land reverted to "a range for bears, beavers, bisons, and deer."[18] The survivors retreated to Labrador. In one go, he both made a pitch for the importance of the Norse and also denigrated the Native Americans, who were in his view incapable of building complex structures. In short, find a fort—credit the Norse!

Just five years later, in 1821, the posthumously published *Travels in New England and New York*, written by Timothy Dwight, postulated varied origins for those who, in antiquity, had discovered America, and included in this "from the north of Europe."[19] While not an endorsement of Vikings, it was a nod in their direction. The podium of original discoverers was getting rather crowded, but the Norse kept getting a mention. And that trend was about to accelerate decisively.

In 1837, the Danish historian, translator, and antiquarian, Carl Christian Rafn, published the medieval *Vinland* sagas, translated into Danish and Latin, with an English summary "for the benefit of American readers."[20] His *Antiquitates Americanae, sive Scriptores Septentrionales rerum Ante-Columbianarum* (*Antiquities of America, or the Writings of the Historians of the North about Pre-Columbian America*) led to what has been termed "the Viking Revival" in the

USA.[21] Furthermore, he claimed to have identified Viking-Age artifacts along America's eastern seaboard to corroborate the idea of Vikings as discoverers of America.[22] Interestingly, Rafn never visited the USA.

Nevertheless, this was a century before anyone found archaeological proof of the Viking settlement on Newfoundland. It is evidence of a growing focus on the Vikings and North America, which led to something of a Viking-frenzy of "finds" long before archaeologists could definitively prove the sagas to be correct. This search for Vikings was fueled by an increased awareness of the saga-claims. And it was an increased awareness which enabled these claims to rapidly expand beyond the relatively small number of people who both spoke a Scandinavian language and could also read Old Norse and knew something about the sagas. American Vikings were about to massively expand their supporter base—and this was a century before the discoveries at L'Anse aux Meadows. In this process, they benefitted from the crisis in the origin-myth-creation situation in the USA in the nineteenth-century. Columbus was about to discover a very tenacious set of competitors.

In the late 1830s, as the two Old Norse sagas which were relevant to the *Vinland* voyages were published in English, they were commented on in both academic circles and in the popular press.[23] This further popularized the Viking-American connection. The place *Vinland* was suddenly on the mental map, although nobody at that point could prove it archaeologically. Rafn's ideas reached a wider audience via an abridged version, titled *The Discovery of America by the Northmen* (1841), by North Ludlow Beamish. Beamish also used the book to "advance the prior claims of the Irish to have discovered America."[24] Additionally, he claimed that continental America was known to the Vikings as "White Man's Land," from references to a place named *Hvitramannaland,* which Norse sources (that appeared in Rafn's book) indicated lay near *Vinland*.[25] This was picked up in the southern states, prior to the Civil War, since the idea of a land named from its white men appeared to be consistent with their own view of the world. The novelist William Gilmore Simms even went so far as claiming that this land was none other than "our own dearly beloved region of South Carolina and Georgia."[26] The Vikings were thus coopted by white supremacists in a location far to the south of anywhere they had actually reached.

Then, in 1874, Rasmus Bjørn Anderson, a professor of Scandinavian studies at the University of Wisconsin-Madison, published *America Not Discovered by Columbus*. This encouraged the idea that the Vikings had visited New England repeatedly from the tenth to the fourteenth centuries. In addition, it connected the Norse and the New England cultural elite in a common ethnic bond of white north Europeans. This underscored the idea of a northern European basis of settlement older than the voyage of the Mayflower and the earlier arrival of the southern-European Columbus. The book was very popular among the non-academic public, and, although reactions to it by academics were mixed, it proved influential in publicizing the Viking claim to a wide readership.

Vikings were now firmly in the American mind, if not yet on the American map. It was an idea that would eagerly be taken up by nineteenth-century Scandinavian-American politicians.[27] Icelanders who migrated to Canada and to the USA, particularly in the period 1870–1914, sought to establish an "ancestral connection" to their new home.[28] Other Scandinavian settlers did the same. The saga place known as *Vinland* had been "transfigured into an imagined landscape for the projection of dreams."[29] Vikings were on a roll.

That the Christian Norse would have been Catholics like Columbus was overcome by the reassuring assertion that Scandinavia had finally become firmly Protestant. By a process of cultural back-transmission this helped make the Vikings acceptable.[30] After all, in time they had developed into the sturdy—and Protestant godly—Norwegians, Danes, and Swedes who emigrated to the United States in the nineteenth century. While not as theologically sound as the Mayflower Pilgrims, this helped the image of Leif Eriksson, in the minds of many who promoted him. In this sense, the Vikings stood out from Columbus and from Italian-Americans who were pleased to promote him as the "discoverer of America." The latter and the former were and remained staunchly Catholic. In this construct, Leif Eriksson was the true "discoverer" of America, not Christopher Columbus.[31] And Leif's heirs were Protestants.

The idea of the eleventh-century Norse as discoverers was "coupled with the idea of northern Europeans as racially and culturally superior, and so the legitimate owners of Native American lands."[32] This idea brought together settlers who were descended from the English, such as the Mayflower and later Puritan immigrants, and the Norse, in "a fusion of Anglo-Saxon and Viking blood," that has been tapped as a myth from the nineteenth to the twenty-first century. To put it frankly: "the Norse discovery of America was to become entangled with racist notions of 'Anglo-Saxon' superiority and exceptionalism, fortified by 'Viking blood.'"[33]

From the US rediscovery of the saga-evidence to the present world of white supremacists and QAnon, the idea of muscular Germanic superiority has been used as justification for dispossession of Native Americans, discrimination against Irish (despite Brendan the Voyager), Italians (despite Columbus), Jews, Americans of African descent, and Hispanics. Indeed, anyone who was or is not white North European. We shall return to this shadowy legacy of American Vikings in a later chapter but suffice it to say at this point that there have been examples of it from the time that the Vikings first made it onto the cultural radar of nineteenth-century America.

As we shall see, when we examine the Scandinavian discoverers of the Kensington Runestone in the next chapter (chapter 8), they did so in the generation after the Dakota War of 1862, following which many in the new Scandinavian pioneer communities were keen to emphasize their title to land that had been taken from the eastern Dakota (also known as the Santee Sioux). White warrior ancestors were attractive forebears to claim in such a contested situation. Swedish settlement of the area accelerated after the defeat of the Native Americans in the 1860s. Consequently, Vikings could be used to compete with the land claims of Native Americans, as well as the Catholic supporters of Columbus, and the descendants of the Mayflower Pilgrims in affluent (and influential) New England. The Viking heritage was rapidly "weaponized" by some people in such a situation of ethnic competition.

At the Norse-American Centennial in honor of the one-hundredth anniversary of the arrival of the first official group of Norwegian immigrants in the United States, at the Minnesota State Fair, in 1925, President Calvin Coolidge hailed Leif Eriksson as the discoverer of America. This was largely due to work by Norwegian-American scholars such as Knut Gjerset and Ludvig Hektoen and built on the earlier interest in the *Vinland* voyages. Then, in 1930, Wisconsin became the first US state to officially promote a Leif Eriksson Day as a state holiday. In 1931, Minnesota followed suit. By 1956, Leif Eriksson Day had been made an official holiday in seven states (California, Colorado, Illinois, Minnesota, South Dakota, Washington, Wisconsin) and the Canadian province of Saskatchewan. The federal US government has observed the day on October 9 since 1964, by annual proclamation.

In 2009, President Obama declared that it was a day "to honor Leif Erikson and celebrate our Nordic-American heritage."[34] In 2020, President Trump described it as being "Accomplished in the face of daunting danger and carried out in service of Judeo-Christian values, Leif Erikson's story reflects the fundamental truths about the American character."[35]

In 2022, President Biden's proclamation stated that "Widely believed to be the first Europeans to set foot on this continent, he and his crew embodied traits that would come to define a uniquely American spirit—restless and bold, brave and optimistic, and in search of a better future." Furthermore, "It remains ingrained in the hearts of roughly 11 million Americans who trace their ancestry to Nordic countries today."[36] This conjunction of Viking adventurers with perceived US values helps explain the cultural attraction of the Vikings that we will explore in greater detail in later chapters, as we chart their modern progress and supporters. In this, they have become players in the "Culture Wars" of the twenty-first century. But that is getting ahead of our story.

While Leif Eriksson Day is enthusiastically celebrated in many communities with Scandinavian ancestry and is especially popular in the upper Midwest, the day is designated an *observance* and not a federal public holiday in the United States.[37] In contrast, Columbus Day is a state holiday in twenty-two states, a state legal holiday in Tennessee, and a federal holiday in twenty-eight states.[38] So, the Italian explorer has managed to fight off a significant part of the Viking challenge, even while losing ground to increasing recognition of Native American history and culture on that day. Nevertheless, the Vikings are now on the US holiday calendar.

This rather obscure holiday (well, obscure to many US citizens who do not have Scandinavian heritage) gained additional publicity when it featured in an episode of the Nickelodeon animated series SpongeBob SquarePants in 2001.[39] We are told that "Every day is a holiday for SpongeBob, even if he has to make one up." Dressed as a Viking (wearing a horned helmet of course), with red beard (as in Erik the Red?) and plaited moustache, the aquatic hero greets the viewers with "Hey everybody, it's Leif Eriksson Day," and some allegedly Norse sounding noises (*Hinga dinga durgen*),[40] which do not represent any genuine Scandinavian terms. Arguably, the implication of how the episode is introduced would appear to be that the holiday is so obscure that viewers may consider that SpongeBob has invented it. This is not how Congress and Scandinavian-American communities had envisaged it being celebrated.

Even as the Vikings were making a play for attention in 1892, something more solid than renewed awareness of the sagas and their claims was about to emerge. And when it did so, it sparked a search on the ground for American Vikings that continues unabated. L'Anse aux Meadows may have become the poster-site for Vikings in North America since the 1960s, but its discovery was way behind the curve in the hunt for physical evidence. That had started long before any spades were wielded and turf was cut on that Newfoundland site. The widely publicized celebration of Vikings leaving behind solid evidence of their presence first started far from the eastern seaboard of the USA, in the unlikely location of Minnesota. Although, as we turn to examine that ground-breaking, debate-starting phenomenon, we will see that, maybe, such a discovery in the Midwest was not quite as unlikely as it might first appear.

CHAPTER EIGHT

VIKINGS IN THE MIDWEST?

The part played by the Norse in the origin-myths-debate of the early United States helps explain why a search was soon under way to discover traces they may have left behind. The beginning of this search long predated the twentieth-century excavations at L'Anse aux Meadows and went well beyond it in terms of the geographical scope of the search, as we shall see.

The Norse "Wild West"

For Viking adventurers of the tenth and eleventh centuries, what we now call North America was their "Wild West." Situated beyond the furthest settled Norse communities on Iceland and Greenland, this frontier was on the very edge of their known world.

In common with the more recent use of that western term, it also involved long and perilous journeys, conflict with native peoples, heroic—sometimes mythical—events, larger-than-life characters, high drama, and tragedy. It was the original "Wild West."

It is therefore perhaps not surprising that people living in the nineteenth-century US "Wild West" were some of the first to declare that they had found physical evidence of Vikings who had explored westward in the distant past. Two concepts of the "Wild West" were about to come together in the most extraordinary way. And when that occurred, it provided a basis for an explosion of interest in American Vikings that long predates the finds at L'Anse aux Meadows and is still ongoing.

However, before we dive further into this exploration of the search for Viking penetration of America, it will be helpful just to briefly remind ourselves of the route by which we have come to this point. What comes next is built on that and takes it onward in time.

The Foundation for What Comes Next . . .

So far, we have explored the way in which the "Viking World" stretched far beyond the Scandinavian homelands in, what are today, Denmark, Norway, and Sweden. From the eighth century onward, raiders, traders and settlers carried a complex and contrasting mixture of destruction, trade, and Norse culture far beyond their original homelands. As we have seen, in the ninth century Danish and Norwegian Vikings devastated the communities and monasteries of the Anglo-Saxon kingdoms and seized control of large areas in the east and north of England. At the same time, they brought fire and destruction to the Irish lands—but also founded the trading settlement of Dublin. The northern and western isles of Scotland saw Pictish culture obliterated by this same wave of raiders and settlers. Down the North Sea coast of Europe, trading centers were looted and burnt. Paris was besieged and Brittany devastated.

Early raiders were followed by later settlers. Then the first Viking colonists took Norse culture from Norway and Ireland to Iceland and began to explore even further westward; the start of a movement that would eventually take them to Greenland and then, even further west, to North America.

During the tenth century, the expansion continued. The kings of France were forced to cede Normandy (the province of the "North men") to settlers who could not be dislodged. New waves of incomers turned England into an "Anglo-Norse" land. Islamic Spain and North Africa, and also Italy, were raided. Originating from these Mediterranean communities, unfortunate captives (termed *bluemen* by Norse-speakers) appeared in the slave markets of Dublin. There they mingled African DNA with the Irish DNA being spread throughout the northern Viking world, as slaves accompanied the exploration of their new masters and mistresses, including to North America.

In the east, we have seen how Vikings from Sweden pushed down the rivers of Russia—into the Slavic lands and beyond. The first Russian state of *Kyiv/Kiev Rus* was established in Ukraine by the middle of the tenth century. Constantinople was besieged, but the raiders were fought off. Islamic sources refer to Viking traders appearing at Baghdad in modern Iraq in a far-flung trading venture.

This was all made possible by a complex mixture of warriors, traders, pirates, and adventurers. It was muscular free enterprise that traded when the opposition was strong and raided where it was weak, disunited, and vulnerable.

As we have seen, "going Viking" was a complex and flexible business. In its broadest sense, it involved women and children, as well as the testosterone-fueled young men of popular imagination. We will need to bear this in mind as we consider the evidence for its North American manifestation. We have already seen how women and children played a role in the legendary exploration of *Vinland* (see chapter 4), which we now know was based on real events of the early eleventh century. As we saw there, evidence from as recent as October 2021 means that we can now accurately date the short-lived Viking settlement that was built at L'Anse aux Meadows on Newfoundland (see chapter 5). "American Vikings"—in all their complexity—definitely made it to the New World five hundred years before Columbus (and he, of course, only made it to the Caribbean islands, and Central and South America).

Everywhere these Vikings went—whether they rapidly assimilated or held out as identifiable Norse communities—they often transformed the cultures of the lands in which they settled. Again and again, they became part of what we can call the "deep stories" and myths of modern nations. Global culture is scattered with references to these intrepid explorers and their mythology.

At times the Viking myth has been politically "weaponized." In central Moscow stands a huge monument to the Viking-Slav ruler Saint Volodymyr/Vladimir the Great, credited with the introduction of Orthodox Christianity to the proto-Russian state of *Kyiv/ Kiev Rus* in the tenth century. His life is part of the "deep story" of both Russia and Ukraine. The statue was unveiled in 2016 by Vladimir Putin. Many Ukrainians considered it a hijacking of history in the service of Russian nationalism. They had good reason to be concerned. In 2022, the unleashing of war on Ukraine by Russia had its roots in a shared Viking/Slav past and a desire to restore Russian control over an area deeply enmeshed in its ancient history.

As we continue to explore the Viking impact on America, we will come across other examples of that history and myth being actively engaged with and sometimes "weaponized."

History can have "attitude." Myths are potent. They help explain who we think we are. At times this can be benign, but sometimes it can be lethal, as in Putin's Russia and in US white supremacy. We use, and also sometimes misuse, history all the time, and Vikings offer a rich quarry for such activities.

Which brings us back to North America and the search for physical evidence of Vikings there . . .

The "Viking Wild West"?

How far did Vikings explore after reaching North America at the beginning of the eleventh century? And for how long? Starting to answer these questions involves a return to the name of that mythical land, far to the west: *Vinland*. For this will help frame something of the location of our ongoing search.

The name *Vinland* is first recorded before the thirteenth-century compilation of the Icelandic sagas and is found in the writings of the medieval German chronicler, Adam of Bremen, in Book IV of his history of the Hamburg-Bremen church, written c. 1075. In this book, the place name appears in the German form *Winland*. Adam implied that it referred to "wine," which links it to grapes. It is this name which later appears in the thirteenth-century Icelandic account, *Saga of the Greenlanders*, we explored earlier. But can this be used to give us a geographical fix on how far Vikings traveled into North America? The answer is: possibly.

The use of the word in *Saga of the Greenlanders* suggests that the reference was to the Old Norse word *vinber* (wineberries), the name for several plants from which wine could be made. This included grapes, of course, but could also encompass currants and bilberries. This opens up the geographical possibilities considerably, since these plants have very different growing ranges. The matter has been thrown even further open by the suggestion that the term *vinviður* (grapevines) found in *Saga of the Greenlanders* should actually have been the word *viður* (wood). If this is correct, then *vinber* need not have referred to grapes at all. Instead, it could have been a reference to any berries observed growing on trees.[1] Consequently, we cannot be entirely sure whether the thirteenth-century Icelandic accounts refer to wild grapes growing in North America—using a word derived from the wine-making plants mentioned earlier by Adam of Bremen—or some other wild berry capable of being fermented to make wine. As a result, we cannot be sure how far down the eastern coast of North America the eleventh-century Vikings reached.

What is clear is that they certainly did not find wild grapes growing at L'Anse aux Meadows on Newfoundland.[2] The northern range of North American wild grapes does not extend further than New Brunswick.[3] So, if it was wild grapes that defined *Vinland*, then Viking exploration went much further south down the eastern seaboard.

We can conclude that L'Anse aux Meadows, important as it is, was not *Vinland*. *Vinland* must lie further south. As we saw earlier (in chapter 5), it is possible that the site at L'Anse aux Meadows may correspond to the camp called *Straumfjord* in *Erik the Red's Saga*. In which case, *Vinland* lay beyond it.

Tantalizingly, the dig at L'Anse aux Meadows unearthed indisputable clues concerning more-southerly journeys by the Viking settlers who built the houses and workshops there. These clues take us beyond discussion over the meaning of terms for wine-making fruits. This archaeological evidence was in the form of remains of butternuts or white walnuts, which grow in the eastern United States and south-eastern Canada. Its coastal range stretches from New Brunswick to Connecticut, although they are not present continuously along the coast. These butternuts provide hard evidence regarding Viking activities further south.

A cautious conclusion can therefore be reached that *Vinland* may have been as far south as the St. Lawrence River and parts of New Brunswick. This is because this is the northernmost limit for *both* the growth of butternuts (white walnuts) and *also* of wild grapes. However, a more expansive reading of the evidence of those butternuts could stretch the Viking exploration down as far as Connecticut. The butternuts are unlikely to have reached Newfoundland via trade as they are not high enough status goods to have been traded so far.

Furthermore, given that the Vikings were adventurous users of river systems, their inland "reach" was considerable. In England, their shallow-draft ships penetrated deep inland by moving far up rivers. In Russia, such boats carried explorers from the Baltic to the Black Sea and the Caspian. In North America, any exploration of the St. Lawrence (and the wild grapes and butternuts may reveal they got at least this far south) opened up the possibility of reaching the Great Lakes. From there, exploration into what is now Upstate New York, Ohio, Indiana, Illinois, Wisconsin, and Minnesota was possible. Possible, but did it happen? How far west did the Vikings get? Just reaching Newfoundland was a stretch, that had taken them far beyond the established Viking Age settlements in Greenland. But how far did the "Viking Wild West" extend beyond that? And how might we recognize it?

The interest in Norse adventurers playing a part within the nineteenth-century US origins-myth debate explains why a search for evidence of their presence started in the second half of the nineteenth century. But what form might such Viking-evidence take? One possible answer soon became apparent—and it was located in Minnesota.

The Kensington Runestone,
Minnesota

One way we might recognize Vikings is if they left a written record where they visited. In which case it would be akin to finding something that said, in effect: "Vikings were here!" This is not as ridiculous a suggestion as it sounds.

Viking Age Norse peoples left written records on objects that used the runic alphabet. Originally derived from the Latin alphabet of the Late Roman Empire, the angular letters known as runes—devised among Scandinavian communities—were designed for easy carving on objects made from metal, bone, or stone. They appear on objects from as early as the year 200 c.e. and continued in use well into the Middle Ages, centuries after the conversion to Christianity. The runic alphabet is often referred to as the *Futhark*. There is what is termed an "Elder" and a "Younger" version of it.

Many runic inscriptions were simple statements denoting ownership, such as: "Nithijo made this" on a shield found near Skanderborg in Denmark.[4] Some were thought to have magical powers such as: "I give good luck" found on a gold disc in Denmark.[5] Many were grave markers and, especially in Sweden, could be quite extensive in their information. One example from Gripsholm Castle in Sweden also reveals the distant travels of Vikings: "Tola had this stone raised in memory of her son Haraldr, Ingvarr's brother. They traveled valiantly far for gold, and in the east gave [food] to the eagle. [They] died in the south in Serkland [Saracen land, the Islamic caliphate]."[6] Some were travelers' graffito such as: "Crusaders broke into Maeshowe. To the north-west is a great treasure hidden. It was long ago that a great treasure was hidden here. Happy is he that might find that great treasure." This is from Maeshowe on Orkney, UK.[7] One, the Hønen Runestone from Norderhov in Norway, may even record a man who traveled to North America since part of it can be read as *Vínlandi á ísa* (from Vinland over ice). However, it may be better interpreted as *vindkalda á ísa"* (over the wind-cold ice).[8] Now, finding something in North America like the Maeshowe runes or the first reading of the Hønen Runestone would be amazing . . .

In late 1898, a farming family from the rural township of Solem, in Douglas County, in the west-central part of Minnesota, claimed to have done just that. It was in that year that Swedish immigrant, Olof Öhman, was clearing land, that he had recently acquired, of trees and stumps before ploughing it. Öhman had settled in the area in 1879 and was one of several Scandinavian immigrant farmers and their families in the region.

The work on that day was focused on the crest of a small knoll rising from the surrounding wetlands. A little way below the top of the knoll, about a quarter of the way down the slope, there was a heavy growth of underbrush around a stunted aspen or poplar tree. Later estimates suggested that the tree, like those growing nearby, was between thirty to forty years old. This is relevant to the story, as we shall shortly see. This spot lay about 11 feet (3.3 m) from the summit of the 55-foot-tall (16.7 m) hill.

Olof was assisted that day by his ten-year-old son, Edward, and the two of them were straining to shift a large slab of greywacke sandstone which was wedged within the tangled roots of the stunted tree. While hauling the rock out, young Edward noticed something odd about the stone and drew the attention of his father to it. The top half of one side of the stone was inscribed with runic script. It was a quite extraordinary find and had the potential to rewrite the history of European settlement in North America. The rock is now known as the "Kensington Runestone," after the small settlement closest to the site of its discovery. For those who accept its authenticity—and there is a great deal of support for it, particularly but not exclusively, in Minnesota—the "Kensington rock" is of greater historical significance in US history than "Plymouth Rock." This is certainly in terms of historical precedence, as its *claimed* date of inscription predates the Mayflower Pilgrim's arrival at Plymouth, Massachusetts, by 258 years.

The generally accepted translation of the runes reads:

> *We are 8 Goths* [Geats or Swedes] *and 22 Norwegians on an exploration journey from Vinland through the West. We had camp by a lake with 2 skerries* [small rocky islands] *one day's journey north from this stone. We were out and fished one day. After we came home we found 10 of our men red with blood and dead. AVM* [*Ave Virgo Maria*, Hail, Virgin Mary] *save us from evil. We have 10 of our party by the sea to look after our ships, 14 days' journey from this island. Year 1362.*[9]

The story is dramatic and reminiscent of the battles fought between Vikings and so-called *skraelings* (Native Americans) recorded in the *Vinland* sagas. The link to those sagas is also apparent in the name *Vinland* that is found within the inscription. Without explicitly stating it, the inscription seems to suggest continuing knowledge and activity involving Norse explorers of North America from the earlier Viking Age to the fourteenth century.

The stone is about 30 inches (76 cm) high, 16 inches (41 cm) wide, six inches (15 cm) thick, and weighs 202 pounds (92 kg). If it was, indeed, found within the tree's root system, then it had been there well before Öhman set up his homestead in 1879, nineteen years before the discovery. Based on estimates of the ages of similar trees nearby that were examined later, the tree was apparently between thirty and forty years old when they found the stone.

At the time that the tree began to grow its roots round the stone, significant Swedish immigration into Minnesota was underway,[10] but European settlement in the area was greatly disrupted by the Dakota War of 1862, in which the eastern Dakota (also known as the Santee Sioux) attempted to drive out all settlers.

Even if the tree was only ten or twelve years old, as one later witness asserted,[11] it would mean that the stone had been in the tree's root system for some years before it was found in 1898. However, we only have Öhman's word for the stone being grasped by the tree roots and later experts have questioned whether it shows signs of root damage. Some critics have suggested that the site of the discovery, just down from the crest of the hill, should have experienced soil-wash eroding earth *away* from the area and not *depositing it* to the depth found covering the stone. The matter is clearly complex.

The stone remained in Öhman's possession until 1911, when he sold it to the Minnesota Historical Society for ten dollars. They still have the bill of sale. In 1910, the cost to support a working family of five members for one week was approximately fifteen dollars.[12] Consequently, that payment was not massive for such a potentially history-making artifact. There is evidence to suggest that the farmer was disappointed that the initial "enthusiasm for the runestone stalled and Öhman took it back to his farm where he used it as a steppingstone."[13] In which case, he may have considered that ten dollars was a fair price for it.

Today, the runestone takes pride of place in the Runestone Museum, located in downtown Alexandria, Minnesota. Indeed, when the museum opened in 1958, the runestone was the museum's only artifact. Today, though, it shares the space with additional artifacts found in Minnesota that are presented as relating to medieval Nordic explorers. The current forty-piece collection includes the "Climax fire steel," which was found in Climax, Minnesota.

This object was part of the Middle Age Nordic collection at the University Museum in Oslo before the discovery of the Kensington Runestone in 1898. The museum at Alexandria describes the Climax fire steel as "one of the only Middle Age Nordic fire steels on display in North America."[14] However, its signage reportedly describes this as "*said* [author's emphasis] to be found buried in 1870,"[15] which rather leaves open the question of whether this medieval object found its way to Minnesota in the Middle Ages or later. In the same way, with regard to the famous runestone itself, the museum website diplomatically states that "the question of its authenticity has been a lightning rod for debate."[16]

Questions over the authenticity of the Kensington Runestone have divided scholars ever since it was discovered. It was swiftly declared a forgery by most experts after its inscription was studied at the University of Minnesota and by linguists in Scandinavia.[17] However, others were—and are—convinced of its authenticity. Despite this, several problems remain.

The first problem lies within the information found in the inscription itself. It claims that the ships of the explorers lay fourteen days away from the site of the stone. The geography of the region points to this having to be on the shore of Hudson Bay, due north from the site of the stone's location. It is hard to imagine how the eight hundred miles in question could possibly have been covered in just fourteen days. The geography does not seem to add up.[18]

The second problem lies in the linguistics of the inscription. As well as there being no persuasive fourteenth-century context which would explain the presence of such a memorial runestone in Minnesota, aspects of its language, grammar, rune-forms and use of a calendar-date (1362) all argue for it being a nineteenth-century forgery, produced in an area with a strong interest in Scandinavian history, by someone wishing to create a local connection to their original homeland. It is also uncharacteristically detailed in comparison with the evidence from most authentic medieval runic inscriptions.[19]

In support of this suspicion is the discovery in 2004 of documents in Sweden which revealed a nineteenth-century use of a form of runic letters for coded communications between contemporary journeymen (people skilled in a trade or craft) in Sweden. The documents in question dated from 1883 and 1885. These were more closely related to the runic forms found on the Kensington Runestone than to any known medieval inscription. The dating of the documents, compared with the date the runestone was found in Minnesota (1898), makes it clear that they were not influenced by it. On the contrary, the dates in question would suggest that the inscriber of the Kensington stone was indebted to the nineteenth-century form of the runes in question. It is not surprising that this led one writer to conclude that "the Kensington Runestone was carved in the nineteenth century by someone from central Sweden."[20] If so, who this was cannot be conclusively ascertained.

The third problem is the condition of the stone itself. Graywacke is tough stone, but many experts feel that the runic letters lack the kind of weathering one might expect to be seen on a stone that had been engraved over five hundred years prior to its discovery.[21] One expert, in 2016, went as far as stating that "the inscription is about as sharp as the day it was carved."[22] This conclusion has been contested, though, and the matter is clearly complex, with arguments for its genuine nature still being presented.[23]

What is clear is that the area in which the stone was found was a region of Minnesota where many Scandinavian immigrants had recently settled. Öhman himself, it is reported, owned a small library which included information on runes. At the time, many settlers of Scandinavian origin were struggling to gain acceptance in a US society that was still dominated by east coast English speakers, with their history of Virginian and New England settlement, and a condescending view of rural Minnesotans.[24] And any earlier tradition than that was eclipsed by Columbus' famous voyage of 1492. In the 1890s, this dominant narrative was being contested. The "Romantic Nationalism" movement was inspiring interest in Vikings in Scandinavia and among Scandinavians settled abroad. The claims of the medieval *Vinland* sagas concerning North America were getting increasing attention in this context, both in Scandinavia and in the USA. Just five short years before the "discovery" of the Kensington Runestone, Norway had participated in the World's Columbian Exposition by sailing the *Viking*, a replica ship, to Chicago. This seems a context which would explain a nineteenth-century forgery of the stone. It is not surprising that some have concluded that "the Kensington Runestone was dug up during a suspiciously convenient period, when there was a general public appetite for all things relating to Vikings in America."[25]

However, belief in its authenticity continues in some quarters despite the strength of the academic evidence against this.[26] Displayed variously at the Smithsonian Institution, and the 1965 New York World's Fair, today the Kensington Runestone is displayed just twenty-three miles from the "discovery" site. In Minnesota, many believe passionately that it is genuine,[27] and "in that region it is a very real emblem of Scandinavian pride."[28] This investment in it as a cultural emblem makes objective assessment rather difficult and some extraordinary efforts are made to support its authenticity.

The stone is sometimes claimed to be connected to an alleged exploration of Hudson Bay associated with Nicolas of Lynn, a fourteenth-century English astronomer.[29] There is, though, no convincing evidence to support this and the assertion that Nicolas was an explorer was not made until the late sixteenth century, by Richard Hakluyt. Since Hakluyt was a promoter of English colonization of North America, his claim is likely to have been prompted by a desire to pre-empt Columbus by an Englishman and to date this a century earlier than 1492. We have seen how this also assisted the promotion of Madoc ap Owain Gwynedd at about the same time (see chapter 6).

While the jury is still out regarding the final verdict on the Kensington Runestone, the overall view among most archaeologists and historians is that it is probably a fake.[30] However, even if the inscription on the stone was carved by Olof Öhman, it tells us a great deal about the power of cultural identity and the use of it to affirm the importance of a community, especially among marginalized groups; and the ways in which "American Vikings" could contribute toward the formation of identities in the USA of the 1890s. The runestone seemed to confirm the right to possession of the land for nineteenth-century Scandinavian immigrants in Minnesota.[31] That tendency to co-opt Vikings, by modern causes, would run and run; and it is still running in the twenty-first century in many areas of life and culture. However, if the stone is genuine, it offers an astonishing insight into Norse-related exploration of the New World which continued what had started at L'Anse aux Meadows. At the very least, the Minnesota Vikings gained a memorable logo.

The Kensington Runestone is not alone in being claimed as archaeological evidence of continuing Viking involvement with North America in the centuries after the failure of the settlement at L'Anse aux Meadows in the eleventh or early twelfth centuries. There are other finds that are also argued to be clues pointing to the activities of American Vikings. Several claim to be from Viking expeditions later than the settlement at L'Anse aux Meadows, but earlier than the venture asserted to be behind the Kensington Runestone. It is to that other evidence that we shall now turn and decide what it can tell us about Vikings in America.

CHAPTER NINE

NEW ENGLAND VIKINGS?

The Kensington Runestone is, arguably, the most famous contender for being evidence of the furthest Viking penetration into the North American continent. If it is accepted as genuine, it is part of the routeway of Viking exploration that connected Greenland with Labrador and Newfoundland . . . and beyond. The implication being that—while some Norse adventurers hit the North American continent and turned left, to follow the coast down the eastern seaboard—some hardy sailors turned right and followed the shoreline until they reached the entrance of Hudson Bay. From there they traveled up the rivers which flowed into the southern section of the bay, using these as entry points into the heart of the Midwest. Either that, or they used the St. Lawrence to access the Great Lakes. From there, they explored further south and west.

Neither are particularly plausible ways to reach Minnesota, and both would have required a huge degree of effort, including porterage of ships from river system to river system. But it is just possible that this travel occurred via one of these routes. There is certainly a growing body of evidence which indicates Norse activity on the periphery of this possible routeway into the heart of North America.

"Turning Right . . ." the Vikings of the Canadian Arctic

There is persuasive evidence that Norse explorers and traders were active in Arctic Canada. On Ellesmere Island, finds of cloth woven in Scandinavian style and patterns, along with pieces of mail, often mistermed "chain mail," on sites occupied by indigenous peoples, indicates the presence of Vikings or, at least, is evidence of trading with Vikings. Ellesmere Island is Canada's most northern, and its third largest, island. It lies within the Arctic Archipelago, and is separated from Greenland to the east, by the Nares Strait. It is easy to imagine how Greenland Vikings could have visited its barren tundra coast in search of walrus ivory, polar bear skins, and seals. The find-spots are very revealing, as is the dating evidence associated with the artifacts.

Mail and cloth, the base of a barrel, iron knife blades, an iron ship rivet, and other iron and copper fragments were found among indigenous sites on Buchanan Bay, eastern Ellesmere Island.[1] All are indicative of contact with Vikings and their technologies. These sites may date from as early as the twelfth century.

On the western coast of Ellesmere Island, archaeologists discovered part of a bronze balance—an object associated with Scandinavian traders—in an indigenous settlement.[2] This suggests an actual Norse presence in the area, rather than traded goods.

An indigenous site at Port Refuge, on Devon Island, situated between Ellesmere Island and the northern coast of Baffin Island, was the find-spot of part of a cast bronze bowl and some smelted iron.[3] As with the other—more detailed—evidence, this indicates Norse activity. The context has been dated to the fifteenth century.

Further south, on Baffin Island, lying between the mouth of Hudson Bay and Greenland, the discovery of a wooden figure, 2.1 inches (5.4 cm) tall, appears to depict a Scandinavian wearing a characteristic hooded robe. Open at the front and with a cross on the chest, this is reminiscent of medieval garments from northern Europe. It is assumed that it was made locally, probably by an indigenous person who was very familiar with the newcomers.[4] It is even possible that such an apparently formal costume represented a bishop. In which case one is reminded of Bishop Erik Gnupsson,[5] and his expedition in 1121 (see chapter 5). Appealing though this identification would be, it is speculation—but remains a possibility. The find-site appears to date from "a fairly early date in the Thule period" in the development of Inuit culture. This suggests that the figure may have been carved as early as the twelfth century. However, a thirteenth-century date has also been suggested for the building within which it was discovered.[6]

This is not the only example of such an object. On Kingiktorsuag Island in northern Greenland, other carved figures found in indigenous sites dating from the thirteenth and fourteenth centuries, also clearly depicted Norsemen.[7] Not far from where these figures were discovered, three cairns and a runestone were also found, dating possibly from the fourteenth century. The runestone has been read as "Erling Sigvatsson, Bjarne Tordsson and Eindride Oddsson erected these cairns on Saturday before Rogation Day [the fifth Sunday after Easter Sunday] and runed well."[8]

Less dramatic than these finds, is the spun cordage and other artifacts, similar to those found on medieval European sites, which were recently recognized during a reexamination of an archaeological collection excavated from Baffin Island. Since this discovery, similar material has been identified from two other sites on Baffin Island and another one in northern Labrador.[9] These various sites span a coastal distance of over 932 miles (1,500 km) which indicates the widespread nature of the Norse interaction with native peoples in the Canadian Arctic. These join a growing list of artifacts, from tally-sticks to willow baskets, which suggest they were made by Greenland Norse.[10]

Although this evidence is fragmentary and scattered, it indicates trade over a long period of time, particularly in the twelfth and thirteenth centuries, between Scandinavians and indigenous peoples of the Canadian Arctic. This probably was based on the exchange of Norse metal objects for animal products of the Arctic. Some of these Norse artifacts may have changed owners several times over an extended trade network via indigenous middle-men and -women, while others may indicate the presence of Viking traders visiting these native sites. This clearly supports the idea of "Norse hunters who had come as far north [and west] as this, and who traded [with indigenous peoples]."[11] It is also highly likely that they traveled west in search of timber, which was not available in Greenland. And this wood was certainly not traded via a series of exchanges. Viking lumberjacks sailed directly to *Vinland* and cut down these trees. There is no other way that the Greenlanders could have maintained their maritime shipbuilding activities over several centuries. Other sources of such wood—in Norway—were just too far away.

This is evidence to support the idea of Vikings who explored round the shores of Greenland, or who reached the North American continent and, basically, "turned right." By this roundabout route, they *could* have reached the Upper Midwest. But what of the other option?

What If the Vikings
"Turned Left"?

More plausible than routes into the heart of the continent via
Hudson Bay or the St. Lawrence, are the claims regarding Viking
sites on the eastern seaboard southwest of Newfoundland. This is
especially so, given hard evidence for Viking voyages down the
eastern coast, as seen in some of the finds from L'Anse aux Meadows.
These sites on the eastern seaboard include the Yarmouth Rock
(Nova Scotia), the Maine Penny, Spirit Pond runestones (Maine),
carvings at Dighton Rock (Massachusetts), the Stone Tower at Newport (Rhode Island), and the Narragansett Runestone (Rhode Island).

These raise two important questions. Do they *really* constitute
evidence of North American Vikings moving down the eastern
coast of North America? Or do these tell us more about the grip
of Vikings on later imaginations? It is to this "evidence," that we
now turn.

Yarmouth Rock, Nova Scotia

Yarmouth Rock, also known as the Fletcher Stone, is a slab of
quartzite on display at the Yarmouth County Museum. It first came
to public attention in the early part of the nineteenth century.[12] It
appears to have an inscription carved into it, consisting of thirteen
characters, which have been interpreted as Norse runes of the kind
found on the Kensington Runestone. As a result, there has been
much speculation regarding whether this area of Nova Scotia was
visited by Viking explorers around the same time as settlement
occurred at L'Anse aux Meadows. However, the matter has been
contested—as in the stone from Kensington—with some asserting

that the "runes" were a hoax or may even have been created by natural forces leaving marks on the rock.

The purported runic inscription can be found near the top of a naturally smooth face of the rock, which does not appear to have been dressed. The "runes" are between 1 and 1½ inches (25 mm to 40 mm) high. The small patches of green paint on the stone were caused by earlier display arrangements. The date "1007" (rather an assumption, one might add) has been marked on it to the left of the inscription.

The modern history of the object begins with a retired British military surgeon, Richard Fletcher, who settled in Yarmouth in 1809. He found the stone on land, near the Chegoggin Flats, on the western side of Yarmouth Harbor.[13] This location was near the Salt Pond, part of which had been a salt marsh since 1799. In 1812, he revealed his discovery of the stone, and ownership passed to the Yarmouth Public Library in the early twentieth century. From there it passed to the Yarmouth County Museum.

The stone became known to a wider audience in 1884. It was then that Henry Phillips Jr., who was the corresponding secretary of the Numismatic and Antiquarian Society of Philadelphia, published a paper in the *Proceedings of the American Philosophical Society* claiming that the inscription was in a runic script. Furthermore, he believed that it could be made to read "*Harkussen men varu*," which he translated as "Hako's son addressed the men." Phillips identified Hako as one of the men of Thorfinn Karlsefni's expedition.[14] This was based on information in *The Saga of the Greenlanders* and *Erik the Red's Saga*. Looking at the way he came to this conclusion— "word after word appeared in disjointed forms, and each was in turn rejected until at last an intelligible word came forth"[15]— does not exactly inspire this writer with confidence concerning the identification. It rather smacks of looking at a cloud long enough until an apparent pattern or picture, appears.

Phillips's "translation" is not the only contender. In 1934, Olaf Strandwold claimed that the stone was inscribed by command of Leif Eriksson, in honor of his father. He thought that the inscription could be read as: "Leif to Eric raises [a monument]."[16]

This illustrates several points: the difficulty in identifying the marks as runic; and, if runic, the variety of words and meanings that might be represented by such an abbreviated form. The latter can be a problem, even when dealing with runestones where the provenance and nature of the markings are much more persuasive.

Despite these complexities, in the 1930s, there was even talk of establishing a small national park at the site and a "Yarmouth Leif Eriksson Society" was formed. The president of both the local history society and the "Leif Eriksson Society"—Reverend Gordon Lewis—even suggested that the Norse had established a village at the site. It should be noted that there is no archaeological evidence to substantiate this claim. More worryingly, it has been claimed that:

> Lewis believed in the stone so passionately that he took the bold step of "improving" it. The recalcitrant markings were allegedly "clarified" under his ministrations with hammer and chisel, transforming the faint tracings described in the nineteenth century into the much more emphatic text of the twentieth. (Herein lies one possible explanation for the striking difference between pre- and post-1930s images of the artifact.)[17]

Others were also unconvinced regarding the stone's purported Viking origins. Professor of archaeology A. D. Fraser suggested that it might have been an old quarry block. As significant, he concluded that he did "not see anything here that is more runic than Roman or Cypriote or of any other system that one might name."[18]

Today, most are skeptical regarding its authenticity, and it has been remarked that "the [Yarmouth] Historical Society wisely makes no claim for it."[19] Nevertheless, we cannot reject it outright. There are some aspects of the find which may keep it within the bounds of possibility. The most important of these being its relative proximity to the authenticated site in Newfoundland, which had been unknown in 1812 when Fletcher revealed the stone.

Spirit Pond Runestones, Maine

In 1971, three stones were allegedly found on state land at the edge of Spirit Pond, near Popham Beach, near Phippsburg, Maine. One of the stones features a roughly scratched map, accompanied by runic letters on one side, with a few runes and some crude drawings on the other. The second of the stones has twelve runic letters on one side. The third stone has a long message of fifteen lines (some accounts add another line, but this seems far from certain), neatly inscribed on both sides of the stone.[20] The Spirit Pond runestones are handheld objects, which are similar to the authentic Kingittorsuaq Runestone, which was discovered in Greenland in 1824. The stones are now in the Maine State Museum, in Augusta.

Intriguingly, the "map" contained the place names *Hop* and *Vinland* on it. On one hand, this might appear to be an extraordinary vindication of the search for American Vikings because these names are so familiar from the saga evidence. On the other hand, it is their very familiarity which may point to the stones being fakes.

After all, what better than an object that carries a label saying what it is? It all sounds just a little too tidy.

Investigation of the site found no further evidence of a Norse presence.[21] More tellingly, as with many such alleged runestones, the form, content, and structure of the inscriptions are noticeably different from the usual pattern on such stones. Not surprisingly, most rune experts are not persuaded of their authenticity.[22]

The finder was a Maine carpenter named Walter J. Elliott Jr. He took the stones to the Bath Maritime Museum, where the director, Harold Brown, suggested that the marks might be runic.[23]

The stones were then studied by Einar Haugen, professor of Scandinavian languages and history at Harvard. He published an evaluation which described the find as being "a few Norse words in a sea of gibberish."[24] Most other experts have tended to agree with Haugen's assessment.

An exception was Professor Cyrus Gordon, an orientalist at Brandeis and New York Universities, in his 1974 book *Riddles of the Past*, who adopted a more positive approach to the possibility of the authenticity of the stones. Another is Suzanne Carlson, of the New England Antiquities Research Association (NEARA). NEARA mostly represents the views of nonprofessionals in the field of archaeological study. Carlson has suggested a possible translation of the long inscription as follows:

> *See—pay heed to* [this]—*Odin cries*
> *To see seventeen dead—praise them*
> *We prayer our prayer—year twenty*
> *The company picked twelve companions*
> *Twelve began west*
> *Ten north, they tell of young*

bearded doomed man that Haakon
found surrounded in the water
the man adrift was handed over as a hostage
We prayer our prayer—year twelve
A gale breaks forth, wind blows up
On the sea. Oh! Fainthearted those that sail the ship
From Ægir, seventeen made red with blood
Gushing, cut the course that caused death
Praise them
We pray our prayer—year M-two [25]

As can be seen, several numbers appear in the inscription. These are: (year) 20, (year) 12, and (year) M2. It has been suggested that Year 20 refers to the twentieth year of the reign of King Magnus VII (Eriksson), of Norway, or 1339. This is the time period in which a visit occurred to the abandoned western colony in Greenland, amid reports that the dwindling settlement had reverted to pagan beliefs. Carlson, who has suggested this date, has also asserted that linguistic forms on the stones are consistent with a less-than-sophisticated Greenland culture when compared with practices in Norway at the time. In 1974, the excavation of two small houses on the edge of Spirit Pond produced only Colonial-era artifacts but with a carbon-14 date of 1405 plus or minus seventy years. This led Carlson to conclude that: "The evidence of runic style and language use weighs heavily on the side of the stones being authentic 14th-century artifacts deposited in Maine."[26]

Most academic researchers would be far more skeptical about the authenticity of these stones, with many considering them to be fakes.[27] At the end of this short examination, they will be placed in the "hoax" category.

The "discovery" of the stones, and the eagerness of many to accept them as authentic, is reflected in the gently satirical novel *Runestruck* (1977), by Calvin Trillin.[28] The novel is set in a fictional Maine coastal town, where an engraved rock is discovered during clamming. Soon the fictional community is planning a "Viking Village and Beach Recreation Area," and locals start calling the town's "Yankee Café" by the new name of "Leif's Lair."[29]

Dighton Rock, Massachusetts

Dighton Rock juts out of the Taunton River at Assonet Neck, opposite the town of Dighton, Massachusetts. It measures c. 10 feet (3 m) long and 5 feet (1.5 m) high. When Harvard graduate John Danforth made a copy of some of the marks on the rock in 1680, he concluded that it was the work of Native Americans and depicted an encounter and battle with visitors who arrived by ship.[30] In 1963, the rock was removed from the river and has since been housed in a small museum located within Dighton Rock State Park.

In 1690, the New England Puritan leader, Cotton Mather, recorded in *The Wonderful Works of God Commemorated* that:

> *Among the other Curiosities of New-England, one is that of a mighty Rock, on a perpendicular side whereof by a River, which at High Tide covers part of it, there are very deeply Engraved, no man alive knows How or When about half a score Lines, near Ten Foot Long, and a foot and half broad, filled with strange Characters: which would suggest as odd Thoughts about them that were*

here before us, as there are odd Shapes in that Elaborate Monument.[31]

The marks on the rock have been variously described as being Carthaginian, Hebrew words written in Phoenician, and runic.[32] Which is where Vikings enter the story.

The Danish scholar, Carl Christian Rafn, and his associate, Finn Magnusen, claimed that here was evidence regarding the location of the place called *Hop* in the sagas (see chapter 4). They believed that they could decipher runic characters which spelled out "*NAM THOR-FINS*" accompanied by the Roman numeral CXXXI. They interpreted this rather enigmatic message as: "Thorfinn and his 151 companions took possession of this land." The number CXXXI would normally be read as 131, but Rafn suggested that the C might represent a "great hundred" or 120. The mention of this number of settlers in the saga material seemed to corroborate this suggestion. Furthermore, a whole Viking-geography seemed to be established, for if this was, indeed, *Hop*, then *Helluland*, *Markland*, and *Vinland* could be postulated as being Newfoundland, Nova Scotia, and either Cape Cod or Nantucket.[33] In short, the route of Viking exploration could be traced down the eastern coast of North America to New England.

However, this "identification" is rather a stretch, given the lack of clarity in the markings and is not assisted by the fact that "CXXXI" should mean 131 and not 151. More significantly, the supposed "runes" that were read by Rafn only existed because he had adapted the characters that were apparent on the copy of the rock sent him by the Rhode Island Historical Society. To put it bluntly, Rafn's runes did not—and do not—exist. This was conclusively pointed out as long ago as 1916–18, by Professor Edmund B. Delabarre of Brown University.[34] Delabarre then added his own suggestion that the rock bore witness to a Portuguese exploratory party which originally reached the area in the late fifteenth century. According to this theory, the inscription should be read as: "1511 *MIGUEL CORTEREAL V. DEI HIC DUX IND*," or "Miguel Cortereal, by the will of God, here leader of the Indians."[35] Many would argue that Delabarre's suggestion is no more persuasive than that of Rafn. Either way, Vikings seem well out of the frame.

The Newport Stone Tower, Rhode Island

The structure—also known as the Old Stone Mill, the Viking Tower (clues in these names regarding competing theories)—is a round stone tower, located in Touro Park, Newport, Rhode Island. While tree growth now obscures the view from the spot to Narragansett Bay, eighteenth-century paintings show that it was once visible from the sea. The question is: what is it and when was it constructed?

The tower features on the service patch of the "landing ship tanks" (LST 1179) USS Newport, commissioned in 1968, but controversial theories seek to connect the stone structure with a much older set of seaborne warriors: the Vikings. The earliest example of such a claim appears to date from 1837. It was then that the Danish archaeologist, Carl Christian Rafn (who commented on Dighton Rock), proposed this in the book *Antiquitates Americanæ*.[36] This identification was partly based on work that he had carried out on the inscriptions found on Dighton Rock.

Rafn's theory inspired Henry Wadsworth Longfellow's poem *The Skeleton in Armor*. This connected with the discovery, in Fall River, Massachusetts, in 1832, of a skeleton with a triangular brass plate on the chest, a broad belt of brass tubes, and several arrowheads made from brass or copper. From the 1840s onward, most experts concluded that this was the body of a Native American, whose metal objects were probably derived from repurposed European metal trade goods. However, as with many finds involving metalwork or complex building structures (which clearly had Native American origins) there was a tendency among some early commentators to ascribe such objects to nonnative influences. This was part of a process whereby things showing signs of cultural sophistication were denied as being of Native American origin. Those thought to be responsible in this case ranging from Phoenicians and Carthaginians to Viking explorers. An example of Phoenician identification was made by John Stark, a lawyer from Illinois, in the *American Magazine of Useful and Entertaining Knowledge* (1837). But Vikings would soon be on the scene, and this linked the skeleton to the tower at Newport.

When Longfellow published his poem in 1841, his evocation of the discovery of the body of a Viking warrior appears to combine awareness of the find from Fall River, with the ideas of Rafn regarding the alleged Norse-origins of the tower at Newport. Within the poem, we find assertions such as "I was a Viking old!"; the warrior flees with his love from pursuit; and "Three weeks we westward bore," which allows for a North American adventure.

Having landed on a western shore marked by "the vast forest":

> *There for my lady's bower*
> *Built I the lofty tower,*
> *Which, to this very hour,*
> *Stands looking seaward.*[37]

The destruction of the skeleton and accompanying metalwork in a fire, which occurred in 1843, means that the matter of cultural identity cannot now be categorically resolved. However, there was, in fact, no obvious connection between the skeleton and the tower.

To return to the Newport tower, it seems clear that it was built as a windmill in the seventeenth century. In 1677, Benedict Arnold (his grandson was the Benedict Arnold who switched sides to fight with the British) mentioned "my stone built Wind Mill" in his will.[38] A document, dating from 1741, describes it as "the old stone mill," which would seem fairly clear. In 1767, it was described as being used as a powder store "some time past." A plan of Newport, which was published in 1776, identifies it as the "Stone Wind Mill."[39]

In 2003, it was concluded that carbon dating of mortar used in construction made it likely that the tower was constructed in about 1680. This all seems very persuasive and there is no room for Vikings. That there ever appeared to have been a space for them tells us more about the romance of the sagas (which were known in the early part of the nineteenth century), when combined with a desire to "find" evidence for pre-Columbian sophistication which did not involve Native Americans. In this case, a Colonial-era building was pressed into service as a Viking-Age monument.[40]

The Narragansett Runestone, Rhode Island

The Narragansett Runestone, also known as the Quidnessett Rock, is a large slab of metasandstone, 7 feet (2.1 m) long, and 5 feet (1.5 m) high, discovered in Rhode Island, in the mud flats of Narragansett Bay, in 1984. The stone was located roughly 60 feet (18.2 m) off-shore and was visible only during extreme low tide. Unauthorized removal of the stone occurred in 2012 but it was recovered in 2013 and is now displayed in Wickford, North Kingstown, Rhode Island.

It carries seven clear, rune-like marks, with several others less visible.[41] Researchers who originally visited the site documented ten runic-looking characters carved into the stone—eight on one line and two just below.[42] At that time the suggestion was made that these represented a runic form of a "Vulgar Latin" inscription which read: "Registered Boundary Line. The Owner."[43] In the 1991 issue of the *New England Antiquities Research Association* (NEARA), Suzanne Carlson suggested it was Icelandic in origin and represented *skraumli* or "screaming river."[44] Another suggestion is that it should be read as "Four victorious near river." There are other suggestions, more complex and even less convincing. As with the alternatives possible with the Yarmouth Rock, even if genuine, the range of possible interpretations from runic inscriptions can be very varied indeed. And this is if they are genuine, which is far from certain in this case.

As if all this was not complex enough, a man named Everett C. Brown Jr. has claimed that, in 1964, as a teenager, he carved the runestone while on vacation at Pojac Point with his family. According to this claim, he used a sledgehammer and an awl or punch to carve runic characters that he had read about in an encyclopedia. He has claimed that he was trying to spell out the Viking word for "Indians" phonetically. But local residents then responded by saying they had seen the markings prior to 1964.[45] So, as they say, the plot thickens.

As with all the runic finds in the USA, the lack of archaeologically attested support means that even the best of them is impossible to verify. Many are undoubtedly modern hoaxes. Others, if "hoax" is too hard a word, are part of a process which has existed since the nineteenth century in the USA, of attempting to forge a link with the Scandinavian past as an expression of Nordic pride and identity. In neither case can such "evidence" tell us anything about how far Vikings sailed into the lands of America. But they certainly can tell us a great deal about how far they have sailed into imaginations there.

That brings us to the Maine Penny . . .

The Maine Penny

It many ways, this is saving the best until last. This concerns a genuine silver coin, dating from the reign of Olaf III Haraldsson, also known as Olaf Kyrre, king of Norway 1067–93. Minted by 1080, the coin is of a type that was widely circulated in the twelfth and thirteenth centuries. Its presence in Maine is, therefore, intriguing and thought-provoking. If it found its way to the site within a generation of its minting, it would be consistent with the century or so of Viking occupation at L'Anse aux Meadows, which may have sporadically occurred until into the early twelfth century. A longer journey to its find-spot would still easily fall within the date-range of Norse settlement in Greenland, from the tenth to the fifteenth century, during which they almost certainly visited North America on several occasions.[46]

While discussing it at this point in our investigation is geographically out of place in our journey down the eastern coast of North America, its importance makes it very appropriate that this is our final evidence for east-coast Vikings to be examined in this chapter. As a result, its finding and its location are crucial in this investigation.

Guy Mellgren, a local amateur archaeologist, and old-coin collector, said he found this coin in August 1957, at the so-called "Goddard Site," what had once been a Native American settlement. This is located at Naskeag Point, near Blue Hill Bay, Brooklin,

Hancock County, Maine. In the fall of 1956, Mellgren and Ed Runge—both amateur archaeologists—were searching for shell middens (ancient refuse sites). A contact named Goddard invited them to explore his shoreline property. There, on a natural terrace about 8 feet (2.4 m) above the high tide line, they found stone flakes, stone knives, fire pits, and other Native American artifacts. Over many years, Mellgren and Runge returned to excavate what became known as the "Goddard Site," with little assistance from professional archaeologists. In the second summer of exploration, they found the coin.[47] The exact circumstances of the discovery are unclear, and it did not occur as part of a methodical archaeological dig. However, Mellgren did not make any major effort to publicize the find (which strengthens the case for authenticity) and widespread interest only occurred after his death. Eventually, the coin was donated to the Maine State Museum in 1974. Dark gray, well worn, and fragmentary, this object has significance far beyond its initial appearance.[48]

The lack of archaeological data gives cause for concern regarding such a significant artifact. This in no way imputes dishonesty on the part of Mellgren, or others involved in the finding of the coin and its promotion as an artifact which was lost at this spot during the Viking Age. It is simply to assert that any artifact that is reported as a stray find, lacks a stratified, dateable, archaeological context, and is not found as part of a formal archaeological investigation, poses a set of serious problems when evaluating it as evidence. The most obvious concern is that its presence at the site, assuming that it was found there, as claimed, *could* have been a hoax. If so, it would not be the first time that a site was "salted" with bogus evidence. Or, some argue, the whole "discovery" may be suspect.

It has been pointed out that 1957 was "a bumper year for Viking fakes."[49] In 1956, Hjalmar Holand had published *Explorations of*

America Before Columbus. Holand was a staunch defender of the authenticity of the Kensington Runestone. Then, in 1957, Frederick J. Pohl published *Vikings on Cape Cod*. That same year a London book dealer publicized the so-called *Vinland Map*, said to date from the fifteenth century and now dismissed as a twentieth-century forgery (see chapter 5).[50] Holand had imaginatively described the Viking Thorvald Eriksson exploring as far as Maine's Mount Desert Island. Since this lies just over the bay from the Goddard Site, it is quite a coincidence that the coin of Olaf Kyrre, king of Norway, was found there and in the year 1957.[51]

It is not surprising that some experts have dismissed the find as a fake designed to encourage the idea of Norse exploration of North America and to include the USA in that venture. However, the matter might not be as simple as that and there is a very real possibility that the coin was as described: found on a Native American site, as deposited there in the Middle Ages. If so, the nature of the find-spot is highly significant.

If the coin was found where it was lost in the medieval past, it does not necessarily imply the actual presence of Norse explorers at this place in Maine. It is surely significant that the penny in question was the only Norse artifact found at the site. This suggests that it may have been a cultural oddity, which had been traded south due to its curiosity value. The fact that it appears to have been perforated, to use as a pendant, would support this interpretation. This assumption is consistent with other evidence from the Goddard Site, which reveals that it was a hub in a large Native American trading network, in the period c. 1180–1235.[52] Many stone artifacts were found there, whose geological signatures indicate that they came from places a significant distance from where they were discovered. Worked copper artifacts were also discovered at the site, indicating it was an exchange-point of prestige trade goods.[53] Pottery shards, of types found as far away as New Jersey and Nova Scotia, were also found there. The absence of shell middens also points to it being a place of periodic gatherings, rather than a settlement site, although there was evidence of a long house.[54] The idea of far-flung trading networks, which extended into areas frequented by the Norse, is further supported by the finding of an object—generally identified as a Dorset Culture burin, a type of handheld stone flake, with a chisel-like edge—at the Goddard Site. Like the coin, it was probably brought to the site through trade-networks which extended to Newfoundland and Labrador. Other tools found at the site were made from chalcedony, a form of silica found in the Bay of Fundy region of Nova Scotia, and Ramah chert from northern Labrador.

All of this suggests that the coin probably was a genuine find from the site.[55] The recent research that encourages this conclusion, is based on the actual coin and its place within the known corpus of this minting. Known as a "class N" coin, it is a rare type. Of 2,301 coins found in the hoard at Gressli, Norway, in 1879, only 41 were "class N" pennies of the type found at the Goddard Site, and the coin found by Mellgren was a particularly rare variant of the type. This suggests that Mellgren had not purchased the coin from the numismatic market which traded in coins from known Viking hoards.[56] Finally, scientific evidence indicates that the coin had been in situ for a very long time, where it had lain in a horizontal position, subject to water draining round it.[57]

The latest in-depth analysis of the coin concludes that: "Based on the numismatic and archaeological evidence, I am inclined to believe that this was a genuine find."[58] Traded from Norse settlements further north, it eventually reached the site at a date we can no longer exactly assess, but probably no later than the early thirteenth century and possibly during the twelfth century.

The Maine Penny is persuasive evidence of the connection between the medieval Viking explorers and New England, even if the coin had been brought to the Goddard Site by traders, rather than by the Scandinavians themselves.

The sites and finds that we have explored so far are not the only ones claimed as evidence for Viking penetration of North America. It is now time to explore others, whose persuasiveness as evidence is far weaker than some of the east coast ones that we have recently examined. And this involves us looping back into the continental heart of the USA and looking again at the influence of Scandinavian settlers there and their impact on the "discovery" of Viking "evidence."

CHAPTER TEN

A NORSE HOME
FROM HOME?

As we have seen, there are a variety of clues which may suggest that Vikings penetrated further south and west into North America than Newfoundland. Some of these are faint possibilities, such as an expedition which may have lain behind the Kensington Runestone. While very skeptical regarding this artifact, we may keep open the very slight possibility of its authenticity. This is more so regarding the Yarmouth Rock and the Narragansett Runestone. Their location makes them more likely to be authentic than Kensington, although they are not without their problems, some of which are serious. When it comes to the Maine Penny, we are on much surer ground, even if its routeway to its eventual find-spot was probably via Native American trade networks rather than any direct Norse presence at the site.

In this chapter, we will move the story on to what are, clearly, forgeries and hoaxes; or possibly Native American monuments which have been culturally hijacked in the search for evidence of Vikings. And in this, they mark an acceleration-point in the history of the search for American Vikings which takes us beyond a search for historic penetration of the continent and, instead, reveals penetration of the minds and imaginations of later Americans. This was prompted by three main factors.

The first was increasing awareness of the saga-claims regarding exploration of North America; awareness which accelerated during the nineteenth century and continued through the twentieth century to today. While there had been knowledge of them in Scandinavia and Iceland for centuries, this increased in North America after 1800 and particularly after 1850. Heightened awareness led to a search for corroborative evidence which was connected to the events narrated in the sagas.

The second was the increasing presence of Scandinavian pioneers and settlers in the western expansion of the United States in the nineteenth century. Some pioneers sought validation of their ownership of the newly taken land through references to ancient saga-claims. By no means were all of these Scandinavian, but latter-day Norse played a major part in this process. For the most skeptical twenty-first-century commentators, the Kensington Runestone is an example of this process at work in the Midwest in the second half of the nineteenth century.

The third factor was the urge to assert European prior-claim to land, which pre-dated the Columbus expedition of 1492 and, furthermore, gave it a *northern European* character. At times, this involved the expropriation of Native American monuments as part of a process which sought to belittle Native American cultural and monumental achievements, by claiming Viking ancestry for them—and, at times, claimed that those responsible were *just about anybody*, so long as they were not Native Americans. This has echoes of the annexation of Viking themes by modern US white supremacists that we will return to in later chapters. As with so much in the search for American Vikings, the strands are tangled and have quite a history.

Scandinavian Pioneers in the New World

Between 1820 and 1920, more than 2.1 million Scandinavians emigrated to America. Just over half were Swedish, almost a third were Norwegians, and a seventh were Danish. About 125,000 Scandinavians came to the US before the start of the Civil War in 1861, but most arrived between the end of that war, in 1865, and the outbreak of World War I, in 1914.[1]

Many came because they saw opportunities for personal advancement in the USA as the western frontier opened, even though Scandinavia saw significant industrialization and economic growth in this period (1865–1914). Several political and economic factors combined to encourage emigration. Some young Finns left Finland, then part of the Russian Empire, to avoid tsarist conscription. Denmark was defeated in war with Prussia in 1864 and lost territory to the unifying German state; consequently, some young Danes living in what is now southern Denmark wanted to avoid conscription into the kaiser's army of the German Empire. Problems in agriculture, official corruption, restrictive powerful state churches, and the increasing gulf between rich and poor encouraged many thousands of Scandinavians to seek what they believed would be a better life in the USA.[2] Letters sent back home by pioneering family members, which extolled the opportunities and the wide-open spaces in the USA, were sometimes accompanied by prepaid shipping tickets, and spurred family members to emigrate and join those already in North America.

Most Scandinavians eventually settled in rural areas of the Midwest and the Great Plains, especially in Illinois, Iowa, Minnesota, North Dakota, and Wisconsin. Before the 1870s, few Scandinavians settled on the West Coast, with just sixty-five Norwegians reported in Washington Territory in 1870; and forty-seven in Oregon. This changed after the 1880s, as railroad construction made it easier to reach the Pacific Northwest, where the topography was reminiscent of lands back home; about 150,000 Scandinavians settled in the Pacific Northwest region between 1890 and 1910.[3]

However, this did not diminish the Scandinavian character that had developed in the Midwest. This explains several "Viking finds" that were later made there. The first Swedes on the US Census in the Minnesota Territory were recorded in 1850 and it would be one of the Minnesota Swedes who would later discover the Kensington Runestone in 1898. The Norwegian Kleng Pedersen Hesthammer (also known as Cleng Peerson) made two trips to the USA in 1821 and 1825; he moved through the Midwest and eventually settled in Texas where his gravestone reads: "Cleng Peerson, the first Norwegian Emigrant to America."[4] The evidence from the sagas undermines this bold claim. There had been Norwegians (by way of Iceland and Greenland) who had made it to America by the 1020s at the latest. In addition to this saga evidence, the many supposed North American runestones would insist that he was not the first to arrive.

Together, these Scandinavian settlers made a distinctive contribution to the development of the cultural character of the USA.[5] They also had a sizeable impact on the search for American Vikings, as can be seen in the discovery of the Kensington Runestone and then the discovery of other clues believed to be artifacts left behind by medieval Norse explorers and settlers in the Midwest.

The new Norse arrivals had a strong incentive to seek legitimacy in their new homes. Scandinavian farmers—struggling to make a living in Minnesota, in Wisconsin, and in the Dakota Territory—were often regarded with condescension by the New England cultural elites who appeared to dominate society in the northern part of the expanding nation. For the latter, it was the Mayflower settlement from 1620 onward which had laid the foundations for what became the United States. It was very much a Yankee origin myth, and one that appeared to gain even greater legitimacy following the northern victory in the bitterly contested Civil War. However, this had unexpected consequences in the push-back that it prompted. The increased Scandinavian presence in the USA encouraged (both consciously and unconsciously) these Norse newcomers to promote an alternative origin myth, one that long predated the arrival of the Mayflower off Cape Cod in 1620. Theirs would stimulate a search for Viking roots to substantiate the saga-claims and would go far beyond what these early written sources claimed in terms of geographical reach.

In 1893, the World's Columbian Exposition, held in Chicago, celebrated the four-hundredth anniversary of the first voyage of Columbus. The new Swedish and Norwegian communities, aware of the saga evidence, found this celebration rather provocative. In fact, the matter was discussed in many newspaper articles read by Norwegians and Swedes, in the USA and in Scandinavia. In this context, money was raised on both sides of the Atlantic to pay for the construction of a full-sized replica of the Viking-Age "Gokstad ship"—excavated in Norway in 1880—to prove that a Viking voyage across the Atlantic as described in the sagas was possible. The replica ship successfully sailed from Norway and was moored in Lake Michigan, on Chicago's shore, throughout the activities of the world's fair.[6] Its presence constituted a strong argument against the supposed preeminence of Columbus. And, anyway, he had not made it to North America. The Scandinavian citizens of the USA were contesting the triumphalism of their Italian fellow-citizens. Just five years later, the Kensington Runestone was discovered, which accelerated the movement countering Columbus (and, for that matter, the New England Mayflower Pilgrims) with the Vikings. The runestone, like the Gokstad replica, was a Midwestern expression of this competition over US origin myths.

In the Midwest, the Viking assertion soon gained real traction. By 1900, it was apparently possible to find Viking-themed restaurants in Chicago whose menus were written in runes! A runic inscription was included in a mural in the hall of Chicago's Norske Klub, founded in 1911.[7] The Vikings of Illinois were set to try to rival those of Minnesota.

Since 1900, many US Scandinavian communities take for granted that Vikings explored the Midwest. In 1952, a drinking horn engraved with runes was found during roadwork at Waukegan, near the shore of Lake Michigan, north of Chicago. Studies suggested it contained a date: 1317. It seemed corroboration of the Kensington Runestone and of the *Vinland Map* that hit the headlines a few years later. However, it soon transpired it was of a type familiar as a tourist keepsake from Iceland, and the runes were identified as a poem composed by a twentieth-century Icelander.[8] It is testimony to the growth in interest in "Viking finds" from the 1880s onward. This interest has continued unabated, as evidenced in the horned-helmet worn by the determined-looking warrior on the logo of the Minnesota Vikings football team since 1961. We will return to this in chapter 15, when we explore the use of the Viking "brand" in modern publicity and marketing. But suffice it to say at this point, in Minnesota the claimed Viking heritage is now well established.

The Viking origin myth would also eventually acquire supporters from beyond the community of Scandinavian US citizens and the Midwestern areas within which they made up a sizeable proportion of the nonindigenous population. Vikings were getting into the contested cultural DNA of the United States in a more general way. A new mythology was being created and it had appeal beyond the Scandinavian immigrant communities. It was this phenomenon of searching for Viking clues which led to many of the New England "finds" that we have recently explored; and then circled-back to produce more of the same in areas which had more in common with the find-spot of the Kensington Runestone. These new finds, like that at Kensington, were in the heart of the continental USA, where it was hard to imagine Vikings exploring. They were, however, areas which had acquired a Scandinavian character since 1850.

The Ave Maria Stone, and the Mooring Stones: More Minnesota Evidence?

In May 2001, another stone was found near the site of the original 1898 Kensington discovery. The new stone was 43 inches (109 cm) long and was located on an island which lay about a quarter of a mile from where the original runestone was unearthed. Members of a group known as the "Kensington Runestone Scientific Testing Team" discovered a boulder which was claimed to have the letters "AV" faintly carved into it. It was suggested that the letters stood for "*Ave Maria*," and might have marked the burial place of a Viking explorer connected to the original stone. As a result of this suggestion, it has become known as the "Ave Maria Stone," or the "AVM stone." In addition, the AVM Stone apparently also carries the runic date of 1363, which would conveniently connect it to the same event alleged to be recorded on the original Kensington stone. It also appears to have some runic letters, which the team speculated might stand for "Christ the Savior conquers." The coincidence of dates—1362 on the Kensington Runestone, 1363 on the AVM Stone—is either remarkable corroboration, or should set alarm bells ringing.

However, archaeological excavation at the new site failed to find anything which supported the idea of a medieval Viking presence. All that was discovered were two quartz flakes that had probably been chipped from arrowheads. This accompanied some other evidence pointing to a Native American presence at the site. All in all, the new find failed to persuade experts regarding its authenticity. Many feel it belongs to the same hoax-tradition which produced the original find at Kensington. Or—if judgement is suspended regarding that earlier find—was produced sometime between 1898 and 2001 to provide corroboration for the earlier runestone. Many would agree with the view expressed in 2001, by state archaeologist Mark Dudzik when he commented that the original runestone theory "has not held up well under professional scientific scrutiny." With regard to the new "find," many would feel that it came under the same category as the original runestone, the authenticity of which Dudzik challenged with the rhetorical question: "Why would they [Vikings] all of a sudden happen to end up in a Scandinavian-settled state, in a Scandinavian farmer's back yard?"[9] It is a good question.

The same skepticism should be applied to other alleged corroborative evidence from Minnesota. For example, Hjalmar R. Holand, the leading advocate for the Kensington Runestone from 1907 until his death in 1963, suggested that holes chiseled into large rocks, apparently found along western and west-central Minnesota lakeshores and former lakeshores, were clues pointing to the presence of Vikings. He proposed that there were ten of these "mooring stones" but, in fact, there are many more than this. In the early 1980s, the matter was examined in detail by the Minnesota Statewide Archaeo-logical Survey of the Minnesota Historical Society.[10] They found that there was no evidence of sufficiently raised water levels in the fourteenth century that would support the idea that the locations of the stones indicated mooring sites and no plausible route which would take Viking longships into Minnesota from Hudson Bay. The difficult river routes could only have been traversed using small boats; and such small vessels would have no use for the "mooring stones," as they would just be hauled ashore.

The very large number of such stones would argue for them most definitely not being used for this purpose. They are found on lakeshores, in fields, on hillsides, and are widely scattered across the landscape—at various elevations. Plus, it would be easier to just tie a rope around the stones, rather than laboriously chisel out a hole. The total absence of any similar stones at any documented Viking sites in Greenland and Newfoundland caps it.[11]

The conclusion regarding the Viking hypothesis was: "The combined weight of the evidence and common sense thus led us to the inevitable conclusion that the Vikings were not responsible for making these holes."[12] The actual explanation, which the team was convinced best explained the stones, was that the holes were chiseled out to take black powder, to blast and break up the stones when clearing fields. In short, they dated from no earlier than farming methods of the nineteenth century.[13]

The "mooring stones" and the more recent "AVM Stone" are best regarded as well-meaning attempts to corroborate an original find, the authenticity of which is suspect. Overall, the Minnesota evidence is far from persuasive regarding actual Viking travels. The same can certainly be said about the following items. These seem geographically even less convincing than the Minnesota examples. And, on close examination, are anything but persuasive.

The Oklahoma "Evidence"

If one was searching for evidence of Vikings, then Oklahoma is not a very likely place to start looking. Located huge distances from the sea, this state seems short of Viking potential. At least Minnesota is in some proximity to the Great Lakes. But this has not stopped Oklahoma from featuring in the search for American Vikings. These examples are so unconvincing that we shall not spend a great deal of time in examining them.

The **Heavener Runestone** was first recorded in 1923 and is located in Heavener Runestone Park, which is in Le Flore County, near Heavener, Oklahoma. Runes carved on the stone belong to a runic alphabet known as the "Elder *Futhark*," a variant out of use long before the Viking voyages to North America, a fact apparently unknown to the person who carved them in Oklahoma. However, it seems that the second runic character is a short-twig "A" from the "Younger *Futhark*." The inscription has been taken to read *gnomedal* (probably meaning "Gnome Valley"). It has also been described as a land-ownership marker meaning "Glome's Valley."

Archaeologist Ken Feder concluded that no evidence of Vikings has been found anywhere near Heavener and that "It is unlikely that the Norse would get significantly more fastidious about leaving any evidence behind of their presence in Oklahoma."[14] We can safely conclude that it is a modern fake and certainly not the product of a Viking settler naming a newly acquired plot of land.

The **Poteau stone** was found by schoolchildren in 1967 near Poteau, in Le Flore County, Oklahoma, and ten miles from the location of the Heavener Runestone. It is similar in several ways to that earlier "discovery" and was clearly based on it. Carved into sandstone, it is 15 inches (38 cm) long and shows little signs of weathering, which supports the conclusion that it is a modern fake.

Like the other stone it carries a mix of runic scripts and may read: "*GLOIEA*(?)(?)." Of its eight letters, five are runes from the Elder *Futhark*, identical to those found on the Heavener Runestone, one is from the Younger *Futhark*, and two are of no runic form. It is clearly a fake.

In 1991, Carl Albert State College in Poteau changed its mascot to a bearded Viking, wearing a horned helmet, apparently inspired by the local "runestones." Its website invites new students to find out more about the college via tabs labeled "Start Your Viking Journey" and "Viking Helpline."[15] In such ways do recent myths inform present realities. It is an intriguing insight into the attraction of the Viking image, and we shall return to this in later chapters.

The **Shawnee stone** was found in 1969 by three children in Shawnee, Oklahoma. It lies one mile from the North Canadian River, a tributary of the Arkansas River. It is a soft red Permian sandstone, and the carving was clearly recent. Nearby, the same Permian sandstone which carries graffiti dates as modern as "1957," shows more sign of weathering than this supposedly medieval inscription. Once again, the runes are from the Elder *Futhark* (it looks like someone locally had a book containing this runic alphabet) and seems to read either *Mildok* or *Mldok*. This is meaningless and the stone appears to contain a random selection of the wrong kind of runic alphabet.

Despite the clear nature of these stones as modern fakes, there is now a Heavener Runestone State Park, which underscores the completely unlikely Viking connection with Oklahoma. Plus, there is a group of supporters of the authenticity of these stones. These are clearly examples of Vikings sailing into American imaginations, not adventuring deep into the continent itself.

A little closer to the coast—but clearly also imaginative rather than historical—are the final stones we will examine. They hail from West Virginia, a state not otherwise known for its Viking connections.

The Braxton Runestone, West Virginia

The Braxton County Runestone—also known as the Wilson Stone and the Braxton County Tablet—was found in 1931, on the Triplett Fork stream, about eight miles west of Gassaway, in West Virginia.

It is a piece of micaceous sandstone, just over 4 inches (10 cm) long, just over 3 inches (7.6 cm) wide, and just under 1 inch (2.5 cm) thick. Its inscription is similar to that found, almost a century before, on a stone at Grave Creek Mound, in Moundsville, in 1838.

The inscription at Braxton features three horizontal lines, which divide three sets of similar characters, with a cross-like symbol placed at the bottom. The state authorities purchased the Braxton Runestone in 1940 and sent it to an archaeologist, Dr. Emerson F. Greenman, at the University of Michigan. He concluded: "It has not been demonstrated that the Wilson tablet is a fraud, but the preponderant evidence points in that direction."[16]

Today, most archaeologists consider the Braxton Runestone to be a hoax. It is on display in the West Virginia State Museum.[17]

The Grave Creek Runestone, West Virginia

The Grave Creek Runestone was discovered in 1838 during the excavation, by non-professional archaeologists, of the Grave Creek

Mound, in Moundsville, West Virginia. This is located on the Ohio
River, about ten miles south of Wheeling. The stone was a small,
inscribed sandstone disk, which measured just under 2 inches (5 cm)
wide, and about 1.5 inches (3.8 cm) high. The reverse side of the
disc was uninscribed.[18] The location of the original Grave Creek
Runestone is unknown, but a copy survives.

The Grave Creek Mound itself was constructed by members
of the mound-building Native American "Adena culture," which
existed from about 500 B.C.E. to 100 C.E. This cultural group was
centered on Ohio, and extended into northern Kentucky, eastern
Indiana, West Virginia, and areas of western Pennsylvania.

By 1868, the stone was in the collection of a man named
E. H. Davis, before most of his collection was sold to the Blackmore
Museum, Salisbury, UK. This museum was founded in 1863 and
amalgamated with the Salisbury and South Wiltshire Museum in
1902. Its collections were dispersed to other museums in the 1930s
and 1960s, including the British Museum. Today, the only known
photograph of the stone, is from a photograph of Items 60–65 of the
Davis collection. In 1868, a plaster cast was made of the stone and
deposited in the Smithsonian Institution.[19] The original item is lost.

No convincing interpretation of the markings on the stone have
been made. Nor can it be described as runic in its character, despite
the name often used to describe the stone. It has even been described
as "Iberian Script Punic," a claim rejected by many other scholars.
However, there may be something in this unlikely identification.

At a meeting of the West Virginia Archaeological Society in
2008, anthropologist David Oestreicher postulated that the inscription was probably a forgery perpetrated by James W. Clemens, who
had financed the excavation of the Grave Creek Mound through
loans. Oestreicher believed that he had found the source of the
inscription. This was in an eighteenth-century book entitled *An*

Essay on the Alphabets of the Unknown Letters That are Found in the Most Ancient Coins and Monuments of Spain. He suggested that all the characters on the stone were copied directly from this book.[20] In which case, Vikings do not even appear on the radar.

It seems clear that the Grave Creek Stone is a forgery (by whom must remain unknown).[21] What is certain, is that this is not a "runestone" and is, in no way, evidence of the presence of medieval Norse or any other ancient explorers.

There is a strong likelihood that what underlay the claims for the Grave Creek Stone were assumptions that impressive archaeological sites in North America could not possibly be the work of Native Americans. This anthropological ethnic elitism was a common underpinning feature of much nineteenth-century archaeology and taints aspects of some of the speculation regarding American Vikings in the twenty-first century.

The Relevance of These Claims to the Search for American Vikings

While it is safe to assume that none of the aforementioned stones were inscribed and set up by Vikings, they still tell us a lot about the penetration into, what is now the USA, by the *idea* of Vikings.

By this point it will be clear that the idea of Vikings has entered the cultural DNA of the USA in a way that is quite remarkable. It started before the excavation of verifiable archaeological evidence at L'Anse aux Meadows and—while bolstered by the discoveries there—is not dependent on them when it comes to exciting enthusiasm. A runic inscription, found in Brooklyn in 1924, nicely sums this up. This runic version in modern Swedish read: "Leif Eriksson was here."[22] For many supporters of the Viking myth, this sums things up. The Vikings were here in the USA—and their potency as a myth has been grasped and reimagined for modern purposes. It is to some of those modern purposes that we now turn. While some are innocent, if historically lacking in validity, others reveal dark motivations. For all our admiration of Viking adventurers, the so-called *skraelings* would recognize aspects of that dark character of the impact of the Norse on North America.

CHAPTER ELEVEN

A DARKER SIDE
TO THE STORY

As we have seen, the idea of American Vikings appealed to many people in the nineteenth and twentieth centuries, sufficient to cause a number of "finds" to have been discovered or faked as evidence of their presence in the USA. Vikings were used to express something about how people felt about themselves, their community identity, and their relationship to the nation.

However, the matter was even more complex because the subject-matter has been quarried to support ideologies far removed from academic study into historic origins and American Scandinavian cultural identities. Although, it should be noted, the latter—though usually simply expressing a desire to feel "at home" in a new land—*sometimes* included aspects that are more disquieting. There was, at times, a discernible motivation to assert the newcomers' rights against those of Native Americans, by prior claim to the land. This was also linked, at times, with the trend of assuming that any Native American site which exhibited architectural sophistication must, in its origins, have been built by Old World adventurers, particularly northern Europeans.

This racial appropriation of Native American achievements and condescension toward indigenous peoples of North America, was carried out in favor of medieval Viking warriors and their families because they seemed to represent a racially more acceptable claim, and this would accelerate in the future, to cast a shadow over the idea of Vikings in the USA.

This dark side to the story should not be allowed to overshadow the narrative, but neither should it be ignored. This is because it was, and still is, part of the cocktail of disparate features which characterizes enthusiasm for Norse forebears and the Viking exploration in North America.

Then, in the 1930s, some nationalists in the USA became enamored with the supposed link between US "Germanic culture" and ideas of "white Aryan supremacy." This referenced (implicitly and, at times, explicitly) the kinds of racial ideology being promulgated by Hitler and his followers in Germany at the time. The Viking heritage in the USA was taking a dangerous path; and a minority have remained on that trajectory into the twenty-first century.

However, before this occurred, other developments had taken place which served to firmly embed Norse character within emerging ideas of US citizenship. These efforts were a long way from the dark path that would later be trod by exponents of Viking racial superiority, but the later, radicalized extremists were able to do so because they could appeal to the idea promulgated in the period 1900–33 of Scandinavian heritage making a vital contribution to US nationhood and the texture of US life. They clearly hijacked something which, in most of its manifestations, was far from their ideology. Nevertheless, the sense of the US having Norse roots was to prove a useful quarry from which they could extract material and use to their own ends. But before we explore that dark path, it is instructive to examine how the idea of Vikings played a part in US cultural identity before the 1930s.

"American Vikings" Become Ideal US Citizens

As early as 1879, O. L. Kirkeberg, a Norwegian-born Unitarian minister visited Wisconsin and marveled at "how Norwegians have managed to isolate themselves together in colonies and maintain their Norwegian memories and customs." He had to ask himself if he was really in the USA. It felt like a piece of Norway.[1] This continued into the next century, albeit with important adjustments made to combine this distinct character with a new "Norse-US" identity.

Interestingly, when Kirkeberg stopped over in Salina, Kansas, on his way to the appropriately named settlement of Denmark, Kansas, he questioned a local hotel-keeper about whether he knew of any Scandinavians in town. The answer was "Yes." Kirkeberg then wanted to know a bit more. Were there any Danes among them, or Norwegians, or Swedes? Having reflected on this, the hotelkeeper answered "No." He went on to explain: "There don't seem to be representatives of those nationalities, most are Scandinavians."[2]

Clearly, for the hotelkeeper they were all Nordics. This revealed more than just rather generalized geography on his part, since at the time "many of them [US Scandinavian immigrants] remained steeped in cultural traditions that were rooted in landscapes and even parishes rather than nation states."[3] National identities were not as concrete as they would become. And it is also a reminder that, rightly or wrongly, to many outside observers there was a recognizable identity which set all the Scandinavians apart—regardless of their individual national origins.

Each one of the Scandinavian communities had its own experiences, but a brief examination of the Norwegians will give a flavor both of how things developed and the fusion between the American present and the Scandinavian past as the twentieth century opened. As the hotelkeeper's answer suggests, some of this character represented a general "Scandinavian experience," though allowing for the fact that things were always more complex in actual communities.

In the period around 1900, "Old-country traditions in food, festive dress, folk arts, and entertainment were given a powerful boost with the establishment of *bygdelag*, or old-home societies."[4] These old-home societies looked back to specific Norwegian localities and loyalties. This reinforced a connection to the old-country and a home community, while establishing a role in a new American context. Meeting annually, these fifty or so societies were named from a specific Norwegian area and "became grand celebrations of a regional and rural Norwegian cultural heritage."[5]

In one sense, these were backward-looking celebrations which focused on ethnic roots. It was noted how women revived the use of the festive rural costume (the *bunad*) which otherwise might have gone out of fashion in their new homes. This involved the wearing of costumes which celebrated their old-country districts. As part of this process of celebrating Norwegian heritage, heavy silver brooches (*sølje*) were worn. About this time the remembered peasant costume of Hardanger, located on Norway's west coast, inspired the official dress worn by the society known as the Daughters of Norway. Such colorful traditional costumes were worn at Norwegian-American public events and continue to be worn at such gatherings.[6] It was a process whereby the newly established immigrant community magnified its Norwegian-ness, even as it proclaimed its new US loyalties.

However, things were more complex than just the creation of Norse cultural enclaves. In larger urban areas such as Brooklyn, Chicago, Minneapolis, and Seattle, the Norwegians lived and expressed themselves within the established multicultural environment of the cities in question, "while constructing a complex ethnic community that met the needs of its members." In short, a hybrid Norse-US identity was being established, which broke down barriers between different groups of Scandinavian citizens. As a result, "a Scandinavian melting pot existed in the urban setting among Norwegians, Swedes, and Danes,"[7] as evidenced by inter-marriage between the different Scandinavian communities which promoted interethnic assimilation between these nationalities, even while reinforcing a more general "Scandinavian distinctiveness." This first occurred between the different Scandinavian groups but then extended into the larger American society as the process of wider assimilation accompanied a continued sense of Norse ancestry which was now intermingled with other ideas of American-ness. Consequently, it has been asserted that "There are no longer any Norwegian enclaves or neighborhoods in America's great cities. Beginning in the 1920s, Norwegians increasingly became suburban, and one might claim, more American."[8] Between 1900 and 1930, Danes and Norwegians seemed more likely to marry outside their own national group than did the Swedes.[9] In time, however, a general pan-Scandinavian character emerged,[10] which continues into the twenty-first century. It was a flexible approach to Norse identity that the Vikings—who drew membership from across diverse Scandinavian communities—would have recognized.

This process of assimilation—but mixed with an awareness of Nordic roots—accelerated through the 1920s. The historic connection of Norwegians with the United States was celebrated at the Norse-American Centennial in the twin cities of Minneapolis and

St. Paul, in June 1925. A century had passed since the first modern Norwegians had landed in New York Harbor in 1825. But the event celebrated roots than ran even deeper into the past. For it was at the Norse-American Centennial that President Calvin Coolidge honored the Norwegians for being good modern Americans *and* also publicly validated their claim of having a shared nationality with the original discoverer of America in the Viking Age.[11]

As part of this event, a pageant was enacted which celebrated the life of Colonel Hans Christian Heg, a hero of the American Civil War. Heg was an abolitionist who led the Scandinavian 15th Wisconsin Infantry Regiment on the Union side. He died of wounds received at the Battle of Chickamauga in 1863. Before the outbreak of the war in 1861, he had been a leading member of Wisconsin's "Wide Awakes," who were an anti-slave-catcher militia. Hans Heg was aged eleven years when his family arrived in Muskego, Wisconsin, from Norway in 1840. With Scandinavians fighting on both sides in the civil war, the conflict meant that those involved could say that they were truly committed to their new homeland. The Heg Pageant—when combined with Coolidge's separate recognition of the actions of Heg's medieval forbears—illustrated the way in which the Norse were becoming integrated into US self-awareness and the national story.

The Norse-American Centennial was an early example of several Norse-related festivals that occurred at the time. Many other Nordic folk festivals followed it in areas of Scandinavian settlement and, like it, they celebrated the Scandinavian contribution to the USA that, while rooted in historic events, was also very malleable when it came to mythmaking.

Language continued to play a significant role in the emerging Scandinavian-US identity. Spoken Norwegian, as with all the Scandinavian languages, was most prevalent in rural communities in the interwar years from 1918–41. This was consistent with a more conservative society, which was less likely to be influenced by the multi-culturalism experienced in urban centers.

At the same time, the Norwegian Lutheran Church in America established several Lutheran congregational schools, which continued into the 1930s. These operated during the summer months and reinforced the Lutheran faith and provided basic teaching in the Norwegian language.[12] In addition, six Norwegian colleges were founded before 1900 to provide a Scandinavian context for higher education. Of these, Luther College, Decorah, Iowa, was the first college founded by Norwegians in America Three other colleges continue to operate in Minnesota. These are St. Olaf College in Northfield, Augsburg College in Minneapolis, and Concordia College in Moorhead. In addition, Augustana College can be found in Sioux Falls, South Dakota; Pacific Lutheran University is in Tacoma, Washington State. At the same time, responses to the Scandinavian presence in the Midwest explains why the Department of Germanic Studies began offering courses in Norwegian, Swedish, and Scandinavian Studies in 1894, just one year after the University of Chicago was founded.

Like the Norwegians, the Swedes also combined references to the past with creating a new US identity. Furthermore, by 1910 the Midwest was not the only area with a significant Swedish population. It was true that about 54 percent lived in these states, primarily in Minnesota and Illinois, but 15 percent now lived in the East, in the industrial areas of New England. On the east coast, New York City and Worcester, Massachusetts, were two settlements that attracted Swedish incomers. There was also a fairly large Swedish-American community on the West Coast, with almost 10 percent of all Swedish-Americans living there, mostly in Washington State and California. In Washington, most lived in the Seattle-Tacoma area.[13] And this growing Swedish community was served by between 600 and 1,000 Swedish language newspapers.

While benefitting from the continued interest in Viking-related matters, the absence of a specific Swedish contribution to the events referred to in the sagas meant that Norwegians were often preeminent in the assertion of Viking roots in the USA. But it would be wrong to assume that it was only Norwegian-Americans who were seeking to root their present experience in what one might call "the *Vinland* past." It should be remembered that Olof Öhman, of Kensington Runestone fame, was Swedish. The inscription there was careful to note that "*We are 8 Goths* [Geats or Swedes] *and 22 Norwegians on an exploration journey from Vinland through the West.*"[14] Sweden, it seems, would not miss out in the mythmaking.

There is plenty of other evidence to support the assertion that, among those seeking roots for the Scandinavian presence in the USA, the history that was appealed to—in affirmation of general Scandinavian group identity and the benefits it brought to the United States—could be very old indeed. Two striking examples will suffice. And both fed into a darker and racially charged approach to Viking heritage. The first contribution did so more by implication; the second contribution did so explicitly.

The Vikings Co-opted as Part of Ethnic and Racial Theories

In the two-volume *History of the Scandinavians and Successful Scandinavians in the United States* (1893–97), edited by the Norwegian-American O. N. Nelson, a connection was made to the period when the Goths from Scandinavia poured into the Roman empire, and to the events of the later Viking Age. In this study,

Nelson characterized Scandinavians as "courageous, freedom-loving individualists who not only exhibited a special predilection for migration, but who in fact also were the energetic representatives of a brave new world, adding fresh vigor to the classical, decaying civilizations of Southern Europe."[15] It was such vigorous Viking Age characteristics which, in the view of the author, so fitted Scandinavians to be Midwestern pioneers.[16]

In case anyone had missed the Viking-connection, Nelson went on to explicitly claim that Norwegians were "bold sailors" and "daring adventurers," who particularly resembled the Vikings more than did the other Scandinavian nations of the Danes and the Swedes.[17] This was a piece of special pleading for his own ancestry and was, very possibly, encouraged by the Norwegian characters of the *Vinland* sagas, although he did not specifically make this point.

Then, in *The Scandinavian Element in the United States*, written by Kendric Charles Babcock in 1914, we find it confidently stated that the most desirable immigrants into the USA were those arriving from the regions "where the purest Baltic stock now exists, that is, north of a line running east and west through Brussels, and especially in north-central Germany and the Scandinavian peninsula." In Babcock's opinion, these contributed to American progress, unlike others who "lower its standards and retard its advancement."[18] It may be of interest to note that Babcock was not himself of Scandinavian stock, so his racist assertions were not due to an attempt to justify his own racial superiority. As far as he was concerned, this was just how it was.

The ideas outlined in Babcock's book were consistent with widespread ideas about racial typologies and eugenics that gained a great deal of traction in the early twentieth century. Twentieth-century racism was running in favor of Vikings and their descendants. Christopher Columbus had already suffered damage as a result of this and, in the 1930s and 1940s, this racist promotion of things Nordic would escalate and, in time, take on increasingly sinister characteristics. These were characteristics that have never been fully shed by some. It was explicitly utilized by US Nazis in the 1930s and echoes of it can, arguably, also be heard in the outlook of some members of the America First Committee in the 1940s. But first, the US Nazis.

Vikings and the "Friends of the New Germany"

The rise to power of Adolf Hitler (appointed chancellor of Germany in January 1933) energized sympathizers in the USA. Between 1933 and 1936, when it was dissolved, the *Bund der Freunde des Neuen Deutschland* (Federation of Friends of the New Germany) promoted Nazi-style German nationalism in the USA. After it was dissolved, following protests by the State Department concerning its pro-Nazi views, another organization—the *Amerikadeutscher Bund* (American German Federation)—was formed, which lasted until December 1941, when Germany declared war on the USA.

Using uniformed parades and other public events, the *Amerikadeutscher Bund* promoted Nazi ideology. On Washington's birthday in 1939, 20,000 supporters gathered in Madison Square Garden, New York, for an event billed as celebrating "True Americanism." On its poster and program, a striking illustration featured a Viking warrior spearing a snake. It was clearly a reference to the Norse myth of Thor's conflict with the *Midgard* Serpent (see chapter 2). But this latter-day Viking was portrayed as a "true American," with the US flag proudly displayed on his shield, and its thirteen starts

representing "the original founding states of Germanic/Nordic settlers in the Northeast."[19]

The *Amerikadeutscher Bund*, though fairly marginal in terms
of membership and influence, illustrates the way that a number of
German or Nordic Americans sought to identify themselves with
a Viking and Aryan mythical past (as they constructed it) which
aimed to bring together Germans and Scandinavians in a unified racial block of these considered racially superior—and "True
American."[20] It was a co-opting of Viking Age imagery in the service
of white supremacy and antisemitism. It was not a unique effort,
and it would not be the last attempt to do this.

The "America First Committee" and "Nordicism"

The America First Committee (AFC) was a US isolationist pres-
sure group during World War II. It was formed in September
1940, and surpassed 800,000 members, grouped in 450 chapters
at its largest extent.[21] It was led by Robert E. Wood, a retired
US Army general, and its members included Henry Ford, who
combined automotive innovation with antisemitism, [22] and the
aviator Charles Lindbergh.

The AFC lasted until 1941 and was dissolved just four days
after the Japanese attack on Pearl Harbor brought the United
States into the war. The Japanese attack was swiftly followed by
Nazi Germany declaring war on the USA.

While it included many from different walks of life and areas of
the country, it is no surprise to discover that a large contingent lived
in the Midwest,[23] where the sense of Viking heritage was strong. In
the AFC, conservative and nationalist politics mingled with some

celebrations of Germanic heritage that, at times, found the Germanic activities of the Third Reich rather too attractive. A number of its members held antisemitic and pro-fascist views; although not all subscribed to these ideas, and it officially opposed efforts by the *Amerikadeutscher Bund* to recruit for it.[24] While it existed, the group strongly opposed US involvement in the war that tore Europe apart after 1939. It seems clear that this was motivated partly by a desire to keep the US out of the carnage, and partly (in the case of some of its members) by sympathies for Nazi Germany under Hitler. Lindbergh, for example, defended Nazi aggression as "the right of an able and virile nation to expand" and also accepted a medal from Hitler's government in 1938.[25]

Charles Lindbergh's father, Charles Augustus Lindbergh Sr. was a Swedish immigrant and Lindbergh Jr. clearly had a loyalty to things Nordic and Germanic that took him in very dangerous directions given how Nazi Germany, and its version of things Germanic, dominated Europe at the time. Lindbergh's outlook was combined with strident anti-communism which resonated with many in the US. Similarly, his belief in eugenics and "Nordicism" enjoyed considerable social acceptance at the time.[26]

1930s Nordicism is a reminder of the dark side of the fascination with Nordic culture which could easily become intertwined with concepts of race hierarchies and even the elimination of so-called inferiors and inferior characteristics (Germans and Nordics, of course, being regarded as superior). Such views came straight from the playbook of *The Scandinavian Element in the United States*, and is a reminder of the reach of such ideas. In these constructions, Vikings exemplified the apex of dominant and energetic manliness which was due to the (alleged) purity of their blood.

Several observers considered that Lindbergh's views on race, faith, and eugenics, sounded too similar to those of the Nazis.[27] Consequently, he was suspected by some commentators of being a Nazi sympathizer,[28] although this has been contested by some biographers.[29] However, there seems some corroboration for these concerns in his friendship with the notoriously antisemitic Ford. Ford remarked that "When Charles comes out here, we only talk about the Jews."[30] Such was an outlook all too common in the US and across Europe at the time, and it is understandable that many who have studied Lindbergh have concluded that, whatever else motivated him, it also included sympathies for Germany and even for Nazism.[31] While many members of the AFC were conservative patriots, there was always a whiff of racist ideology associated with the organization, even when it was hard to categorically track it down. Such was the kind of Nordicism and fascination with things Germanic (even Nazi) that was found in sections of the radical right of the USA in the 1930s.

With regard to American Vikings, the relevance of this is the way in which such right-wing nationalist movements plugged into the most extreme version of "Nordicism." This was a racial concept which originated in nineteenth-century anthropology and saw in an idealized Nordic type—characterized by blue eyes, pale skin, tall stature, and skull shape—a form of superior human being. These physical characteristics were claimed to be accompanied by character traits of honesty, competitiveness, and individualism.[32] All in all, these were the "super-men" and (though very much to be kept within their gendered place) "super-women," so central to the racial theories of the time. It is reminiscent of the alleged "courageous, freedom-loving [Viking] individualists" so admired by Nelson in *History of the Scandinavians and Successful Scandinavians in the*

United States and "the purest Baltic stock" promoted by Babcock in *The Scandinavian Element in the United States.*

It is a reminder of how the search for Viking roots could be hijacked in the service of very dark ideologies indeed and how this gained increased traction in the 1930s and early 1940s. The search for American Vikings and their modern influence had taken a turn into a bleak and threatening landscape.

CHAPTER TWELVE

VIKINGS READING COMIC BOOKS

B y the 1950s, the popularity of Vikings had been well established in US culture. They were no longer simply the preserve of Scandinavian immigrants who had sought to validate their role in the emerging nation of the nineteenth century. The saga accounts had become increasingly well known, as the Norse became contenders for the role of founders of European settlement in North America as part of ongoing myth making. Indeed, as we have seen, some had been reflecting on this possibility ever since Benjamin Franklin wrote to the Boston minister, Reverend Samuel Mather, in the late eighteenth century.

Even though hard evidence for their presence would have to wait until the discovery of the Maine Penny in 1957, and the even more convincing excavations at L'Anse aux Meadows in 1961–68, plenty of other searchers had claimed to have found Viking Age clues, as interest in the Norse explorers of North America had steadily grown. Yarmouth Rock had been extolled as a Viking artifact as far back as 1812, long before Olof Öhman discovered his runestone at Kensington, in 1898.

Then, during the first four decades of the twentieth century, American Vikings had gone from being cultural competitors of Columbus and the Mayflower Pilgrims, to being coopted in the service of right-wing nationalists in the 1930s and early 1940s as part of an aggressive promotion of alleged Nordic virtues in their deeds and their biology. It had been quite a journey and it had occurred before convincing archaeological evidence had been unearthed—let along dated—to support it.

What this meant was that Vikings were very visible on US cultural radar as the post-war period dawned after 1945. And, along with fascination with tracing evidence for historic explorers, had developed a parallel interest in Norse mythology and its cast of dramatic and colorful characters. This fascination was rooted in a nineteenth-century promotion of Germanism which brought the myths before an ever-widening audience, both in Europe and in the USA.

The dramatic adventures, supernatural feats, and weaponry, made the Norse myths very attractive to the emerging comic culture of the 1960s. And in seizing on, adapting, and repackaging these myths, the characters could be presented as super-heroes and super-heroines whose cultural roots, even after a huge amount of imaginative reworking, were a lot deeper than those of Superman, Batman and Robin, the Hulk, or Captain America. The Norse pantheon provided a cast of heroes and villains, conflicts, and worlds of being, that had been generating interest since the Middle Ages. Vikings were about to come of age in a new imaginative world and genre.

Consequently, Viking-related "heroes" have played a major role in the genre of US comic books. These include ones as diverse as: Jon Haraldson (also known as the Viking Prince), created by writer

Robert Kanigher and artist Joe Kubert, in *The Brave and the Bold #1*;
Thor, seen in the Marvel Universe as both an alien and a god
depending on who is writing the character; Odin and Loki, who
first appeared in the same Marvel issue as Thor in 1962; the goddess
Frigga first appeared in the Marvel comics as Thor's mother (and
Loki's adoptive mother) in 1963; then a separate character (Freya)
appeared in 1993 but, after 2011, both characters were combined.

   Charting the way these mythic characters have been used, and
their roles developed, in US comic culture, helps explain much of
how Vikings (already embedded in the US imagination) are viewed
today. The last sixty years have been a very successful time for
Viking public relations in the USA!

Old Characters
in a New Genre

The phenomenon of superhero comics is now well embedded in US
and world culture. One of the most famous of these comic-book
publishers, DC Comics, is one of the largest and oldest of all the
US comic-book companies. The first comic under the DC banner
was published in 1937. It was DC Comics (then named Detective
Comics, Inc) who first published the exploits of Superman (in
Action Comics Issue #1, in 1938). Arguably, DC invented the concept of the "comic superhero." The company used the brand name
"Superman-DC" from the 1950s. In 1977, it officially changed its
name to DC Comics, although it had colloquially been known as
"DC Comics" for many years. While it was DC Comics who had
a seminal role in establishing the superhero concept, it was a rival
company—Marvel Comics—which brought Vikings (via aspects
of their mythology) into the genre.

Marvel Comics (aka Marvel) is a primary imprint of Marvel Worldwide Inc. and part of Marvel Entertainment (the parent company was acquired by the Walt Disney Company in 2009). Marvel was started in 1939 as Timely Comics but it was in 1961 that the Marvel era really started when the company launched "The Fantastic Four" and several other superhero titles. These were famously created by Stan Lee, Jack Kirby, Steve Ditko, and other groundbreaking comic-book writers and artists. Among such superheroes as Spider-Man, Iron Man, and Captain America, Thor and his role in the superhero universe is most of interest to us.

Thor is known in the Old Norse pantheon as the god of thunder—the English word "thunder" is derived from his name. He first appeared in Marvel's *Journey into Mystery #83* (August 1962). This version of the Viking god of weather, a creation of artist Jack Kirby, writer Stan Lee, and scripter Larry Lieber, appeared during, what has been termed, the "Silver Age" of comic books. Today, "not only is Thor a recognizable superhero like Spider-Man, but the whole Norse pantheon has proven to be an endless source of inspiration for movies, TV shows and books."[1] In the comic books, Thor's superhero attributes and activities include his use of his mighty hammer, called *Mjolnir*, which enables him to both fly and control the weather.

Named as a founding member of the superhero team known as "the Avengers," in 1963,[2] the stories involving Thor have drawn in a range of supporting characters and opponents. Since his first appearance, he has featured in all volumes of the Avengers series, as well as other stories. As a result, the Marvel character of Thor has been deployed in animated television, films, video games, clothing, toys, and other merchandise. A whole generation of those influenced by comic-book culture are now familiar with a deity whose popularity in the Viking Age arguably surpassed that of Odin. Many of these readers and viewers will never have read one of the Icelandic mythical sagas, but they are now cognizant of at least one version of the thunder god.

The original concept was aimed at creating a character stronger than the Hulk. This prompted the idea of co-opting a god. The Norse myths were delved into in preference to the more familiar Greek and Roman pantheon. The one selected—Thor— would be depicted as a Viking warrior.[3] A form of this depiction had earlier appeared in 1957, when Jack Kirby did a version of Thor for DC, which appeared in *Tales of the Unexpected #16*. But it was the Marvel version which was to achieve huge publicity and impact. In September 1963, Lee and Kirby included Thor in *The Avengers #1*. A Viking-Age superhero had appeared in comic book culture and, in time, "the adventures of Thor were gradually transformed from stories about a strange-looking superhero into a spectacular saga."[4] Given the original significance of sagas in the building of the medieval Viking image, this choice of words was appropriate.

The selection of Thor for this comic-book role was clearly prompted by the image that is found in Norse mythology but the positive reception it received, it can be argued, owed something to the special place that Vikings had already forged in US consciousness. Scandinavian myth and US cultural history combined with Marvel's creative skills to ensure the enduring success of this Viking superhero. One of the North American saga sources (*Erik the Red's Saga*) referred to one of the original explorers of America as being a follower of "Old Redbeard" (Thor). That follower was named, appropriately, "*Thor*hall the Huntsman."[5] As the publisher's blurb on one study of medieval figures in US comic-book culture neatly put it: "The Mighty Thor reflects the legacy of Germanic migration into the United States."[6] Medieval history and myth, nineteenth-century immigration and mythmaking, have met in the comic book superhero based on the Norse prototype.

In this reimagined comic-book form, Thor battles not only the Frost Giants of Norse mythology, but also aliens, other super-villains, and dark supernatural enemies. Loki too plays a part as Thor's rival, although in the 1980s they were depicted as fighting alongside each other in an uneasy alliance. This ambiguity reflects something of the complexity of their relationship in the original medieval traditions.

Jason Aaron presented a memorable version of Thor, in *Thor: God of Thunder* (2012) and "then went on to shepherd the lightning lord through a series of ongoings, travels through time, an identity crisis, a new person wielding the hammer, and even a war across all ten realms!"[7]

Very different is *Thor: Vikings* (July 2003 to February 2004). This is a five-issue comic book limited series. It was published by MAX Comics, which is an imprint of Marvel Comics and was very much geared for adult audiences. Written by Garth Ennis and illus-trated by Glenn Fabry, this particular series tells the story of Thor's battle with a band of thousand-year-old undead Vikings, attacking New York City. It is an adult and US comic fantasy story, which involves rape and slaughter carried out by this group of Vikings.[8] In the story, a murderous, atrocity-causing Viking gang is first por-trayed in AD1003 on the coast of Norway. They then decide to sail to the New World (a clear connection to the *Vinland* sagas). How-ever, they are cursed (with the aid of a runestone) for their crimes and become undead. As a result, their journey lasts one thousand years, until they reach New York, where they embark on more atrocities. In the end, Thor leads a resistance which destroys them.

Loki and Other Norse Deities
in the Comic Books

Loki first appeared in the 1949 comic book *Venus,* but it was not until Stan Lee and Larry Lieber adapted him in 1962's *Journey into Mystery #85* that he became a prominent comic-book figure. In that issue Loki is presented as the complex enemy—but occasional ally—of his brother, or foster-brother, Thor. As in the sagas, Loki can change gender at times. He is a very complex character. Chris Bishop, author of *Medievalist Comics and the American Century,* has pointed out that the Loki-Thor dynamic of the comics and the later movies is a "classic, formulaic archetype," in which Thor represents the "big, hunky, handsome (but slightly dumb) hero" and Loki acts as "his slight, quirky but super-smart frenemy."[9] In short, "Thor is that dumb jock who everyone looked up to at school, but Loki was that cool, quiet kid who went on to found a tech-empire."[10] There is something quintessentially American, as well as Viking, about this dramatically imagined image.

However, while the contemporary feel is there in the comic image, the medieval original is also present in this characterization of Loki. This is because "despite the fact that the narrative details between the medieval Loki stories and their contemporary versions vary, the main idea remains the same—the trickster mercilessly attacks those in power and nearly causes the end of the world."[11] The world needs rescuing from Loki. The trickster-god appears here as "one of the greatest comic book villains of all time."[12]

In this sense, the idea of the trickster mischief-maker resonates with the modern turbulent and conflicted world. Something in this characterization of American Vikings in their mythic representation seems to speak to a polarized contemporary society. There are echoes of the anarchic threat of QAnon in this, and to that we will return shortly. However, in the comic world, it has been suggested that "There's still hope that Loki will prove to be good and that the other superheroes will save the world from whatever mayhem he's caused."[13]

The *Mighty Thor* series of comics proved highly successful for Marvel. As a result, many other figures from Norse mythology appeared in various other places in the Marvel universe. These included Loki as well as the Norns, the weavers of human fate. In opposition to Thor, Loki's followers, the Frost Giants, initiate the movement leading to *Ragnarok*. Loki has also appeared in Spider-Man.

Odin (Thor's father in the comics) first appeared in 1962, as did Thor, where he is described as Odin Borson, the All-Father (*Journey into Mystery #85*, October 1962). He has appeared in several stories since then. In one of the later series, he was even depicted as part of an ancient Avengers team (reflecting something of his son's role in the current one).[14]

Hel, Loki's illegitimate daughter with a giantess, also features in the comic books. In the original Norse mythology, she rules over the realm which contains the dead not chosen for Odin's hall in Valhalla. In the Marvel comics she is named Hela, first appearing in a 1964 issue as the daughter of Loki.[15]

Another notable mythological character is Freya. Along with her twin brother Frey, they both are members of the family of Norse deities called the *Vanir*. Freya is goddess of love and beauty and renowned for her chariot drawn by cats. Freya is also sometimes conflated with Frigg, the wife of Odin and queen of the gods. As "Frigga" she first appeared in the Marvel comics as Thor's mother—and Loki's adoptive mother—in 1963. Freya made a separate, short appearance in 1993. After 2011, "both these female characters were more or less considered the same person" in the comic books.[16]

In the 1990s, Marvel sold the rights to notable comic-book characters. This was part of a series of changes facing the comic book industry that decade. The key to survive this was "trying to figure out how to recoup money and so they licensed their characters to film studios."[17] It was to prove a momentous moment in the developing "careers" of fictional superhero characters, Norse among them. For American Vikings—at least in their mythic form—it hugely increased public awareness, a matter we will address in the next chapter.

Before we leave Marvel comics, it should be noted that DC Comics—while not creating an impact as large as *The Mighty Thor*—nevertheless also promoted Viking heroes. *The Viking Prince* began a series which first appeared in the earliest issue of *The Brave and the Bold* in 1955. He accompanied two other heroic figures: the "Golden Gladiator" and the "Silent Knight." The DC Comics *Viking Prince* stories were fantasy tales of high-seas adventures. Interestingly, it has been noted that "They came out just one year after Fredric Wertham's book *The Seduction of the Innocent* was first published—a book that blamed all the problems of American youth on the corrupting influence of comics."[18] It has been suggested that this may have been partly responsible for the more lighthearted tone of this series. However, "it left an indelible mark on the comics industry,"[19] which added to that later made by Marvel's contribution to the fascination with Viking themes. Most relevant to the idea of American Vikings was the publication of *Birds of Prey #29* (July 2001), in which a female superhero, Black Canary, travels back in time to twelfth-century America. There she meets Jon Haraldson (aka "the Viking Prince"), one of the *Vinland* Viking explorers. At this point, we have come full circle to the medieval adventurers of the *Vinland* sagas and the journeys to North America.

Other Comic-Book Vikings

DC and Marvel have not been the only publishers quarrying the Vikings for modern tastes. *Hägar the Horrible* is a very popular US cartoon which manages to comment on modern US life and society; but does it via a caricature that purports to be based on Viking Age life.

It was first published in 1973, the creation of Dik Browne, and was syndicated by King Features Syndicate. In 1988 Browne retired and died in 1989 and the cartoon was continued by his son Chris Browne, with artwork provided by Gary Hallgren.

One of its modern exposures came in 2020. It was then that the Viking character was spotted in a publicity photo used to announce Joe Biden's selection of Kamala Harris as his running mate in the presidential election, via a Zoom call. The cartoon—which could be seen in the photograph—was actually first printed in March 1986. It depicts Hägar the Horrible caught in a terrible storm and shouting heavenward "Why me?" To which God replies, "Why not?" The cartoon was given to Biden by his father in the early 1970s, shortly after the road traffic accident in which his first wife and little daughter were killed.[20] It illustrates the way that cartoons can be used to make profound points. As Biden described it: "My dad was always saying to us when we were down about something, 'Where is it written that the world owes you a living, pal? Get up.' This cartoon was his way of saying there is no way to rationalize what has taken place. It can happen to anyone, at any time."[21]

ABOVE: *Leiv Eirikson* [aka Leif Eriksson] *discovering America* by Christian Krohg (1893). *The National Museum (Nasjonal Museet), Oslo, licensed under the Creative Commons.* BELOW: Artist's reconstruction of a battle between Vikings and Native Americans, as described in the saga evidence. *Artwork by Angus McBride, from* The Vikings (Elite Series), *text by Ian Heath, color plates by Angus McBride, Osprey, 1985* © *Osprey Publishing, part of Bloomsbury.*

ABOVE: L'Anse aux Meadows site, Newfoundland, footprint of large building. *Clinton Pierce, licensed under the Creative Commons.* BELOW: L'Anse aux Meadows site, Newfoundland, reconstructed longhouse. *Copyright David J. Francis, used with permission, accessed from flickr.com/photos/professor126.*

Kensington Runestone, Minnesota. *Courtesy of August Schwerdfeger.*

ABOVE: Maine Penny/ Goddard coin, Maine. *Collections of the Maine State Museum (72.73.1/ME 30.42.1).*
BELOW: Yarmouth Rock, Nova Scotia. *Courtesy of the Yarmouth County Museum and Archives.*

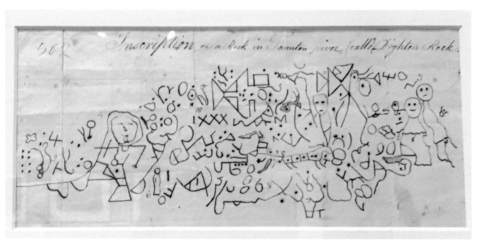

TOP: Dighton Rock, Massachusetts (marks on rock reconstructed). *Courtesy of Helena Meijer.* CENTER: Narragansett Runestone, Rhode Island. *Courtesy of Michael Derr/The Independent.* BOTTOM: Heavener Runestone, Oklahoma (with marks labeled). *From wikipedia, Holly Montgomery.*

ABOVE: Stone Tower, Rhode Island. *Courtesy of Darrell Nieberding.* BELOW: One of the Spirit Pond Runestones, Maine, showing alleged map. *From the collections of the Maine State Museum (72.19.2, Side 1).*

ABOVE: One of the Spirit Pond Runestones, Maine, with long inscription, side 1. *From the collections of the Maine State Museum (72.19.1, Side 1).* BELOW: One of the Spirit Pond Runestones, Maine, with long inscription, side 2. *From the collections of the Maine State Museum (72.19.1, Side 2).*

ABOVE: One of the Spirit Pond Runestones, Maine, with short inscription. *From the collections of the Maine State Museum (72.19.3, Side 1).* BELOW: Viking Centennial Stamp, 1925. *From wikimedia.*

The continued appeal of this cartoon strip, with its ability to communicate both serious comments humorously expressed and send-ups of human foibles, has contributed to its enduring popularity. How much of this is dependent on a cultural image of Vikings is open to question, but clearly something of the Viking caricature—drinking, adventuring, blundering—allows for comments on life to be communicated through the antics of a scruffy, overweight, red-bearded Viking. Let us not forget that a Viking linked to the American adventure was Erik *the Red*.

However, Vikings are not just there for wry humor. The image has been taken up by more serious publications too. The comic book series *Black Road* was written by Brian Wood, a US writer, illustrator, and graphic designer, with artwork by Gary Brown and its story takes place during the Christianization of Norway, "exploring concepts like honor, battle, regret, vengeance, and the struggle between the new Christian faith and ancestral polytheism practiced by the Scandinavian peoples."[22]

Also written by Brian Wood, and illustrated by a rotating cast of artists, the comic book series *Northlanders* features Viking Age stories to provide the background to a crime comic. Themes of injustice and retribution are major aspects of its plotlines. *Northlanders* ended in 2013.[23] The geographical spread of the stories extends from Russia to Orkney, via Norway. There is also "a glory-seeking tale of exploration following a crew rowing west across the endless sea."[24] For those of us focused on *Vinland*, this westward movement is a major feature of the Viking story.

Explicitly so is the appropriately titled *Vinland Saga*, a manga by Japanese artist Makoto Yukimura. The manga stories offer a Japanese take on the style of writing made famous by the US comic books. In it, the young warrior Thorfinn travels with the mercenary group who murdered his father; but he is plotting his revenge.

Unlike many of the comic story approaches to Viking history this account of the westward adventure "prides itself on a level of historical accuracy."[25] It draws imaginatively on the *Vinland* sagas as its hero is based on Thorfinn Karlsefni, who the sagas recount traveled to *Vinland*.[26] Leif Eriksson also makes an appearance in this manga series, portrayed as a friend of Thorfinn's father.[27] *Vinland Saga* was adapted into an anime series by Wit Studio; and Japanese animation studio MAPPA announced plans to animate its second season from January 2023.

Also, in the Japanese manga genre, but not historical in its portrayal of events, is the *Ah! My Goddess* (or *Oh My Goddess!*) series, which is written and illustrated by Kōsuke Fujishima. The series of stories is based on the Norns (those who weave the fates of humans) and the World Tree, *Yggdrasil*, which unites the different realms of being.

An example of Viking fantasy, of which many could be cited, is *Head Lopper*, "a fantasy Viking comic that's a mix of Samurai Jack and Dungeons and Dragons, with a dash of Adventure Time mixed for good measure."[28] Written and drawn by US comic book creator Andrew MacLean, with colors by Mike Spicer, the storyline follows a Viking named Norglund who fights injustice and battles monsters. It was originally self-published but was then taken on by Image Comics.[29]

Another popular Viking fantasy is the short graphic novella titled *Eternal*, by Australian Ryan K. Lindsay (writer), Eric Zawadzki (artist), Dee Cunniffe (colors). In it, a woman warrior leads other women from her village to victory against a malevolent warlock. However, his vengeance revisits her from beyond the grave.[30] Dramatically depicted, there are pages with no text at all.

All these Viking comic-book stories and graphic novels underscore the popularity of the Norse genre—rooted in the wider US comic books concept—and its role in communicating dramatic tales featuring Vikings. While this now has a global dimension (the Japanese manga being particularly striking examples of this), the original inspiration for the genre was in the USA and made use of characters and motifs already popular due to an American fascination with Viking themes. The idea of American Vikings, as it developed between 1800 and 1930, also played a major part in the growth of that Norse-focused fascination. The end-product of this process is still with us in the twenty-first century, as seen in the continued interest in comic book and graphic novel Vikings, and the influence of these on other genres. This phenomenon is closely related to films and TV series, to which we will now turn.

CHAPTER THIRTEEN

THE VIKINGS GO TO THE MOVIES . . . AND WATCH TV

T his chapter examines how and why the ideas of Vikings, and of Norse mythology, have influenced cinematic representations as diverse as the *Avengers* movies and the plot of the TV series *American Gods*. Why has this resonated with aspects of modern culture in the USA and globally? How has this influenced how we view the Viking heritage?

In this we will see how, as it were, Vikings have come to go to the movies, watch TV, stream programs, in which they and their mythology play a significant part.

Spoiler alert! Some of this will reveal the characters from the superhero comics appearing via another medium. Same "Nordic superheroes," similar plotlines, just a different form of communication. However, other representations go far beyond this. As we shall see in due course, some of the most recent representations offer a very different take on the Vikings and their mythology and, furthermore, firmly connect this with the febrile and contested subject of what constitutes "American Vikings" and their legacy in the modern USA, with its culture wars and battles for the "soul of America."

The Marvel Universe

After his Marvel debut in 1962, Thor—the Norse god of Thunder—was included in the first issue of *Avengers* in 1963. He was a founding member of this superhero team. Following this, he has appeared in many comic books, animated series, and in video games. However, the international success of the character hugely increased with Chris Hemsworth's portrayal of "Thor Odinson," in *Thor* (2011),[1] where we see the *Asgardians* battling the Frost Giants. The *Asgardian* concept imagines the Norse deities as "a humanoid race of extradimensional beings that hail from *Asgard*, a small pocket-dimension adjacent to Earth." In this reimagining of the Norse myths, "They travel around the Nine Realms including Earth via an interdimensional nexus known as the Bifrost."[2] This takes themes and motifs central to Norse mythology—*Asgard*, the home of the gods; the tiered realms of being; Bifrost, the rainbow bridge connecting *Asgard* to the human world—but envisages them in a fantasy sci-fi way. The idea is that these extraterrestrial superheroes became mythologized in human culture; but fell out of favor with the rise of Christianity. This seeks to loosely root mythology in an historic continuum; albeit framed in a fantastic way. There is, as we shall see, something of this in *American Gods*, but there it is envisaged in a grittier way.

Thor then became part of a large movie franchise created by Marvel Cinematic Universe (MCU), which involved the establishment of what has been termed "shared universes," in which the running storyline brings in a range of characters in an ongoing (loosely connected) narrative. This has involved the cross-over of common plot features, story-settings, cast members, and fictional characters. For Thor, this cinematic exposure (in addition to *Thor*, 2011) consisted of *The Avengers* (2012); *Thor: The Dark World* (2013); *Avengers: Age of Ultron* (2015); *Thor: Ragnarok* (2017); *Avengers: Infinity War* (2018); *Avengers: Endgame* (2019); *Thor: Love and Thunder* (2022).[3] This is a remarkable run of films and clearly indicates how Thor, the well-known comic-book character, has become a major player in this fictionalized universe.[4] As one commentator memorably put it: "this mighty god of thunder has really put in the work."[5] At the end of *Thor: Love and Thunder*, we are told that Thor will return, but in what form, we do not know. However, a mid-credit sequence "gave us a glimpse of a future adversary."[6] But will the character of this later Thor be Hemsworth's version? Only time will tell.

The same character also appeared in *Doctor Strange* (2016), as a cameo in the film's mid-credits scene. In this, Dr. Strange assists Thor, who has come with his brother Loki to Earth, engaged in a search for their father, Odin.

Additionally, an alternative version of this character appeared in 2021, in the US animated web TV series, produced by Marvel Studios and released on Disney+, *What If . . . ?* Thor appeared in the seventh episode of the first season. *What If . . . Thor Were an Only Child?* explores what would have happened if the central events of the film *Thor* (2011) had been different. In this animated alternative, Thor grows up without his adopted brother, Loki. In contrast to his usual character, Thor becomes the self-styled "party prince."[7] Thor was voiced by Chris Hemsworth, which provided continuity with the film character.

Reflecting on the process leading to this important step in the portrayal of the myths, it has been suggested that "They [Marvel] were trying to figure out how to recoup money and so they licensed their characters to film studios. That's when they licensed Spider-Man to Sony Pictures and Fantastic Four, X-Men, and Daredevil to 21st Century Fox studios."[8] It was the start of a winning idea. Then, "Upon the realization that they could create a movie franchise from their characters, they began filming successful box office movies."[9] The whole process has accelerated from there, with Marvel creating "their own film universe," and "not just sequels, but what we call film franchises."[10] The rest is cinematic history and Viking mythology played a major part in its emergence; and in a way that was very much in line with the US comic-book version of the Norse myths.

In this Marvel-inspired "cinematic universe," Odin too has played a part and has been portrayed in the movies by Sir Anthony Hopkins. We see him acting as the mythic Norse "All-Father" in *Thor*, *Thor: The Dark World*, and *Thor: Ragnarok*. At the same time, it has been asserted that, in this particular version of Odin, "many of the character's morally grey aspects have been hushed up."[11] This can be contrasted with the way that Odin is portrayed in *American Gods*, where Ian McShane plays the "enigmatic Mr. Wednesday."[12] Wednesday being the day named from Odin (from the Old English form Woden).

As we have seen, Loki too has been included in the movies. In the MCU films, Tom Hiddleston first portrayed Loki in 2011 and has delivered, what has been described as "a wickedly flamboyant performance ever since."[13] Outside the MCU, the trickster-god has also appeared as a character in CW Network's *Supernatural*. This series was created by Eric Kripke. It was first broadcast in 2005, on The WB Television Network, before becoming part of the output of its successor CW. In this presentation, Loki was portrayed by Richard Speight Jr. It has been remarked that while "this version of Loki is less glamorous and more gritty [than sometimes played], it stays true to the Trickster spirit of the Norse myths."[14]

In addition, the Marvel Studios and Disney+ series *Loki* was released in 2021 and explores more "antics of Thor's trickster brother as he attempts to fix the timeline he helped break in *Avengers: Endgame*."[15] This is a reminder both of how Thor and Loki form a complex duo, and of how the character of Loki is as ambiguous in the twenty-first century as in the medieval material.

Hela—who is portrayed by Cate Blanchett in *Thor: Ragnarok*—is presented as being Odin's first-born child; and is locked in conflict with Thor over the control of *Asgard*, the realm of the gods. It is a reminder that "pop culture doesn't always follow the original mythology,"[16] since in the Norse mythology Hel/Hela is daughter of Loki.[17] The myths and the semi-mythical history are mutable and never more so than in popular culture, as the next example vividly illustrates.

Vikings in a Sitcom: *Ghosts* and the Connection to *Vinland*

American Vikings can appear in surprising places. A recent example is in *Ghosts*, the American TV sitcom, adapted for CBS in the US from the British series of the same name. It first aired in October 2021 and in January 2023, the series was renewed for a third season.

The storyline is based on the idea that several ghosts inhabit a country mansion which is inherited by New Yorkers Samantha and Jay Arondekar, played by Rose McIver and Utkarsh Ambudkar. After a near-death experience, Sam finds she is able to see and hear them. The Viking connection comes in the form of a ghost named Thorfinn, played by Devan Chandler Long. Having sailed to North America over a millennium ago, the fictional Thorfinn was abandoned by his Viking shipmates and died after being struck by lightning. This character is based on Robin the caveman, who appeared in the original British series.[18] The substitution with a Viking is a clear nod to the *Vinland* sagas and the Viking exploration of the eastern seaboard of North America. In the sagas, Thorfinn Karlsefni (husband of Gudrid Thorbjornsdottir) shares a name with the character in this TV sitcom.

Vikings

A portrayal of Viking activities which has been widely viewed is the series *Vikings*, which first appeared in 2013 on History Channel (a Canadian network) and has gone on to appear on Amazon Prime. The series concluded in December 2020, although a sequel series—entitled *Vikings*: *Valhalla*—was first broadcast on Netflix in February 2022. The series is inspired by the activities of a Viking leader named Ragnar Lothbrok, who led raids on England and Francia in the ninth century.

There is also a North American connection since, in season 6, Ragnar's second-eldest son (Ubbe) is shown embarking on a perilous journey to Newfoundland, via Greenland. In so doing, the series places the North American adventure over a century before it occurred and involving a man who never actually sailed there. It illustrates how modern portrayals of historic events often adapt the traditional narrative for dramatic effects. In this case, "The Norse people's discovery of North America was accelerated in the *Vikings* timeline for the sake of bringing the show's themes full circle." This was because "The story began with Ragnar Lothbrok's dreams of exploring land that Vikings had never been to before, and season 6 saw the sons of Ragnar fulfilling his ambitions in different ways [including voyaging to North America]."[19]

This portrayal also edits out the violence against Native Americans that is so apparent in the saga evidence which recounts the voyages to *Vinland*. In *Vikings*, the Norse "settlers first encounter the Mi'kmaq people, leaving gifts for them as a gesture of good intent and working with the Mi'kmaq's leaders to try and cultivate peace between their people."[20] History—if the *Vinland* sagas are correct, and they almost certainly are—was much more violent than this portrayal.

It seems that more North American adventures are planned for the series *Vikings: Valhalla*, as this will feature Leif Eriksson among its cast of characters. We can expect more connections made in this series to the theme of American Vikings.

This brings us to a series which is explicitly set in America—in fact in the modern USA—and offers a very particular take on the idea of American Vikings.

American Gods—and a Battle for the "Soul of America"

American Gods is a dramatic and unusual American fantasy drama TV series. It was based on Neil Gaiman's 2001 novel of the same name and was developed by Bryan Fuller and Michael Green for the cable network Starz. It was distributed by Lionsgate Television, having been produced by Fremantle North America. The first season was broadcast in 2017. After three seasons, the series was cancelled in March 2021. By that time, it had attracted a lot of attention due to its highly unusual take on Viking mythology and a reimagining of it being played out in the modern United States.

Among other stars, it featured Ian McShane as the enigmatic Mr. Wednesday (a modern Odin or Woden), who leads the "old gods"; Ricky Whittle as Shadow Moon, a former convict who becomes the bodyguard and minder of Mr. Wednesday; Emily Browning as Laura Moon, the wife of Shadow Moon and a revenant (an animated corpse); Crispin Glover as Mr. World, the new god of Globalization, the leader of the "new gods"; Bruce Langley as Technical Boy, the new god of Technology; Yetide Badaki as Bilquis, a goddess of love; Demore Barnes as Mr. Ibis;[21] and others who represent different divinities and spiritual beings residing in the modern USA.

The plot is complex and unusual—in its combination of Americana, reflections on spirituality, and reworkings of ancient and modern mythologies—but we can reduce it to its main points by reference to the author's own website which sets the scene:

> Released from prison, Shadow finds his world turned upside down. His wife has been killed; a mysterious stranger offers him a job. But Mr. Wednesday, who knows more about Shadow than is possible, warns that a storm is coming—a battle for the very soul of America . . . and they are in its direct path . . . American Gods is a kaleidoscopic journey deep into myth and across an American landscape at once eerily familiar and utterly alien.[22]

It transpires that "Mr. Wednesday" is a god, one of the "old gods." These are "scratching a living in America"[23] because (and this is the central theme), each wave of immigrants to North America is envisaged as bringing their ancestral gods and goddesses with them. These include pagan deities and spiritual beings from across the varied pantheons of the Old World, along with US mythical folk heroes like Johnny Appleseed.

However, as people cease to believe in them, so their power dwindles. "Worse than that, there are new gods in America, and they have plenty of worshippers—the gods of TV and the internet, of shopping malls and credit cards, technological gods."[24] In the war for the soul of America, the Norse deities face another *Ragnarok*, but this time the demise they face is at the hands of twenty-first-century US materialism, consumerism, and technology, personified as the "new gods."

What is most striking is the lack of a strong presence of Christianity as a major force in this conflict. The novel never depicts Christ himself. There are just a few references to Jesus, but he never makes an appearance, nor does he directly interact with anyone in the story.[25] On the other hand, the Starz series eventually presents encounters with different Jesuses, beginning in episode 6, in 2017.[26] As a consequence, the series was written to include a Mexican Jesus, Hippie Jesus, White Jesus, Black Jesus, and Asian Jesus.[27] In the episode, titled "Come To Jesus" (the season finale), at least twelve different versions of Jesus travel to the estate of the goddess Easter, to celebrate the holiday that they all share.[28] Most Christians would not accept the view of Jesus presented in this episode. This raises the question of Viking Christians and the way that most who focus on the Norse seem reluctant to engage with the fact that conversion to Christianity rapidly replaced or hugely diluted faith in the old pagan pantheon. As we have seen, the triumph of the new faith is apparent in the *Vinland* sagas; but this is rarely seen in much popular reflection on Viking Age beliefs—which were not static.

Many of the original Viking Christian explorers of *Vinland*—not to mention the Mayflower Pilgrims, Columbus, and waves of Christian Scandinavian immigrants—would surely challenge this lack of a clear emphasis regarding the predominance of Jesus, considering

the religious outlooks they carried to America (even given conflicting versions of the faith, as pointed to by the TV series).

There is, it might be argued, an answer to this in the fictional
narrative theme of *American Gods* and that is that, because Jesus
is still worshipped by millions of Americans, he is not really part
of the battle going on between "new gods" and "old gods." He is,
in this construct, largely interacting with his huge number of followers and their expectations.[29] How well such a view explains the
absence of Jesus in the book and the emphasis on multiple Jesuses
in the series, only readers can judge. It clearly sidesteps a vast area
of historic and contemporary US faith culture; and this includes the
culture of the Christian Vikings who sailed to *Vinland*.

The book paints a dark picture of a hidden America, that lurks
beneath the surface of the visible, around the corner in the street
of the here-and-now. There are echoes in the situations faced by
Shadow of the Arthurian hero Sir Gawain, who is honor-bound
to face death at the axe of the Green Knight; or Orpheus, braving
Hades to rescue the woman he loves.[30] Ancient and modern myths
intertwine in the book and in the series.

Today—in a world that has seen the claims of QAnon about dark
forces at work in politics and society, social-media dissemination
of conspiracy theories, and the recourse to violence among those
who oppose what they consider to be the trajectory of modernity
and politics generally—there is something prescient in the novel's
portrayals of a battle between the past and present in small-town
America, as well as on the wider canvas of modern technological
developments. And in this, the mythology of the Vikings plays a key
part. It is a significant addition to the multidimensional character
of American Vikings.

We may consider these themes as signposts pointing the way
toward our next chapter, where we will explore the way in which

conspiracy theorists and white supremacists have taken on the Viking mantle as they seek to influence the narrative in the modern US culture wars. This is very different to the fantastic mythological picture painted by Gaiman, but in some ways there is, perhaps, something worryingly similar—in the modern dark web and the violent polarization of the contemporary world, as some in modern society seek to use the Norse as totems in today's culture wars and battles for "the soul of America." Arguably, Mr. Wednesday's warning that "a storm is coming" strangely anticipates the QAnon claims of a "coming storm," when hidden conflicts will finally break to the surface,[31] in a violent battle reminiscent of *Ragnarok* itself. It is to that we now turn.

CHAPTER FOURTEEN

AMERICAN VIKINGS MEET QANON

T he search for American Vikings—their origins and their impact—has been a complex one. However, this long and varied history has reached one of its most extraordinary, shocking, and surprising milestones in the twenty-first century. It is not without some precedence in the history of the past two hundred years, but its current manifestation is, nevertheless, still striking and disturbing. For this is where the history of American Vikings meets QAnon and the culture wars that beset the USA in the 2020s.

A Viking at the Capitol?

On January 6, 2021, QAnon follower, Jake Angeli (aka Jacob Chansley), joined in the storming of the Capitol Building in Washington, DC. Photos of the bison-horned headdress and face paint of the bare-chested person, who became known as the "Q-Shaman," were some of the defining images of the event and were seen around the world. At first glance, it looked as if only Native American cultural traditions were being appropriated by him. The bison-horn headdress seemed reminiscent of those worn by some members of Plains tribes in the nineteenth century. However, on closer investigation, it became clear that Vikings were very much in the mix on that dramatic day and in the worldview of this person who, for many, came to personify much of it. This is because Angeli was seen to have three "Viking" tattoos clearly visible on his body: the intersecting three triangles of the *valknut*; an apparent depiction of *Yggdrasil*, the World Tree; and *Mjolnir*, Thor's hammer.[1]

We have come across two of these already in this exploration of the Vikings. *Mjolnir* has been seen on items as varied as Viking Age pendants from archaeological sites, and the modern film depictions of Thor in action. It is a weapon closely associated with the Norse god of Thunder. Those who wore these pendants in the early medieval period were signaling their devotion to this deity. Those who wear it today no doubt do so for a wide range of reasons but, at the very least, it evokes some form of claimed Viking identity and an appeal to the mythology of the Norse peoples.

Yggdrasil was the connecting point between the different realms of being in Norse mythological cosmography and symbolized the worldview of the pagan Viking Age. It is sometimes now used by those who wish to signal sympathy with—or belief in—pagan Norse mythology. As with the Thor's hammer symbol, it is linked to modern "Viking identity."

The *valknut* is formed from three interlocking triangles and has been found on several objects from the Viking Age and the early medieval Germanic world. These include: the Anglo-Saxon Nene River Ring, from eastern England; the wooden bed in the Oseberg ship-burial, from Norway; and it is also found on fragments of tapestry from the Oseberg ship-burial. The *valknut* is also depicted on two picture-stones from Gotland, Sweden, the Stora Hammars I stone and the Tängelgårda stone. Some experts have suggested that, in the Viking Age, it was associated with the god Odin and it has been compared to markings found on the Danish Snoldelev Stone.[2] Snorri Sturluson—the thirteenth-century Icelander who did so much to preserve earlier Norse mythology—recounted in his composition entitled *Skaldskaparmal* (*Language of Poetry*) that a famous giant called Hrungnir had a stone heart, which was "pointed with three corners." As a result, the *valknut* is sometimes also known as "Hrungnir's Heart."[3]

What is clear is that it—like the Thor's hammer and the World Tree—was derived from Viking Age beliefs and has become closely identified with ancient Norse culture among those seeking to promote this and connections to it. This has been particularly the case among people who, today, believe in some form of the Norse mythology or who seek to draw political or cultural parallels between aspects of modern society and Viking society. Far less controversially, the *valknut* symbol is also used by the Swedish forest products company *Svenska Cellulosa Aktiebolaget*, and the German Football Association (the DFB). However, in the case of Jake Angeli, the Viking symbols apparently conveyed something beyond just an interest in Norse history and culture. This raises the rather obvious questions of why a person involved in the violent events at the US Capitol would have so publicly displayed these tattoos? And whether they have any meaning that is related to the cause that he and others were espousing on that day?

That these symbols were, in some way, connected with his belief in the conspiracy theory known as "QAnon," was made abundantly clear by the fact that he was photographed bare chested, to display the tattoos, in Peoria, Arizona, in 2020, carrying a homemade placard that read: "Q Sent Me!" As an explosive input into apocalyptic right-wing politics, the phenomenon known as "QAnon" first appeared in October 2017, when a "drop" (aka a post) appeared on 4chan from an anonymous account calling itself "Q Clearance Patriot." These posts later shifted to 8chan and then to 8kun. This was the appearance of the infamous "Q." Claiming to be a government insider with high security clearance, what followed was a huge number of cryptic posts—known to followers as "Q-drops"—that claimed that Donald Trump was engaged in an existential conflict with a "deep state" international conspiracy of devil-worshipping pedophiles and cannibalistic child-murderers. The Q-drops claimed that the Trump-led resistance would culminate in "The Storm," when the members of the cabal would be arrested by the military, with some being imprisoned at Guantánamo Bay, and others facing military tribunals and execution.[4] Supporters of QAnon later "deluged social media with false information about COVID-19, the Black Lives Matter protests, and, of course, the presidential election [of 2020]."[5] The last "Q-drop" occurred on December 8, 2020.[6] By this time, the Q-phenomenon had become an integral part of the febrile partisan politics of the modern USA.

This was the shadowy world in which Angeli lived; and which culminated in the events of January 6, 2021. After being photographed taking part in the storming of the Capitol, Angeli was arrested on January 9, 2021, on federal charges of "knowingly entering or remaining in any restricted building or grounds without lawful authority, and with violent entry and disorderly conduct on Capitol grounds."[7] His attire and his highly visible Viking tattoos made him easily identifiable. He pleaded guilty to a single charge in September 2021. Following this, he was sentenced to three and a half years, or 41 months, in prison in November 2021.[8] American Vikings had become entangled with a very dark aspect of contemporary US politics and culture.

What is clear is that, while Angeli exemplified a strange personal connection between Viking pagan symbols, QAnon, and the world of conspiracy theorists, he was not alone. "Many people have similar tattoos which express their neo-pagan belief, Scandinavian heritage, or interest in the myths. But there is no doubt that these symbols have also been co-opted by a growing far-right movement."[9] The question is how and why have some aspects of the Viking myth been co-opted by modern believers in right-wing conspiracy theories? In addition to this, it is clear that the Viking legacy has also become closely associated with white supremacists in the modern USA. Why is this so?

Vinland and the Modern Alt-right

The white supremacist Jeremy Christian—sentenced to life imprisonment in 2020, for the murders of two fellow passengers on a MAX train in May 2017, in Portland, Oregon[10]—had earlier posted on Facebook: "Hail Vinland!!! Hail Victory!!!"[11] For many, the reference to the Norse name for North America will have been incomprehensible. However, it has become woven into a modern narrative which seeks to rewrite the history of the USA and to use that as justification for radical and violent racism in the twenty-first century.

In 2009, the Southern Poverty Law Center (SPLC) reported on the rise of "Odinism." This is more than simply an attempt to revive Norse paganism. Instead, it is a movement designed to draw on Vikings and their North American connection, to promote a radical alt-right political and cultural agenda. This has included the establishment of groups such as the "Holy Nation of Odin, Inc." and the "Vinland Folk Resistance." These groups extol "the virtues of

Odinism and racism" and are dedicated to "the ultimate triumph of a pure, white race."[12]

Such names are not isolated examples of Norse and Germanic references by modern groups, with alleged white supremacist views. In the Pacific Northwest can be found the "Wolves of Vinland" (again that Viking connection to the place known from the sagas) and other groups, such as one, allegedly affiliated, named "Operation Werewolf."[13] With regard to this latter group, it has been reported that "One individual who routinely shares Operation Werewolf social media posts, responded in 2012 to an article about the (untrue) legend of Viking colonization of Minnesota and southern Canada by writing on Facebook, 'Our History is not a hoax. Hail Vinland!!!'"[14] Once again, a reference to *Vinland*. The pattern is becoming difficult to ignore. Clearly, "Vinland is a rallying cry for white nationalists."[15] One Canadian Odinist tellingly described himself as "White and a Nationalist for Vinland" and a "Viking and Patriot."[16] There seems little ambiguity there. Similarly, at the infamous "Unite the Right" rally in Charlottesville, Virginia, in 2017, it was noted that some alt-right protesters there dressed as crusaders, and others as Vikings, and some carried Viking-style shields.[17] Thor's hammer symbols were also apparent there.[18]

The radical right connection with Vikings is not confined to the USA. Anders Breivik, the Norwegian extremist who murdered seventy-seven people in 2011, carved the names of Norse gods into his guns.[19] The perpetrator of New Zealand's Christchurch Massacre, in March 2019, posted on the 8chan message board "I will see you all in Valhalla,"[20] before carrying out mass shootings at two mosques which left fifty-one people dead and forty injured. In 2020, he was sentenced to life imprisonment without the possibility of parole; the first such sentence issued by a court in New Zealand. Closer to the USA, a Finnish white supremacist movement named

the "Soldiers of Odin" have been noted as now having members in
Canada.[21] When the researcher Patrik Hermansson went undercover
among Odinist groups, he reported on "gatherings where extremists drank mead from a traditional Viking horn and prayed to the
Norse god Odin."[22]

The scholar Dorothy Kim, Assistant Professor of English, and
teaching Medieval Literature at Brandeis University, Massachusetts,
commented that "The medieval western European Christian past
is being weaponized by white supremacist/white nationalist/KKK/
Nazi extremist groups."[23] The particularly Neo-Nazi form of the
modern pagan belief described as "Odinism" (and referred to earlier)
is sometimes described using the term *Wotansvolk* (Odin's Folk)[24]
and *Wotanist* (a German form of the Old Norse name Odin). It
should, however, be noted that not every modern neo-pagan group,
that adopts Norse mythology as part of its belief system, is racist.

The Appeal of a Version of
Viking History

The answer to why the Vikings have this appeal to modern radical-
right nationalists in the USA (and elsewhere) is rooted in the belief
held by some members that the early Scandinavian Viking Age
culture represents a primordial European society that was all white
and racially unmixed. Vikings have, once again, become part of
political mythmaking. In this new myth, "American white supremacists want to make Vinland (as they term it) great again, laying out
an imagined past in which Vikings are the rightful conquerors of
North America, locked in eternal battle with the Skraelings, the
Viking slur for indigenous people."[25] Despite "the catastrophic and
bloody failure of Vinland as recorded in the sagas," this has become

"a rallying cry, rewriting history to create a need for the existence of a movement to defend whiteness."[26] This is often linked to "the perception of Vikings as being the ultimate example of masculine ideals," which—it has been argued by one commentator—"is at the root of white supremacists' obsession with this subject."[27]

Those who engage with this use of Viking imagery often subscribe to belief in "The Great Replacement," which expresses fears about alleged white demographic decline. It is a phrase frequently used among white nationalists, both in the USA and globally, and resonates with those who view Viking Age warriors and communities as representing "racially pure" Germanic culture. In 2001, a contributor named "Yggdrasil" started a thread on the white nationalist site Stormfront (founded in the US in 1995 [28]) which sought to establish criteria by which films would be deemed acceptable to white nationalists. These included "Positive portrayal of whites in defense against the depredations of liberalism, crime, and attack by alien races."[29] This is often connected to armed defense of the "*Vinland* cause." It is noteworthy that one prominent *Wotanist* (who founded an organization named the Viking Brotherhood) is reported as having linked the US Second Amendment to a command by Odin "to be armed."[30]

In 2020, Natalie Van Deusen, Scandinavian Studies professor at the University of Alberta, Canada, commented (in an article for the Canadian Historical Association) that current white supremacist movements are "motivated by their belief in a white medieval past and a pure ancestral race they perceive as under threat in the face of immigration and religious and racial diversity."[31] This partly helps explain why the Vikings who are (as we have seen) "prime fodder for comic book superheroes and videogame characters," and dramatic action films, can also get coopted by "White supremacists in the U.S. and elsewhere [who] have seized onto the imagery and iconography of Viking warriors as part of a fascistic appeal to pure bloodlines and social Darwinism."[32] The Viking legacy is complex and has been made more so by those who wish to use them as part of a modern alt-right narrative.

In reality—as Van Deusen and many other Norse scholars have pointed out—Viking Age communities were culturally and ethnically complex and diverse. The Vikings who sailed to *Vinland* did not represent the Germanic monoculture promoted by the modern white nationalists who have coopted them as historical prototypes.[33] This view is often impervious to attempts to challenge it. Although at the London premiere of *The Northman* (distributed by Focus Features in the USA and by Universal Pictures International, internationally) in early April 2022, the director, Robert Eggers, explained on stage that he was seeking to reclaim Viking history from right-wing groups, this did not stop an anonymous post from appearing on 4chan praising its "all white cast" and "pure raw masculinity," and furthermore claiming that such films are "restoring pride in our people" and "The Northman is going to be epic . . . Hail Odin."[34] It is a view of the film strongly challenged by, among others, Danish actor Claes Bang, who appears in the film.[35]

The current situation, with regard to this disturbing use of Viking culture for extreme political purposes, illustrates how the Norse have sailed into some very dark places of the US—and global—imagination. Nevertheless, as one film commentator reminds us: "At the same time, Vikings are legitimately fascinating, and bad people liking a good thing doesn't usually make that thing less good, though it can cloud perceptions."[36] This is a reasonable assertion and reminds us that the study of American Vikings is far broader than this most controversial of their modern manifestations. And, as we have seen in this study overall, "medievalism can be used for positive and negative causes."[37] However, this chapter does remind us of the complexity of the Viking journey from eleventh-century *Vinland* into modern perceptions.

CHAPTER FIFTEEN

MERCHANDISING VIKINGS

W e have seen how Vikings have become interwoven into many highly visible aspects of US culture and politics since the nineteenth century. Alongside this, Vikings have also added to brand identities in many areas of US life and consumption.

What does this reveal about the complex nature of Vikings in the modern USA? How does this relate to the historic story of American Vikings that we have explored in this book? Exploring a little of this evidence will go some way toward providing answers to these questions.

The "Viking Brand"

Vikings appear is a staggeringly large number of ways in US merchandising. What follows here is just a small sample of what is out there! What we might call the "Viking brand" has many facets, as we shall see. However, having looked at the wide range of ways that Vikings are referenced, we will attempt to "see the forest for the trees" by identifying common and repetitive features of this merchandising of Vikings. This will allow us to draw some tentative conclusions regarding the main ways in which Vikings act as commercial references and the role that they play in marketing policies.

One common feature of much of the merchandising is "the fallacious horned helmet,"[1] the axe, the fur jacket, and the longship. This has made Vikings a very recognizable "product," even if archaeology can supply no examples of the horned (nor the winged) helmets that dominate the modern popular imagination.

There are many examples which reference this image, but one of the most famous is associated with the NFL team, the Minnesota Vikings. The fact that the Minnesota Vikings have this evocative name is not surprising, given the location of the Kensington Rune-stone in the state and the high level of interest in the medieval Norse past which has characterized the Midwest since the mid nineteenth century. The striking logo of the Minnesota Vikings consists of a rightward facing Viking warrior, with long golden moustache and plaited hair. The helmet has two backward-sweeping horns and its lower section is purple, the dominant color of the team's Home Uniform. The distinctive logo and uniform has altered over time but the highly recognizable mustached Viking warrior has appeared largely the same, since 1966. Prior to that (1961–65), he faced left, had a white moustache, the horns were yellow, and the style of presentation was significantly different. Nevertheless, he was still very recognizable as an archetypal Viking.[2] This is a remarkable example of how nineteenth-century pioneering settlement—which looked back to the medieval past as settlers established a new identity in the USA—has had an ongoing impact on identities since then. The Minnesota Vikings are a vivid example of this. But they are not alone.

There are other NFL connections to Vikings. During the 2018 Super Bowl, the Dodge company ran commercials for the Ram 1500 truck. "In them, a group of Vikings use the truck to haul their ship,"[3] which underscores the robust nature of the vehicle. Singing a version of "The Wheels on the Bus"—with the word "truck" replacing "bus"—the advert proclaims, "There's tough, and then there's *Viking* tough."[4] As a researcher at the University of Western Michigan succinctly put it: "The target audience for truck ads are typically men. In order to appeal to their target audiences, ads sell you an idealized image of yourself."[5] It is a fair observation. Another version of the Dodge Ram truck advert has Vikings singing "We will rock you!" as they travel in the truck; and then row a Viking longship that is towing the truck across roiling gray waves. At one point, with a humorous nod to health and safety, the ad advises: "Never ride in the bed of a truck unless you are an authentic Viking."[6] In the ad, the Vikings are heading to Minneapolis, Minnesota, before realizing they need to divert to a different location for the night's match.

Vikings can also be used to sell sex. In Durex's "Be Heroes for the Night" campaign, of 2016, a Viking man and woman are used to sell the "Durex Pleasure Ring." As they roll around, before a roaring fire, "they instantly transform into their modern-day selves."[7] The message? Apparently, it is: use this product and have sex like a Viking. It should be noted that what is shown is entirely consensual; unlike much that would have occurred on a Viking raid.

A related kind of thinking rooted in ideas of attractive masculinity probably lies behind the naming of male personal deodorants, hair gel, and shower products. Razors, beard grooming products, and beard conditioner and shampoo, ties into modern ideas of maleness while evoking images of bearded Vikings of the past—although these probably did not put as much time into personal grooming.

But maybe that is doing them an injustice. After all, the English medieval chronicler John of Wallingford (died c. 1258), included an accusation that Viking men had seduced married English women and persuaded the daughters of English nobles to be their mistresses through the (in his view) questionable habits of bathing every Saturday, frequently changing their woolen clothes, and regularly combing their hair.[8] In which case, we must assume that the image of sweating and disheveled Viking warriors, prevalent in TV dramas, needs to be moderated with the thought of them looking to personal hygiene in order to stand out from ill-smelling males who were love rivals! Similarly focused on a perceived appeal of a certain kind of "maleness," a Viking press-attachment for a barbell evokes ideas of muscular Vikings engaged in workouts to improve their toned muscles.

A number of food products are also enhanced by connection with Vikings. A North Dakota brewery—Drekker, in Fargo—styles its product as "hand-crafted beer for the Viking in all of us."[9] Its website references common ideas about Vikings, but with a twist: "Create and destroy . . . create experiences and destroy expectations"; "Do good and give back. UnPillage," alongside information about the brewery's support for charitable causes. One of its "UnPillage Projects" is described as assisting in cleaning out trash from the Red River at Fargo, "then head back to the brewery for some beer and pizza!"[10] It is a striking way in which even the negative image of Viking raiders can be rerouted to positive ends. Other beers also reference the Viking name.

One food producer sources meat from small, local farmers in Missouri and Illinois, in order to produce food labelled "Viking delight." In New Jersey, one can find a deli and grill named from Vikings. "Viking Pastries," in Pennsylvania, sells wedding cakes and other sweet delights. There's a "Viking Bakery" in New Jersey and no doubt in many other places too if one searches. The connection with foodstuffs may be encouraged by the idea that Vikings feasted, alongside the generally positive way that these intrepid explorers are remembered. No doubt there is an individual story behind each one of these enterprises that reference the ancient Norse—often with a longship or a horned helmet visible in order to underscore the connection.

Many other items that have nothing to do with Norse history attract the Viking name; no doubt to convey ideas about their robust nature and reliability. So, an internet trawl, accompanied by a check of US registered traders, produces: Viking cookware (nonstick and stainless steel) and Viking kettles; electrical suppliers; sprinkler systems; trailers; coil tubing; office products; pest control; manufacturing and marketing of professional grade kitchen appliances; drills and tool bits; fire and burglary resistant products; global investors; a fencing company; a supplier of forest products; automotive supplies; a construction company; a collection agency. The list goes on and on. It is interesting how many of these are based in Minnesota or Michigan. Clearly, the regional identification with Vikings encourages this as a known and trustworthy brand name there. But the key point is that Vikings are considered a solid and reliable thing to be associated with, and to be named from.

A number of the specific products—except for the neutral cookware—seem gendered and geared toward traditional male appearance and activities. This is not exclusively so, but the trend that way is strong. The only time that this trend shifts somewhat the other way, is if one searches online for "fancy dress" and then female Viking costumes (often highly inadequate for a cold night out on a longship) accompany the stereotypical male costumes (with plastic horned helmets and axes being much in demand, regardless of the gender identified, or so it seems).

It is also notable that we find "numerous school Junior Reserve Officer Training Corps using Viking branding in their insignia."[11] Given the association of the Viking image with "fearsome warriors and adventurers,"[12] this is understandable.

The continued attraction of Vikings is also seen in the "virtual violence" of video gaming; in a genre sometimes termed "Hack and Slash." For example, *God of War Ragnarök* (released worldwide in November 2022, for the PlayStation 4 and PlayStation 5), was the latest release in the *God of War* action-adventure game franchise created by David Jaffe at Sony's Santa Monica Studio. Having become a flagship series for PlayStation, since its inauguration in 2005, its Norse-based games remind us of the continued attraction of the Viking mythological brand, the mutability of Vikings, and the way that references to them occur across the wide range of available media in the twenty-first century. *God of War Ragnarök* is currently "the fastest-selling first-party launch game in PlayStation history," having sold more than 5.1 million units during its first week.[13] This is testimony to the attraction of "the immersive spell that video games cast"[14] and of the Viking contribution to this.

The Characteristics of the "Viking Brand"

Several characteristics stand out and can be identified as facets of the "Viking brand."

The first is the portrayal of the Viking's rugged masculinity; a "visual shorthand for a masculinity that is synonymous with strength." In marketing terms: "buy this product, and your manliness is confirmed."[15] As we have seen, the Viking brand is often gendered in its application.

The second is less explicitly masculine, but assumes a general sense of robust well-being. This encapsulates ideas of "endurance, adventurousness, joviality, and feasting."[16] This sense of positivity and can-do, means that "the Viking brand itself is so strong it can add commercial value even when the public knows there is no connection to a historical period or indeed to Norse culture."[17] This is an inclusive use of the brand, which sharply contrasts with its use within the excluding community of white supremacists (chapter 14). And, even if this expansive use of the image is bland, at least it is not toxic.[18]

The third is rooting a product or service in an area with Scandinavian roots. This is certainly not always the case, but it is interesting to note how many of the enterprises which reference Vikings are located in the Midwest. For example, it has been estimated that more than three hundred businesses in Minnesota use the word "Viking" in their name.[19] In this, we can chart an oblique, but long-rooted, connection with the *Vinland* sagas because this was an area where nineteenth-century Scandinavian settlers consciously developed and celebrated an identity in the New World which was deliberately linked to the Old World and the *Vinland* explorers.

The fourth is providing a modern product or experience that has an echo of tradition, of longevity, of rootedness. Many people may not be able to accurately place the Viking Age on a timeline, but they are well aware that it is an historic period in the past. That can give a modern product, or experience, the sense of being on a solid foundation. And marketing is, after all, rooted in perception as well as in actuality.

Many of these aspects of Viking merchandising can be found globally, but they also have particular appeal within the US context. That appeal is, arguably, connected with both the reality and the myth of *Vinland*. This is because *Vinland* acts as a dramatic precursor to the better-known arrivals and pioneering that characterized European settlement from the sixteenth century onward. It was this aspect that was consciously celebrated by Scandinavian settlers in the Midwest in the nineteenth century. It said: we were here before Columbus, Jamestown, and the Mayflower. While this commonly presented "pioneering spirit" is a selective construction, which ignores or minimizes displacement and destruction of Native American communities, there is no doubt that it played, and plays, a key role in both historic US self-awareness and mythmaking, and present-day concepts of the confident US nation that overcomes adversity. The simple reality is that something of "Manifest Destiny" still influences modern US culture and identity. To this, the *Vinland* Vikings (again usually excluding memories of the violence) speak strongly. In short, "the *Vinland* sagas have provided the opening for a myth that fits well with America's vision of itself as a nation of pioneers and adventurers."[20] It is frequently this that modern merchandising references, even if in a vague way. Vikings and *Vinland* continue to impact on many modern perceptions and values in North America generally, and especially in the United States.

WHERE NEXT FOR THE AMERICAN VIKINGS?

W e have come a long way—both in time and distance—in the search for American Vikings. It is a story that connects the so-called Old World with the New, the past with the present, the real with the imagined, the ancient myth to the modern, the dramatic Middle Ages with the turbulent twenty-first century. It is a story that ranges across Greenland, the Canadian Arctic, Newfoundland, New Brunswick, the St. Lawrence catchment and its hinterland, the Great Lakes, Maine, Massachusetts, Rhode Island, Minnesota and beyond. It is about remembering, imagining, celebrating, and creating identities. And because it is a mixture of all these ingredients, the "Viking Cocktail" packs quite a punch in terms of controversy. Questions and assertions about the Norse animate discussion, controversy, and heated arguments across the North American continent but, arguably, nowhere more so than in the current United States. So, while the search for American Vikings ranges across the eastern part of the North American continent and its northern islands, it finds its most challenging route to negotiate (a very appropriate term) within the USA itself. Here, especially, the Norse have proved so malleable in the process of mythmaking that Annette Kolodny memorably described them as "The Plastic Viking."[1]

What is clear from all of this is that—in hard-won fact, as in creative fantasy—the search for these Vikings of North America continues in the twenty-first century. As a result, we see Vikings in history-documentaries and blogs; on beer labels and football-team badges; in comic-books, and on the screen (cinema, TV, computer, and phone); as well as in assertions of cultural identity which, at times, have become highly politicized and radicalized.

Alongside the harmless mainstream merchandising which references Vikings, and the more-troubling annexation of the Viking heritage in some corners of modern politics, there is also the legitimate archaeological search for more evidence of Viking settlement in North America.

In 2015, archaeologists working at Point Rosee, a peninsula on southern Newfoundland extending into the Gulf of St. Lawrence, were drawn to a site which satellite images had revealed to contain ground features that might indicate human habitation. The site was located by archaeologist Sarah Parcak of the University of Alabama at Birmingham, and a National Geographic Fellow. Parcak is experienced in the use of satellite imagery to locate lost archaeological sites. Limited excavation there revealed what was tentatively interpreted as an iron-working hearth, partially surrounded by what appears to have been a turf wall. Traces of charcoal found at the site, along with 28 lb (12.7 kg) of what was identified as slag were suggested as possibly indicating that the roasting of bog iron ore had occurred there. This, and the turf-built shelter, initially pointed toward the possibility of Norse activity at the site (rather than Native Americans or Basque whalers).[2]

However, from 2016 to 2018, this tentative possibility has been seriously questioned. The rocky shoreline and lack of fresh water, accompanied by lack of definitive evidence, means it cannot definitely be identified as Viking.[3] Indeed, there was no clear proof of human activity that could be dated earlier than 1800, and the metal (originally suggested to possibly be smelted iron) has since been identified as the kind of bog iron commonly found across Newfoundland. A report submitted to the provincial government in 2018 concluded that the 2016 research "found no evidence whatsoever for either a Norse presence or human activity at Point Rosee prior to the historic period."[4]

However, the discovery of seeds of butternut at the site, points to someone taking part in journeys further south (these do not grow on Newfoundland) and could link the site to L'Anse aux Meadows, where butternuts were also found. So, the site and area may yet surprise.

If Point Rosee had been definitely identified as Norse, then this would have encouraged the use of satellite imagery to locate other Viking Age sites on the eastern seaboard of North America. Even if not identified to be such, the technology may yet reveal sites elsewhere that do turn out to be what is being sought.

Since then, in 2018, Birgitta Wallace—an Atlantic Region archaeologist for Parks Canada—suggested a new site as the possible location of *Hop*, in the sagas. As L'Anse aux Meadows is often considered to be *Straumfjord*, the search for *Hop* has occupied a number of researchers for some time. The site suggested by Wallace is in the Miramichi River-Chaleur Bay area of New Brunswick. In her view, this possible identification is based on a triangulation of wild grapes, salmon, coastal sandbanks, and a native population that used animal-hide boats.[5] However, while this may be correct, the identification was not based on any new archaeological evidence.

This reminds us of the complexity of the topic and of the difficulties faced in the search for new sites. Nevertheless, it is very possible that future research will unearth archaeological clues that connect with the eleventh-century explorers. If L'Anse aux Meadows is not *Vinland* (and this seems a reasonable conclusion), then what sites remain to be discovered that may connect to the places mentioned in the sagas? Given the reasonable assumption that the saga evidence does not represent every Norse site in North America, we may yet find places for which we do not even have a tentative name. And this is before we consider the possibility of discovering more Norse artifacts on Native American sites, to compare with the Maine Penny (Goddard Coin). These are fascinating—and very real—possibilities for the future of American Vikings.

All of this has established the Vikings firmly in American consciousness. When the Smithsonian opened its exhibition *Vikings: The North Atlantic Saga*, in 2000, Hillary Clinton referred to the Vikings being "more than an historical presence in North America; they also represent the spirit of discovery that Americans, especially, can relate to."[6]

At the same time, there is every reason to believe that the celebration of a more modern Scandinavian heritage in the USA will continue to be strong.[7] While this is often linked to specific Scandinavian nations, it also includes pan-Scandinavianism, which celebrates common features of Nordic culture. For example, the largest Scandinavian festival in the USA—*Norsk Høstfest*—was first established in 1978, in Minot, North Dakota. With about 40 percent of the town's population being of Scandinavian descent when the festival started, it soon became very popular and has remained so.[8] According to its website: "The festival features world-class entertainment, authentic Scandinavian cuisine, Scandinavian culture on display, and handcrafted Norsk merchandise."[9] Each year more than 60,000 visitors from the US and Canada visit Minot for the event.[10] Similarly, the event known as Nordic Fest was established in 1967, in Decorah, Iowa,[11] and today attracts 10,000 people per year. Since 1967, more than 1.5 million visitors, from all over the world, have attended this festival.[12] In 2022, the theme of the festival was summed up in the catchy slogan "All Directions Point Norse."[13]

Such modern festivals, and similar events, showcase Scandinavian culture in America in a fun and positive way. It is a tradition which stretches back to the original Midwestern settlers of the nineteenth century. In the past, as the Kensington Runestone illustrates, this tradition has (for many) been validated by a memory of the *Vinland* sagas. For large numbers, we may assume, this continues to be the case. When Scandinavian Americans in Turlock, California, began a Scandinavian-American festival there in 1991, the official opening of the first festival was conducted by the mayor of Turlock, who was dressed in a Viking helmet.[14] One can expect to find these ubiquitous helmets at many Norse-themed events. They are a reminder that Vikings are a potent symbol (though certainly not the only one) in the ongoing celebration of Norse heritage.

However, as we have also seen, alleged connectivity with the Viking past can sometimes have a shadowy side, as was demonstrated on January 6, 2021, at the Capitol. In the febrile atmosphere of contemporary US politics, there is every likelihood that this will continue and increase. As we have witnessed, this aspect of modern culture and politics also references the Viking story in North America—but makes a more explicit, and highly controversial, attempt to link this to the world of (an imagined) *Vinland* and its claimed legacy in subsequent history. It is a reminder of how history generally can provide a complex "quarry," from which material can be wrested in order to construct very different edifices, according to preconceived agendas.

In conclusion, it is clear that—in fact and in fantasy—the Vikings who sailed to *Vinland* have entered into the cultural, (as well as perhaps the actual), DNA of North America, and especially the USA. While this fascination with Vikings is part of a global phenomenon, it certainly also has a particularly American character that has been amplified by later Scandinavian settlement, claims of corroborative archaeological evidence, popular culture and media attention, and (finally) unequivocal archaeological proof. Variously researched, celebrated, manipulated, used, and abused, American Vikings have become part of a "deep story"—and that story continues to be told. As this book's title reminds us, the search for *American Vikings*, involves exploring *How the Norse Sailed into the Lands and Imaginations of America*. Their "journey" is far from over.

ACKNOWLEDGMENTS

I wish to thank Robert Dudley, my agent, and Claiborne Hancock, Jessica Case, Maria Fernandez, Julia Romero, and all the team at Pegasus Books, for their encouragement and assistance. Benjamin Stickney, at Maine State Museum, was particularly helpful regarding the Maine Penny and the Maine runestones. In addition, I am grateful (as always) to my family for the interest they take in my work and for the support shown to me as I embarked on this "American Viking journey."

It goes without saying that all errors and interpretations are my own.

Martyn Whittock

ENDNOTES

INTRODUCTION

1   "America: geographical name," https://www.merriam-webster.com
      /dictionary/America, accessed January 2023. The term "America" can,
      of course, refer to either the North or South American continents of
      the western hemisphere, but in this book, it is shorthand for "North
      America."

2   "American," https://www.merriam-webster.com/dictionary/American#h1,
      accessed January 2023.

CHAPTER ONE: WHO AND WHAT WERE "VIKINGS"?

1   D. Whitelock, *English Historical Documents Volume I, c.500–1042*
      (London: Eyre Methuen, 1979), 180; compare the information found in
      manuscript A, also called the Parker Chronicle, with Manuscript E, the
      Laud or Peterborough Chronicle, of the Anglo-Saxon Chronicle.

2   G. Jones, *A History of the Vikings* (Oxford: Oxford University Press,
      2002), 75–6.

3   M. Whittock, H. Whittock, *The Viking Blitzkrieg AD 789–1098* (Stroud:
      History Press, 2013), 25.

4   N. Price, "Novgorod, Kiev and their Satellites," in *A Comparative
      Study of Thirty City-state Cultures: An Investigation*, ed. M. H. Hansen
      (Copenhagen: Kongelige Danske Videnskabernes Selskab, 2000), 267.

5   Whittock, Whittock, *The Viking Blitzkrieg*, 26.

6   M. Whittock, "The Saint at the Heart of the War in Ukraine," https
      ://www.christiantoday.com/article/the.saint.at.the.heart.of.the.war.in
      .ukraine/138286.ht, accessed July 2022.

7   "Viking Runes at Hagia Sophia," https://www.atlasobscura.com/places
        /viking-runes-at-hagia-sophia, accessed January 2023.
8   Whittock, Whittock, *The Viking Blitzkrieg*, 26.
9   Jones, *A History of the Vikings*, 76–7.
10   Jones, *A History of the Vikings*, 76.
11   M. Whittock, "Vikings: When the Hammer Met the Cross," *Church
        Times* (October 26, 2018), https://www.churchtimes.co.uk/articles
        /2018/26-october/features/features/vikings-when-the-hammer-met-the
        -cross, accessed July 2022.
12   Whittock, "Vikings: When the Hammer Met the Cross."
13   For an overview of the use of the term "Viking" and the names used
        by others to describe them, see: M. Arnold, *The Vikings: Culture and
        Conquest* (London: Hambledon Continuum, 2006), 7–8. See also: *The
        Viking Age: A Reader*, eds. A. Somerville and R.A. McDonald (Toronto:
        University of Toronto Press, 2010), xiii.
14   M. Whittock, H. Whittock, *Tales of Valhalla* (New York: Pegasus Books,
        2018), 2.
15   C. Balbirnie, "The Vikings at Home," *BBC History Magazine* 13, no. 9
        (September 2012), 25.
16   Quoted in S. Brimberg, "In Search of Vikings," *National Geographic*
        (May 2000), 8–27.
17   See: E. Ekwall, *The Concise Oxford Dictionary of English Place-Names*
        (Oxford: Oxford University Press, 1960).
18   Whittock, Whittock, *Tales of Valhalla*, 1.
19   Whittock, "The Saint at the Heart of the War in Ukraine."
20   Whittock, Whittock, *Tales of Valhalla*, 4.
21   Whittock, "Vikings: When the Hammer Met the Cross."
22   See: Whittock, "Vikings: When the Hammer Met the Cross."; and M.
        Whittock, H. Whittock, *The Vikings: From Odin to Christ* (Oxford: Lion
        Hudson, 2018).

CHAPTER TWO: INSIDE THE HEADS OF THE VIKINGS

1   For an overview of this process and its outcome(s) see: Whittock,
        Whittock, *The Vikings*.
2   J. Lindow, *Old Norse Mythology* (Oxford: Oxford University Press, 2021), 2.
3   P. Gilliver, J. Marshall, E. Weiner, *The Ring of Words: Tolkien and the
        Oxford English Dictionary* (Oxford: Oxford University Press, 2009), 104–8.
4   See: Whittock, Whittock, *Tales of Valhalla*.
5   For modern translations of these see: Snorri Sturluson, *Edda*, ed. and
        trans. A. Faulkes (London: Everyman 1987)—often known as the
        Prose Edda; and *The Poetic Edda*, trans. C. Larrington (Oxford: Oxford
        University Press, 1996).
6   Whittock, Whittock, *Tales of Valhalla*, 4–5.

7   *Skaldic* poetry is one of the two main forms of Old Norse poetry and is a highly complicated poetic form usually reserved for writing historical or praise poems.

8   P. Meulengracht Sørensen, "Religions Old and New," in *The Oxford Illustrated History of the Vikings*, ed. P. Sawyer (Oxford: Oxford University Press, 1997), 206.

9   For an accessible overview see: M. L. Colish, *Medieval Foundations of the Western Intellectual Tradition, 400–1400* (New Haven, CT: Yale University Press, 1997), ch. 8: "Varieties of Germanic Literature: Old Norse, Old High German, and Old English."

10   For an overview of the Norse saga literature see: M. Clunies Ross, *The Cambridge Introduction to the Old Norse-Icelandic Saga* (Cambridge: Cambridge University Press, 2010).

11   Whittock, Whittock, *Tales of Valhalla*, 7.

12   See: J. Lindow, *Handbook of Norse Mythology* (Santa Barbara, CA: ABC Clio, 2001), 10.

13   Adam of Bremen, *History of the Archbishops of Hamburg-Bremen*, trans. F. J. Tschan (New York: Columbia University Press, 2002), Bk IV, ch. 26, 207.

14   K. Kunz, "Eirik the Red's Saga," in *The Sagas of Icelanders*, ed. Ö. Thorsson (London: Penguin, 2001), 668.

15   J. Jesch, "The Norse gods in England and the Isle of Man," in *Myths, Legends, and Heroes: Essays on Old Norse and Old English Literature in Honour of John McKinnell*, ed. D. Anlezark (Toronto: University of Toronto Press, 2011), 18–19.

16   M. Osborn, "The Ravens on the Lejre Throne," in *Representing Beasts in Early Medieval England and Scandinavia*, eds. M. D. J. Bintley, T. J. T. Williams (Woodbridge: Boydell & Brewer, 2015), 104; *Old Norse Religion in Long-term Perspectives: Origins, Changes, and Interactions: An International Conference in Lund, Sweden, June 3–7, 2004*, eds. A. Andrén, K. Jennbert, C. Raudvere (Lund: Nordic Academic Press, 2006), 128.

17   "Medieval Women and Gender Index: Pendant Amulet in the Shape of a Woman, Possibly a Valkyrie," https://inpress.lib.uiowa.edu/feminae /DetailsPage.aspx?Feminae_ID=31944, accessed July 2022.

18   P. Parker, *The Northmen's Fury: A History of the Viking World* (London: Vintage, 2015), 130.

19   Lindow, *Old Norse Mythology*, 83–90.

20   See: J. D. Richards, "The Scandinavian presence," in *The Archaeology of Britain: An Introduction from the Upper Palaeolithic to the Industrial Revolution*, eds. J. Hunter, I. Ralston (London: Routledge, 1999), 200; J. Jesch, "Speaking like a Viking: Language and Cultural Interaction in the Irish Sea Region," in *In Search of Vikings: Interdisciplinary Approaches to the Scandinavian Heritage of North-West England*, eds. S. E. Harding, D. Griffiths, E. Royles (Boca Raton FL: CRC Press, 2015), 58.

21   *Anglo-Saxon Chronicle* annal for 878, *English Historical Documents,*
      Volume I, c.500–1042, ed. D. Whitelock (London: Eyre Methuen, 1979),
      195. Referring to this event, the later *Annals of St Neots* (early twelfth
      century) records the tradition that the banner fluttered before a victory
      but hung down before a defeat.

CHAPTER THREE: THE VIKING WORLD

1   See: T. Horne, *A Viking Market Kingdom in Ireland and Britain* (London:
      Routledge, 2022).

2   W. Duczko, *Viking Rus: Studies on the Presence of Scandinavians in Eastern
      Europe* (Leiden: Brill, 2004), 22.

3   *Laxdæla saga, Vatnsdæla saga, Egils saga Skallagrímssonar.*

4   W. I. Miller, *Bloodtaking and Peacemaking: Feud, Law, and Society in Saga
      Iceland* (Chicago, IL: University of Chicago Press, 1997), 15.

5   Miller, *Bloodtaking and Peacemaking*, 15.

6   S. Olafson Furstenau, "Irish and Icelandic," https://www.icelandicroots
      .com/post/2016/03/17/irish-and-icelandic#:~:text=Genetic%20
      studies%20in%20Iceland%20reveal,derive%20from%20our%20
      Irish%20ancestry, accessed August 2022.

7   In the source known as *Íslendingabók.*

8   For an accessible overview of Viking Age Scandinavia see: J. Haywood,
      The Penguin Historical Atlas of the Vikings (London: Penguin, 1995),
      28–33; A. Forte, R. Oram, F. Pedersen, *Viking Empires* (Cambridge:
      Cambridge University Press, 2005), 7–53.

9   Forte, Oram, Pedersen, *Viking Empires*, 51–53.

10   For an expansion of this argument see: K. Randsborg, *The Viking Age in
      Denmark: The Formation of a State* (London: St Martin's Press, 1980).

CHAPTER FOUR: *VINLAND* . . . THE EDGE OF THE WORLD

1   L. Abrams, "Early Religious Practice in the Greenland Settlement,"
      Journal of the North Atlantic (2009–2010), 52–65.

2   See: Kunz, "Eirik the Red's Saga," in *The Sagas of Icelanders.*

3   See: Kunz, "The Saga of the Greenlanders," in *The Sagas of Icelanders*, ed.
      Ö. Thorsson (London: Penguin, 2001).

4   V. Hansen, *The Year 1000: When Explorers Connected the World—and
      Globalization Began* (New York: Scribner, 2021), 34.

5   Hansen, *The Year 1000*, 34.

6   K. D. Goss, A. A. Grishin, *Colonial America: Facts and Fictions* (Santa
      Barbara, CA: ABC-CLIO, 2021), 17.

7   Goss, Grishin, *Colonial America: Facts and Fictions*, 19.

8   W. I. Miller, *Bloodtaking and Peacemaking: Feud, Law, and Society in Saga
      Iceland* (Chicago IL: University of Chicago Press, 1990), 14–15.

9   J. Byock, *Viking Age Iceland* (London: Penguin, 2001), 9.

10   O. Vésteinsson, "A Divided Society: Peasants and the Aristocracy in
      Medieval Iceland," *Viking and Medieval Scandinavia*, volume 3 (2007),
      117.

11   G. Barnes, *Viking America: The First Millennium* (Woodbridge: D. S.
      Brewer, 2001), xvii.

12   A. Kolodny, *In Search of First Contact: The Vikings of Vinland, the Peoples
      of the Dawnland, and the Anglo-American Anxiety of Discovery* (Durham,
      NC: Duke University Press, 2012), 9.

13   Kunz, "The Saga of the Greenlanders," 637–38.

14   Kunz, "The Saga of the Greenlanders," 638–41.

15   Kunz, "The Saga of the Greenlanders," 640.

16   It seems that the term was first used by Ari Thorgilsson in his twelfth-
      century *Book of Icelanders*. It next appears in the thirteenth century, in
      Erik the Red's Saga and *The Saga of the Greenlanders*.

17   Kunz, "The Saga of the Greenlanders," 643.

18   Kunz, "Eirik the Red's Saga," 666.

19   H. Ingstad, A. Stine Ingstad, *The Viking Discovery of America: The
      Excavation of a Norse Settlement at L'Anse aux Meadows, Newfoundland*
      (New York: Checkmark, 2001), 44–5. Previously published in *The Viking
      Discovery of America*, eds. F. Hødnebø, J. Kristjánsson (Oslo: J. M.
      Stenersens, 1991).

20   Kunz, "Eirik the Red's Saga," 667.

21   Kunz, "The Saga of the Greenlanders," 646.

22   See: Ingstad, Stine Ingstad, *The Viking Discovery of America*.

23   E. Wahlgren, *The Vikings and America* (London: Thames & Hudson,
      2000), 159.

24   Wahlgren, *The Vikings and America*, 157 (Fig. 90), 163–64.

25   Wahlgren, *The Vikings and America*, 159–60.

26   Kunz, "Eirik the Red's Saga," 668.

27   Kunz, "Eirik the Red's Saga," 672; "The Saga of the Greenlanders,"
      647.

28   Kunz, "Eirik the Red's Saga," 672.

29   S. S. Ebenesersdóttir, et. al., "A New Subclade of mtDNA Haplogroup
      C1 Found in Icelanders: Evidence of pre-Columbian Contact?" *American
      Journal of Physical Anthropology* 144, no. 1 (January 2011), 92–99. First
      published November 10, 2010.

30   See: K. TallBear, "Predictable Press on PhysAnth Article on Native
      American mtDNA in Iceland," https://indigenoussts.com/predictable
      -press-on-physanth-article-on-native-american-mtdna-in-iceland/,
      accessed February 2023.

31   Kunz, "The Saga of the Greenlanders," 649.

32   See: Ingstad, Stine Ingstad, *The Viking Discovery of America*.

33   Barnes, *Viking America: The First Millennium*, xvii.

CHAPTER FIVE: VIKING NORTH AMERICANS

1   See: K. Kunz, "Eirik the Red's Saga."

2   See: K. Kunz, "The Saga of the Greenlanders."

3   R. H. Clarke, *Lives of the Deceased Bishops of the Catholic Church in the United States*, vol. 1 (New York: R. H. Clarke,1888), 16.

4   T. J. Oleson, "EIRIKR GNUPSSON," in *Dictionary of Canadian Biography*, vol. 1 (Toronto: University of Toronto/Université Laval, 2003), http://www.biographi.ca/en/bio/eirikr_gnupsson_1E.html, accessed August 2022.

5   Oleson, "EIRIKR GNUPSSON."

6   Oleson, "EIRIKR GNUPSSON."

7   Oleson, "EIRIKR GNUPSSON."

8   E. Haug, "The Icelandic Annals as Historical Sources," *Scandinavian Journal of History* 22, no.4 (1997), 263–74.

9   "From the Icelandic Annals," American Journeys Collection, Document No. AJ-059, Wisconsin Historical Society, Digital Library and Archives, 2003, 69, https://www.americanjourneys.org/AJ_PDF/AJ-059.pdf, accessed August 2022.

10   "From the Icelandic Annals", 69.

11   A. Middleton Reeves, *The Finding of Wineland the Good* (London: Henry Frowde Oxford University Press, 1890), 90.

12   Middleton Reeves, *The Finding of Wineland the Good*, 89–90.

13   Middleton Reeves, *The Finding of Wineland the Good*, 90-1.

14   Middleton Reeves, *The Finding of Wineland the Good*, 90.

15   Middleton Reeves, *The Finding of Wineland the Good*, 84.

16   Middleton Reeves, *The Finding of Wineland the Good*, 87–9.

17   For a very accessible overview of the site and the evidence, see: B. L. Wallace, "L'Anse aux Meadows," www.thecanadianencyclopedia.ca /en/article/lanse-aux-meadows, accessed August 2022. The description in this chapter of the site, the finds, and their significance, made use of this valuable online site, along with additional material from other sources.

18   W. A. Munn, *Wineland Voyages: Location of Helluland, Markland, and Vinland* (St. John's Newfoundland: Labour Press, 1929).

19   W. A. Munn, "Wineland Voyages," December 1913, http://newlangsyne .com/articles/vikingdays/wineland.htm, accessed August 2022.

20   Wallace, "L'Anse aux Meadows."

21   See: Ingstad, Stine Ingstad, *The Viking Discovery of America*, 123–27, 135–69.

22   "L'Anse aux Meadows National Historic Site," https://whc.unesco.org/en /list/4/, accessed August 2022.

23   "L'Anse aux Meadows National Historic Site."

24   P. M. Ledger, *et al*, "New Horizons at L'Anse aux Meadows," https ://www.pnas.org/doi/10.1073/pnas.1907986116, accessed August 2022.

25   M. Kuitems, *et al*, "Evidence for European Presence in the Americas in AD 1021," *Nature* 601 (October 20, 2021), 388–91, https://www.ncbi .nlm.nih.gov/pmc/articles/PMC8770119/, accessed August 2022.

26   Wallace, "L'Anse aux Meadows."

27   Wallace, "L'Anse aux Meadows."

28   Kolodny, *In Search of First Contact*, 9.

29   Wallace, "L'Anse aux Meadows."

30   H. Sweet, "The Native Grape Vines of North America," https://eattheplanet .org/the-native-grape-vines-of-north-america/, accessed August 2022.

31   A. J. Winkler, *et al*, *General Viticulture* (Berkeley, CA: University of California Press 1974), 17–20, 59, 166–67.

32   Kolodny, *In Search of First Contact*, 18.

33   Kuitems, *et al*, "Evidence for European Presence in the Americas in AD 1021."

34   B. Handwerk, "New Dating Method Shows Vikings Occupied Newfoundland in 1021 C.E.," https://www.smithsonianmag.com/science -nature/new-dating-method-shows-vikings-occupied-newfoundland-in -1021-ce-180978903/, accessed August 2022.

35   Kuitems, *et al*, "Evidence for European Presence in the Americas in AD 1021."

36   "The Norse Were Definitely at L'Anse aux Meadows in 1021, Study Finds," https://www.medievalists.net/2021/10/norse-lanse-aux-meadows -1021/, accessed August 2022.

37   Kuitems, *et al*, "Evidence for European Presence in the Americas in AD 1021."

38   Ledger, *et al*, "New horizons at L'Anse aux Meadows."

39   Kunz, "The Saga of the Greenlanders," 646.

40   Wallace, "L'Anse aux Meadows."

41   "Vinland—Skálholt Map," https://canadianhistoryworkshop.wordpress .com/group-a/group-a/, accessed August 2022.

42   Ingstad, Stine Ingstad, *The Viking Discovery of America*, 111.

43   Ingstad, Stine Ingstad, *The Viking Discovery of America*, 117.

44   Ingstad, Stine Ingstad, *The Viking Discovery of America*, 118–9.

45   M. Cummings, "Analysis Unlocks Secret of the Vinland Map—It's a Fake," *Yale News* (September 1, 2021).

CHAPTER SIX: SHARING THE STAGE WITH VIKINGS?

1   A. G. MacPherson, "Pre-Columbian Discoveries and Exploration of North America," in *North American Exploration*, ed. J. L. Allen (Lincoln, NE: University of Nebraska Press, 1997).

2   "Nauigatio sancti Brendani abbatis (the Voyage of St Brendan the Abbot)," trans. D. O'Donoghue (1893), https://markjberry.blogs.com /StBrendan.pdf, accessed August 2022.

3   D. Mandal, "Did the Irish Reach America before the Vikings and
     Columbus?" https://www.hexapolis.com/2014/08/04/irish-reach-america
     -vikings-columbus/, accessed August 2022.

4   Benedeit, *The Anglo-Norman Voyage of Saint Brendan*, eds. I. Short,
     B. Merrilees (Manchester: Manchester University Press, 1979).

5   O'Donoghue, "Nauigatio sancti Brendani abbatis (the Voyage of
     St Brendan the Abbot)," iv.

6   https://www.lumebooks.co.uk/book/land-to-the-west-st-brendans
     -voyage-to-america/, accessed August 2022.

7   O'Donoghue, "Nauigatio sancti Brendani abbatis (the Voyage of
     St Brendan the Abbot)," xxviii.

8   O'Donoghue, "Nauigatio sancti Brendani abbatis (the Voyage of
     St Brendan the Abbot)," xxviii.

9   O'Donoghue, "Nauigatio sancti Brendani abbatis (the Voyage of
     St Brendan the Abbot)," xxviii.

10   J. Fritzinger, *Pre-Columbian Trans-Oceanic Contact* (Morrisville, NC:
     Lulu Press, 2016), 58.

11   T. J. Oleson, "Brendan, Saint," in *Dictionary of Canadian Biography*,
     Volume 1 (Toronto: University of Toronto/Université Laval, 2003).

12   T. Severin. "The Voyage of the 'Brendan'," *National Geographic Magazine*,
     152, no. 6 (December 1977), 768–97. Also: T. Severin. *The Brendan
     Voyage: A Leather Boat Tracks the Discovery of America by the Irish Sailor
     Saints* (Chicago, IL: McGraw-Hill, 1978).

13   See: R. T. Reilly, *Irish Saints*, (New York: Avenel Books, 1964), 37;
     G. Ashe, *Land to the West: St Brendan's Voyage to America* (New York:
     Viking, 1962).

14   S. King. "The Brendan Voyage," https://lookingnorth.blog/2020/07/the
     -brendan-voyage/, accessed August 2022.

15   Mandal, "Did the Irish Reach America before the Vikings and Columbus?"

16   P. H. Chapman. *The Man Who Led Columbus to America* (Atlanta, GA:
     Judson Press), 1973.

17   J. D. Anderson, "The Navigatio Brendani: Medieval Bestseller,"
     Classical Journal 83, no. 4 (April–May 1988), 315–22; B. Regal, *The
     Battle Over America's Origin Story: Legends, Amateurs, and Professional
     Historiographers* (Cham, Switz: Springer Nature, 2022), 79–80.

18   Regal, *The Battle Over America's Origin Story: Legends, Amateurs, and
     Professional Historiographers*, 80.

19   Ashe, *Land to the West: St Brendan's Voyage to America.*

20   P. Imbrogno, M. Horrigan, *Celtic Mysteries: Windows to Another
     Dimension in America's Northeast* (New York: Cosimo, 2000), 20–31.

21   Imbrogno, Horrigan, *Celtic Mysteries*, 32.

22   D. D. Fowler, *Laboratory for Anthropology: Science and Romanticism in the
     American Southwest, 1846–1930* (Salt Lake City, UT: University of Utah

Press, 2010), 54; E. Owen, "Prince Madoc's Discovery of America," *The Red Dragon: The National Magazine of Wales*, VIII, no.1 (July 1885), 546–60.

23   M. Stephens, *The Oxford companion to the literature of Wales* (Oxford: Oxford University Press, 1986), 143.

24   H. Llwyd, *Cronica Walliae*, ed. I. M. Williams (Cardiff: University of Wales Press, 2002).

25   Llwyd, *Cronica Walliae*, 168.

26   https://docsouth.unc.edu/southlit/smith/smith.html, accessed September 2022.

27   Owen, "Prince Madoc's Discovery of America," 550.

28   R. H. Fritze, *Legend and Lore of the Americas before 1492: An Encyclopedia of Visitors, Explorers, and Immigrants* (Santa Barbara, CA: ABC CLIO, 1993), 163.

29   Owen, "Prince Madoc's Discovery of America," 550.

30   Owen, "Prince Madoc's Discovery of America," 550.

31   Owen, "Prince Madoc's Discovery of America," 551.

32   Owen, "Prince Madoc's Discovery of America," 551.

33   G. A. Williams, *Madoc: The Making of a Myth* (London: Eyre Methuen, 1979), 76.

34   Fowler, *Laboratory for Anthropology: Science and Romanticism in the American Southwest, 1846–1930*, 55.

35   B. Johnson, "The Discovery of America . . . by a Welsh Prince?" https://www.historic-uk.com/HistoryUK/HistoryofWales/The-discovery-of-America-by-Welsh-Prince/, accessed August 2022.

36   Fritze, *Legend and Lore of the Americas before 1492*, 163.

37   Johnson, "The Discovery of America . . . by a Welsh Prince?"

38   J. Griffiths, "The racist origins of the myth a Welsh prince beat Columbus to America," https://edition.cnn.com/2019/07/20/uk/welsh-americas-history-intl-hnk/index.html, accessed September 2022.

39   Fowler, *Laboratory for Anthropology: Science and Romanticism in the American Southwest, 1846–1930*, 55.

40   Williams, *Madoc: The Making of a Myth*, 86.

41   Johnson, "The Discovery of America . . . by a Welsh Prince?"

42   Williams, *Madoc: The Making of a Myth*, 84.

43   M. A. Mitchell, "Prince Madog of Wales," https://crossingtheoceansea.com/OceanSeaPages/OS-15-PrinceMadog.html, accessed September 2022.

44   T. J. Oleson, "ZENO, NICOLÒ and ANTONIO," *Dictionary of Canadian Biography*, http://www.biographi.ca/en/bio/zeno_nicolo_1E.html, accessed September 2022.

45   Oleson, "ZENO, NICOLÒ and ANTONIO."

46   "Earl Henry Sinclair: The Legendary Atlantic Crossing," http://www.orkneyjar.com/history/historicalfigures/henrysinclair/princehenrytrip2.htm, accessed September 2022.

47   Whittock, Whittock, *The Vikings*, 159.
48   Whittock, Whittock, *The Vikings*, 159–60.

**CHAPTER SEVEN: COMPETING ETHNIC ORIGIN MYTHS OF
"DISCOVERY," IN THE EARLY US**

1   Kolodny, *In Search of First Contact*, 11–12.
2   H. Paul, The Myths That Made America: An Introduction to American
      Studies (Bielefeld: Transcript Verlag, 2014) https://oaresource.library
      .carleton.ca/oa-America9783839414859.pdf, accessed November 2022, 52.
3   C. L. Bushman, *America Discovers Columbus: How an Italian Explorer
      Became an American Hero*, (Hanover, NH: University Press of New
      England, 1992), 40.
4   Paul, *The Myths That Made America*, 53.
5   Bushman, *America Discovers Columbus*, 41.
6   Bushman, *America Discovers Columbus*, 54.
7   Paul, *The Myths That Made America*, 54.
8   Paul, *The Myths That Made America*, 57.
9   M. Dennis, *Red, White, and Blue Letter Days: An American Calendar*
      (Ithaca, NY: Cornell University Press, 2002), 140.
10   Paul, *The Myths That Made America*, 140.
11   Kolodny, *In Search of First Contact*, 11.
12   Dennis, *Red, White, and Blue Letter Days*, 145.
13   See: C. S. Fischer, *Made in America, A Social History of American Culture
      and Character* (Chicago, IL: University of Chicago Press, 2010), chapter 4,
      "Groups."
14   Kolodny, *In Search of First Contact*, 27.
15   Kolodny, *In Search of First Contact*, 29.
16   Kolodny, *In Search of First Contact*, 31.
17   Kolodny, *In Search of First Contact*, 32.
18   Kolodny, *In Search of First Contact*, 32.
19   Kolodny, *In Search of First Contact*, 27.
20   G. Campbell, *Norse America: The Story of a Founding Myth* (Oxford:
      Oxford University Press, 2021), 206.
21   Campbell, *Norse America*, 206.
22   C. Ellis, "Remembering the Vikings: Ancestry, cultural memory and
      geographical variation," https://compass.onlinelibrary.wiley.com/doi
      /full/10.1111/hic3.12652, accessed November 2022.
23   Kolodny, *In Search of First Contact*, 12.
24   Campbell, *Norse America*, 207.
25   Campbell, *Norse America*, 207.
26   Campbell, *Norse America*, 207.
27   J. M. Mancini, "Discovering Viking America," *Critical Inquiry* 28, no. 4
      (2002), 868–907, especially 868, 871.

28   Ellis, "Remembering the Vikings: Ancestry, Cultural Memory and
        Geographical Variation"; T. W. Machan, "Vinland on the Brain:
        Remembering the Norse," in *From Iceland to the Americas: Vinland and
        historical imagination*, eds. T. W. Machan, J. K. Helgason (Manchester:
        Manchester University Press, 2020), 12.

29   Kolodny, *In Search of First Contact*, 18.

30   G. Campbell, "No, the Vikings Did Not Discover America. Here's
        Why That Myth Is Problematic" https://time.com/6076460/vikings
        -discovered-america-myth/, accessed November 2022.

31   I. D. Björnsdóttir, "Leifr Eiriksson versus Christopher Columbus: The
        Use of Leif Eriksson in American Political and Cultural Discourse," in
        *Approaches to Vinland. A Conference on the Written and Archaeological
        Sources for the Norse Settlements in the North Atlantic Region and
        Exploration of America*, eds. A. Wawn, and Þ. Sigurðardóttir (Reykjavík:
        Sigurður Nordal Institute, 2001), 220–26.

32   Campbell, "No, the Vikings Did Not Discover America."

33   J. Jesch, "Who's First? The Norse Voyages to Greenland and Canada
        as Part of a Bigger Story," in a review of G. Campbell, *Norse America:
        The Story of a Founding Myth* (Oxford: Oxford University Press, 2021).
        https://www.historytoday.com/archive/review/whos-first, accessed
        November 2022.

34   Kolodny, *In Search of First Contact*, 231.

35   https://www.presidency.ucsb.edu/documents/proclamation-10097-leif
        -erikson-day-2020, accessed November 2022.

36   https://www.whitehouse.gov/briefing-room/presidential-actions/2022
        /10/07/a-proclamation-on-leif-erikson-day-2022/, accessed November
        2022.

37   https://www.timeanddate.com/holidays/us/leif-erikson-day, accessed
        November 2022.

38   https://www.timeanddate.com/holidays/us/columbus-day, accessed
        November 2022.

39   https://comicbook.com/tv-shows/news/spongebob-squarepants-leif
        -erikson-day/#7, accessed November 2022.

40   "Bubble Buddy," https://www.youtube.com/watch?v=Bjgbv1hHOCk,
        accessed November 2022.

CHAPTER EIGHT: VIKINGS IN THE MIDWEST?

1   Kunz, "The Saga of the Greenlanders," 640, footnote.

2   See: Ingstad, Stine Ingstad, *The Viking Discovery of America*.

3   E. Small, *North American Cornucopia: Top 100 Indigenous Food Plants*
        (Boca Raton, FL: CRC Press, 2013), 332.

4   R. I. Page, *Reading the Past: Runes* (London: British Museum
        Publications, 1987), 23

5   Page, *Reading the Past: Runes*, 30.

6   *The Viking Age: A Reader*, eds. A. A. Somerville, R. A. McDonald
        (Toronto: University of Toronto Press, 2014), 290.

7   "Maeshowe's runes—Viking graffiti," http://www.orkneyjar.com/history
        /maeshowe/maeshrunes.htm, accessed March 2022.

8   P. B. Taylor, "The Hønen Runes: A Survey", *Neophilologus*, 60, no. 1
        (January 1976), 1–7. See also: C. Cavaleri, "The Vínland Sagas as
        Propaganda for the Christian Church: Freydís and Gudríd as Paradigms
        for Eve and the Virgin Mary," Master's thesis, University of Oslo, 2008.

9   P. Nelson, "The Kensington Runestone: Minnesota's Most Brilliant and
        Durable Hoax?" https://www.minnpost.com/mnopedia/2020/05/the
        -kensington-runestone-minnesotas-most-brilliant-and-durable-hoax/,
        accessed March 2022.

10   L. Ljungmark, *Swedish Exodus* (Carbondale, IL: Southern Illinois
        University Press, 1996), 89. As early as 1870, Scandinavians exceeded
        Germans as the largest ethnic group in Minnesota. By 1890 Swedish
        Americans began calling it the "Swedish state."

11   See: M. M. Quaife, "The Myth of the Kensington Runestone:
        The Norse Discovery of Minnesota 1362," *New England Quarterly*
        (December 1934).

12   Calculation of the Pittsburgh Associated Charities, quoted in: K.
        Hillstrom, L. Collier Hillstrom, *Industrial Revolution in America* (Santa
        Barbara, CA: ABC Clio), 2007, 107.

13   M. Sherman, *The Skeptic Encyclopedia of Pseudoscience Volume 1* (Santa
        Barbara, CA: ABC Clio, 2002), 575.

14   https://runestonemuseum.org/about/, accessed November 2022.

15   G. Campbell, *Norse America*, 184.

16   https://runestonemuseum.org/runestone/, accessed 2022.

17   See: I. Hahn, "Linguistic Research on the Kensington Runestone," *Arctic
        Studies Centre Newsletter* 11, Smithsonian Institution, National Museum
        of Natural History, (December 2003), 12–15.

18   Nelson, "The Kensington Runestone: Minnesota's Most Brilliant and
        Durable Hoax?"

19   Hahn, "Linguistic Research on the Kensington Runestone," 12–15.

20   Campbell, *Norse America*, 189.

21   See: Nelson, "The Kensington Runestone: Minnesota's most brilliant and
        durable hoax?"

22   Geologist Harold Edwards, quoted in: "The Kensington Runestone:
        Fascinating Find or Fake News?" https://www.history.co.uk/shows
        /secrets-of-the-viking-stone/the-kensington-runestone-fascinating-find
        -or-fake-news-, accessed March 2022.

23   A. White, "Calcite Weathering and the Age of the Kensington Rune
        Stone Inscription (Lightning Post)," https://www.andywhiteanthropo

logy.com/blog/calcite-weathering-and-the-age-of-the-kensington
-rune-stone-inscription-lightning-post, accessed March 2022.

24   Campbell, *Norse America*, 190, 191.

25   "The Kensington Runestone: Fascinating Find or Fake News?"

26   Hahn, "Linguistic Research on the Kensington Runestone," 12–15.

27   As recently as March 2022 the author discovered this when expressing
        doubts concerning the stone to a Minnesotan, during a conversation at a
        meeting in New York.

28   P. Hancock, *Hoax Springs Eternal: The Psychology of Cognitive Deception*
        (Cambridge: Cambridge University Press, 2015), xv.

29   "The History of Kensington," https://kensingtonmn.com/about-kensington
        -mn/, accessed March 2022.

30   Whittock, Whittock, *The Vikings*, 181; Sherman, *The Skeptic Encyclopedia
        of Pseudoscience*, 575.

31   Hancock, *Hoax Springs Eternal*, 186.

CHAPTER NINE: NEW ENGLAND VIKINGS?

1   See: Ingstad, Stine Ingstad, *The Viking Discovery of America*, 173, 174 (Fig. d).

2   "Viking Contact with the Indigenous Population in the Eastern Arctic,"
        http://viking.archeurope.info/index.php?page=viking-contact-in-e-arctic,
        accessed November 2022.

3   E. Wahlgren, *The Vikings and America* (London: Thames & Hudson,
        2000), 171.

4   See: Ingstad, Stine Ingstad, *The Viking Discovery of America*, 175–6.

5   Ingstad, Stine Ingstad, *The Viking Discovery of America*, 176.

6   A. Beck Kehoe, *The Kensington Runestone: Approaching a Research
        Question Holistically* (Long Grove, IL, Waveland, 2005), 27.

7   Ingstad, Stine Ingstad, *The Viking Discovery of America*, 173, 170 (Fig. a).

8   Ingstad, Stine Ingstad, *The Viking Discovery of America*, 172.

9   "Recent finds," https://www.historymuseum.ca/cmc/exhibitions/archeo
        /helluland/str0301e.html, accessed November 2022.

10   "Other artifacts," https://www.historymuseum.ca/cmc/exhibitions
        /archeo/helluland/str0601e.html, accessed November 2022.

11   Ingstad, Stine Ingstad, *The Viking Discovery of America*, 173.

12   https://www.yarmouthcountymuseum.ca/product-page/runic-stone, has a
        photograph of the stone, accessed October 2022. Photographs can also be
        found at: https://commons.wikimedia.org/wiki/File:Yarmouth_Runic
        _Stone_at_Yarmouth_County_Museum.jpg, accessed October 2022.

13   H. Phillips, "On a Supposed Runic Inscription at Yarmouth, Nova
        Scotia," *Proceedings of the American Philosophical Society* 21, no. 115 (April
        1884), 490.

14   Phillips, "On a Supposed Runic Inscription at Yarmouth, Nova Scotia,"
        490–92.

15 Phillips, "On a Supposed Runic Inscription at Yarmouth, Nova Scotia," 491.

16 C. S. Goldring, "The Yarmouth Runic Stone—or the Fletcher Stone, 1812," https://forum.oakislandtreasure.co.uk/viewtopic.php?f=5&t=366, accessed October 2022.

17 I. McKay, R. Bates, *In the Province of History: The Making of the Public Past in Twentieth-Century Nova Scotia* (Montreal: McGill-Queen's University Press, 2010), 322–27.

18 McKay, Bates, *In the Province of History: The Making of the Public Past in Twentieth-Century* Nova Scotia, 322–27.

19 Goldring, "The Yarmouth Runic Stone—or the Fletcher Stone, 1812."

20 S. O. Carlson, "North Atlantic Rim, Barrier or Bridge?" https://neara.org/pdf/north%20atlantic%20rim%20bridge%20or%20barrier-illust%20for%20web.pdf, accessed October 2022, 3.

21 R. I. Page, *Reading the Past: Runes* (London: British Museum Publications, 1987), 61.

22 A case in point being: Page, *Reading the Past: Runes*, 60–1.

23 Carlson, "North Atlantic Rim, Barrier or Bridge?," 3.

24 E. Haugen, "The Rune Stones of Spirit Pond, Maine," *Visible Language* 8, no. 1 (Winter 1974), 33–64.

25 Carlson, "North Atlantic Rim, Barrier or Bridge?," 4.

26 Carlson, "North Atlantic Rim, Barrier or Bridge?," 5.

27 Kolodny, *In Search of First Contact*, 14.

28 Kolodny, *In Search of First Contact*, 14.

29 See: R. Strozier, "*Runestruck*, book review," *New York Times* (March 6, 1977), 305, https://www.nytimes.com/1977/03/06/archives/runestruck.html, accessed February 2023. See: C. Trillin, *Runestruck* (Boston: Little, Brown, 1977).

30 J. Bills, "The Mystery of Dighton Rock," https://newengland.com/today/travel/massachusetts/the-mystery-of-dighton-rock/, accessed October 2022.

31 E. Brecher, "The Enigma of Dighton Rock," *American Heritage*, 9, no. 4 (June 1958), https://www.americanheritage.com/enigma-dighton-rock, accessed October 2022.

32 A clear impression of the appearance of rock and marks can be gained from Bills, "The Mystery of Dighton Rock."

33 Brecher, "The Enigma of Dighton Rock."

34 Brecher, "The Enigma of Dighton Rock."

35 Brecher, "The Enigma of Dighton Rock."

36 "Vikings, Newport Rhode Island, Newport Tower c.1670," https://buildingsofnewengland.com/tag/vikings-newport-rhode-island/, accessed October 2022.

37 H. W. Longfellow, "The Skeleton in Armor," https://www.poetryfoundation.org/poems/44648/the-skeleton-in-armor, accessed October 2022.

38   "Vikings, Newport Rhode Island, Newport Tower c.1670."

39   See: J. S. P. Buckland, "The Origins of the Tower Mill, with a Note on
      Chesterton," *Proc. 11 Mills Research Conference. Mills Research Group*
      (1994).

40   J. Hale, et al, "Dating Ancient Mortar," *American Scientist* 91, no. 2
      (2003), 130–37.

41   A clear photograph of the rock can be found here: C. Church, "Rock of
      Ages: The Mysterious Rune Stone is Now an Official Tourist Attraction,"
      https://www.independentri.com/independents/ind/north_kingstown
      /article_59f859ac-dfa7-5a46-8072-1c4e1fc12a52.html, accessed October
      2022.

42   Church, "Rock of Ages: The Mysterious Rune Stone is Now an Official
      Tourist Attraction."

43   Church, "Rock of Ages: The Mysterious Rune Stone is Now an Official
      Tourist Attraction."

44   S. Carlson, "The Narragansett Stone Reconsidered," *Journal of the New
      England Antiquities Research Association* (NEARA) (Winter/Spring 1991).

45   "The Great Narragansett Rune Stone Debate," https://sorhodeisland.com
      /stories/the-great-narragansett-rune-stone-debate,17149, accessed October
      2022.

46   P. Sutherland, "The Norse and Native Norse Americans," in *Vikings: The
      North Atlantic Saga*, eds. W. W. Fitzhugh, E. I. Ward (Washington, DC:
      The Smithsonian Institution, 2000), 238–47.

47   S. Laskow, "The Mystery of Maine's Viking Penny. The Coin is the Real
      Deal, but How Did It Get All the Way from Norway?" https://www
      .atlasobscura.com/articles/maine-norse-penny-archaeology-vikings
      -north-america, accessed October 2022.

48   A photograph of it can be found on the cover of *Journal of the North
      Atlantic* 33 (November 2017). https://www.researchgate.net
      /publication/321103808_The_Norse_Penny_Reconsidered_The
      _Goddard_Coin-Hoax_or_Genuine, accessed October 2022.

49   Edmund Carpenter, quoted in Laskow, "The Mystery of Maine's Viking
      Penny."

50   Ingstad, Stine Ingstad, *The Viking Discovery of America*, 121.

51   Laskow, "The Mystery of Maine's Viking Penny."

52   G. Campbell, *Norse America*, 151.

53   See: B. Bourque, *Twelve Thousand Years: American Indians in Maine*
      (Lincoln, NE: University of Nebraska Press, 2004), 83.

54   W. Haviland, *Canoe Indians of Down East Maine* (Charleston, NC: The
      History Press, 2012), 45–46.

55   S. H. Gullbekk, "The Norse Penny Reconsidered: The Goddard
      Coin—Hoax or Genuine?" *Journal of the North Atlantic*, 33 (November
      2017), 1–8. The complete article can be found at: https

://www.researchgate.net/publication/321103808_The_Norse_Penny
_Reconsidered_The_Goddard_Coin-Hoax_or_Genuine, accessed
October 2022.

56   Gullbekk, "The Norse Penny Reconsidered," 3–4.

57   Bruce J. Bourque, formerly Maine State Museum's chief archaeologist,
referenced in: Laskow, "The Mystery of Maine's Viking Penny."

58   Gullbekk, "The Norse Penny Reconsidered," 6.

CHAPTER TEN: A NORSE HOME FROM HOME?

1   https://www.oregonhistoryproject.org/articles/historical-records
/scandinavian-immigration/#.Y1gcM3bMKUk, accessed October 2022.

2   https://www.loc.gov/classroom-materials/immigration/scandinavian/,
accessed October 2022.

3   https://www.oregonhistoryproject.org/articles/historical-records
/scandinavian-immigration/#.Y1gcM3bMKUk.

4   A. Estrem, O. N. Nelson, "History of the Scandinavians and Successful
Scandinavians in the United States," *American Historical Review* 3, no. 1
(1904), 161.

5   See: R. Daniels, *Coming to America: A History of Immigration and
Ethnicity in American Life*, 2nd ed (New York: HarperCollins, 2002).

6   I. Kjaer, "Runes and Immigrants in America: The Kensington Stone,
the World's Columbian Exposition in Chicago and Nordic Identity,"
Nordic Roundtable Papers 17 (Minneapolis: Center for Nordic Studies,
University of Minnesota, 1994), 19–24.

7   Wahlgren, *The Vikings and America*, 112.

8   See: Wahlgren, *The Vikings and America*, 113–4.

9   https://www.deseret.com/2001/8/13/19601254/2nd-stone-found-near
-site-of-minnesota-runestone, accessed October 2022.

10   T. Trow, "Small Holes in Large Rocks: The 'Mooring Stones' of
Kensington," *Minnesota History* (Minnesota Historical Society, 1998),
124, http://collections.mnhs.org/MNHistoryMagazine/articles/56
/v56i03p120-128.pdf, accessed October 2022.

11   Trow, "Small Holes in Large Rocks," 125–27.

12   Trow, "Small Holes in Large Rocks," 127.

13   Trow, "Small Holes in Large Rocks," 127–28.

14   K. L. Feder, *Encyclopedia of Dubious Archaeology: From Atlantis to the
Walam Olum*, (Westport, CT: Greenwood, 2010), 137.

15   https://www.carlalbert.edu/, accessed October 2022.

16   R. F. Maslowski, "Braxton County Rune Stone," *e-WV: The West Virginia
Encyclopedia*, (January 7, 2011), https://www.wvencyclopedia.org/articles
/646, accessed October 2022.

17   https://www.wvpublic.org/radio/2019-04-10/april-10-1931-braxton
-county-rune-stone-found, accessed October 2022.

18   A photograph of it can be found in: J. H. McCulloch, "The Grave Creek
      Stone," https://www.asc.ohio-state.edu/mcculloch.2/arch/grvcrk.html,
      accessed 2022.

19   McCulloch, "The Grave Creek Stone."

20   B. T. Lepper, "Great Find in West Virginia Nothing More than a Fraud,"
      https://eu.dispatch.com/story/news/technology/2008/11/11/great-find-in
      -west-virginia/23788281007/, accessed October 2022.

21   This is accessibly explored in "Awful Archaeology Episode 3: The Grave
      Creek Stone," https://www.reddit.com/r/videos/comments/se43l5/awful
      _archaeology_ep_3_the_grave_creek_stone/, accessed October 2022.

22   Wahlgren, *The Vikings and America*, 121.

CHAPTER ELEVEN: A DARKER SIDE TO THE STORY

1   O. S. Lovoll, "Norwegian Americans," https://www.everyculture.com
      /multi/Le-Pa/Norwegian-Americans.html, accessed November 2022.

2   J. Brøndal, D. Blanck, "The Concept of Being Scandinavian-American,"
      American Studies in Scandinavia, Vol. 34 (2002), 1, file:///C:/Users
      /Martin/Downloads/4397-Article%20Text-17029-1-10-20140827.pdf,
      accessed November 2022.

3   Brøndal, Blanck, "The Concept of Being Scandinavian-American."
      See also: J. Gjerde, "The Effect of Community on Migration: Three
      Minnesota Townships 1885–1905," *Journal of Historical Geography* 5, no. 4
      (1979), 406.

4   Lovoll, "Norwegian Americans."

5   Lovoll, "Norwegian Americans."

6   Lovoll, "Norwegian Americans."

7   Lovoll, "Norwegian Americans."

8   Lovoll, "Norwegian Americans."

9   S. Lindmark, *Swedish America, 1914–1932: Studies in Ethnicity with Emphasis
      on Illinois and Minnesota*, (Uppsala: Laromedelsforlagen, 1971), 58.

10   Brøndal, Blanck, "The Concept of Being Scandinavian-American," 24.

11   Lovoll, "Norwegian Americans."

12   Lovoll, "Norwegian Americans."

13   D. Blanck, "Swedish Immigration to the US," https://www.mnhs.org
      /newspapers/swedishamerican/migration, accessed November 2022.

14   Nelson, "The Kensington Runestone: Minnesota's Most Brilliant and
      Durable Hoax?"

15   Brøndal, Blanck, "The Concept of Being Scandinavian-American," 21.

16   Brøndal, Blanck, "The Concept of Being Scandinavian-American," 21–22.

17   O. N. Nelson, "Characteristics of the Scandinavians and Review of Their
      History," in *History of the Scandinavians and the Successful Scandinavians
      in the United States*, vol. I, ed. O. N. Nelson (Minneapolis: O. N. Nelson,
      2nd ed., 1900), 24.

18   K. C. Babcock, *The Scandinavian Element in the United States*, University
      of Illinois Studies in the Social Sciences 111, no. 3 (September 1914), 11.

19   G. E. Forssling, *Nordicism and Modernity* (New York: Springer
      International, 2020), 174.

20   Forssling, *Nordicism and Modernity*, 174–5.

21   C. Berlet, M. N. Lyons, *Right-Wing Populism in America: Too Close for
      Comfort* (New York: Guilford Press, 2000), 146.

22   Berlet, Lyons, *Right-Wing Populism in America*, 105.

23   Berlet, Lyons, *Right-Wing Populism in America*, 146.

24   Berlet, Lyons, *Right-Wing Populism in America*, 146.

25   Berlet, Lyons, *Right-Wing Populism in America*, 146.

26   See: C. Rosen, *Preaching Eugenics: Religious Leaders and the American
      Eugenics Movement* (Oxford: Oxford University Press, 2004).

27   Berlet, Lyons, *Right-Wing Populism in America*, 146–7.

28   M. Wallace, *The American Axis: Henry Ford, Charles Lindbergh, and the
      Rise of the Third Reich* (New York: Macmillan, 2005), 83–5.

29   See: J. P. Duffy, *Lindbergh vs. Roosevelt: The Rivalry That Divided America*
      (Washington, DC: Regnery History, 2010).

30   See J. Hoberman, "Fantasies of a Fascist America," *The Forward*
      (October 1, 2004).

31   Wallace, *The American Axis*, 358.

32   For an overview of the subject see: Forssling, *Nordicism and Modernity*.

CHAPTER TWELVE: VIKINGS READING COMIC BOOKS

1   D. Christopoulou, "How Pop Culture Revived Norse Mythology,"
      https://theculturetrip.com/europe/norway/articles/how-pop-culture
      -revived-norse-mythology/, accessed December 2022.

2   Christopoulou, "How Pop Culture Revived Norse Mythology."

3   See: S. Lee, G. Mair, *Excelsior!: The Amazing Life of Stan Lee* (New York:
      Fireside Books, 2002).

4   L. Daniels, *Marvel: Five Fabulous Decades of the World's Greatest Comics*
      (New York: Harry N. Abrams, 1991), 124.

5   Kunz, "Eirik the Red's Saga," 668.

6   https://www.upress.state.ms.us/Books/M/Medievalist-Comics-and
      -the-American-Century2, accessed December 2022, concerning: C.
      Bishop, *Medievalist Comics and the American Century* (University Press of
      Mississippi, 2016).

7   T. J. Dietsch, "Read Jason Aaron's Complete Thor Saga," https://www
      .marvel.com/articles/comics/the-full-reading-order-of-jason-aaron-s-thor,
      accessed December 2022.

8   C. Hoffer, "The Five Best Viking Comics," https://comicbook.com/news
      /celebrate-leif-erikson-day-with-these-five-viking-comics/, accessed
      December 2022.

9   Bishop, *Medievalist Comics and the American Century.*
10   S. Durn, "How Loki Shapeshifted from Nordic Folklore to a Marvel
        Icon," https://gizmodo.com/how-loki-shapeshifted-from-nordic-folklore
        -to-a-marvel-1846953783, accessed December 2022.
11   Dr. Helena Bassil-Morozow, Lecturer in Media and Journalism, Glasgow
        Caledonian University, quoted in: Durn, "How Loki Shapeshifted from
        Nordic Folklore to a Marvel Icon."
12   Christopoulou, "How Pop Culture Revived Norse Mythology."
13   Durn, "How Loki Shapeshifted from Nordic Folklore to a Marvel Icon."
14   Christopoulou, "How Pop Culture Revived Norse Mythology."
15   Christopoulou, "How Pop Culture Revived Norse Mythology."
16   Christopoulou, "How Pop Culture Revived Norse Mythology."
17   Curt Hersey, Associate Professor of Communication; Filmmaking
        and Cinematic Arts, Berry College, GA, quoted in: G. Jordan, "Comic
        Culture Influences American Media," https://vikingfusion.com
        /2021/04/08/comic-culture-influences-american-media/, accessed
        December 2022.
18   T. Kogod, "10 Epic Viking Comics Worthy of Valhalla," https://www
        .cbr.com/best-viking-comics/, accessed December 2022.
19   Kogod, "10 Epic Viking Comics Worthy of Valhalla."
20   A. Nelson, "Why Me Why Not: Who is Hagar the Horrible, and Why is
        the Cartoon Strip on President Joe Biden's Desk?" https://www.scotsman
        .com/whats-on/arts-and-entertainment/why-me-why-not-who-is-hagar
        -the-horrible-and-why-is-the-cartoon-strip-on-president-joe-bidens
        -desk-3107776, accessed December 2022.
21   Nelson, "Why Me Why Not"
22   Kogod, "10 Epic Viking Comics Worthy of Valhalla."
23   C. Hoffer, "The Five Best Viking Comics," https://comicbook.com/news
        /celebrate-leif-erikson-day-with-these-five-viking-comics/, accessed
        December 2022.
24   Kogod, "10 Epic Viking Comics Worthy of Valhalla."
25   Hoffer, "The Five Best Viking Comics."
26   Kogod, "10 Epic Viking Comics Worthy of Valhalla."
27   Hoffer, "The Five Best Viking Comics."
28   Hoffer, "The Five Best Viking Comics."
29   Hoffer, "The Five Best Viking Comics."
30   Kogod, "10 Epic Viking Comics Worthy of Valhalla."

CHAPTER THIRTEEN: THE VIKINGS GO TO THE MOVIES . . .
AND WATCH TV
1   D. Christopoulou, "How Pop Culture Revived Norse Mythology."
2   "Asgardians," https://marvel.fandom.com/wiki/Asgardians, accessed
        December 2022.

3   M. Fowler, "How to Watch the Thor Movies in Chronological Order. Here's Thor, from Banished Braggart to Awesome Avenger to Cosmic Crusader," https://www.ign.com/articles/how-to-watch-the-thor-movies -in-chronological-order, accessed December 2022.

4   An overview of this development can be found in: Christopoulou, "How Pop Culture Revived Norse Mythology."

5   Fowler, "How to Watch the Thor Movies in Chronological Order."

6   Fowler, "How to Watch the Thor Movies in Chronological Order."

7   "What If . . . Thor Were an Only Child?" https://marvelcinematic universe.fandom.com/wiki/What_If . . . _Thor_Were_an_Only _Child%3F, accessed February 2023.

8   Curt Hersey, Associate Professor of Communication; Filmmaking and Cinematic Arts, Berry College, GA, quoted in: G. Jordan, "Comic culture influences American media," https://vikingfusion.com /2021/04/08/comic-culture-influences-american-media/, accessed December 2022.

9   Jordan, "Comic culture influences American media."

10   Hersey, quoted in: Jordan, "Comic culture influences American media."

11   Christopoulou, "How Pop Culture Revived Norse Mythology."

12   Christopoulou, "How Pop Culture Revived Norse Mythology."

13   Christopoulou, "How Pop Culture Revived Norse Mythology."

14   Christopoulou, "How Pop Culture Revived Norse Mythology."

15   Durn, "How Loki Shapeshifted from Nordic Folklore to a Marvel Icon."

16   Christopoulou, "How Pop Culture Revived Norse Mythology."

17   Whittock, Whittock, *Tales of Valhalla*, 42.

18   See: "Ghosts TV Series, 2021–," https://www.imdb.com/title /tt11379026/; "Thorfinn," https://ghosts-bbc.fandom.com/wiki/Thorfinn, accessed March 2023.

19   H. Shaw-Williams, "Vikings True Story: Did Ubbe Really Explore North America?" https://screenrant.com/vikings-true-story-real-ubbe-discover -north-america/, accessed December 2022.

20   Shaw-Williams, "Vikings True Story: Did Ubbe Really Explore North America?"

21   https://www.rottentomatoes.com/tv/american_gods, accessed February 2023.

22   https://www.neilgaiman.com/works/Books/American+Gods/, accessed December 2022.

23   D. Barnett, "A Book for the Beach: American Gods by Neil Gaiman," https://www.theguardian.com/books/booksblog/2014/jul/29/book-beach -american-gods-neil-gaiman, accessed December 2022.

24   Barnett, "A book for the beach: American Gods by Neil Gaiman."

25   C. Pulliam-Moore, "'American Gods' Jesus Shows What Happens When a God Becomes Too Popular," https://gizmodo.com/american-gods

-jesus-shows-what-happens-when-a-god-becom-1796255952, accessed
December 2022.

26   E. Bley Griffiths, "American Gods mythology guide: Meet Mexican
      Jesus, White Jesus, and Black Jesus," https://www.radiotimes.com/tv
      /fantasy/american-gods-mythology-guide-meet-mexican-jesus-white
      -jesus-and-black-jesus/, accessed December 2022.

27   Bley Griffiths, "American Gods mythology guide"; and R. Duncan,
      "5 Things Christians Should Know about *American Gods*," https://www
      .crosswalk.com/blogs/christian-movie-reviews/5-things-christians
      -should-know-about-i-american-gods-i.html, accessed December 2022.

28   Pulliam-Moore, "American Gods' Jesus Shows What Happens When a
      God Becomes Too Popular."

29   Pulliam-Moore, "American Gods' Jesus Shows What Happens When a
      God Becomes Too Popular."

30   Kirkus Reviews, "American Gods," https://www.kirkusreviews.com
      /book-reviews/neil-gaiman/american-gods/, accessed December 2022.

31   See, for example: M. Rothschild, *The Storm Is Upon Us: How QAnon
      Became a Movement, Cult, and Conspiracy Theory of Everything* (Brooklyn,
      NY: Melville House, 2021).

CHAPTER FOURTEEN: AMERICAN VIKINGS MEET QANON

1   T. Birkett, "US Capitol Riot: The Myths behind the Tattoos Worn by
      'QAnon Shaman' Jake Angeli," https://theconversation.com/us-capitol
      -riot-the-myths-behind-the-tattoos-worn-by-qanon-shaman-jake-angeli
      -152996, accessed December 2022.

2   *Dictionary of Northern Mythology*, trans. R. Simek, A. Hall (Martlesham,
      UK: Boydell & Brewer, 1993) 163.

3   Birkett, "US Capitol riot."

4   M. Whittock, *Apocalyptic Politics* (Eugene, OR: Wipf and Stock, 2022),
      196.

5   Whittock, *Apocalyptic Politics*, 196.

6   Whittock, *Apocalyptic Politics*, 197.

7   R. Ruelas, "Unsealed Indictment Reveals More Counts against Jake
      Angeli, QAnon Shaman, for U.S. Capitol Raid," *The Arizona Republic*,
      January 13, 2021.

8   T. Jackman, "'QAnon Shaman' Sentenced to 41 Months for Role in
      Capitol Riot," *Washington Post*, November 17, 2021.

9   Birkett, "US Capitol Riot."

10   A. Green, "Judge Sentences MAX Train Murderer Jeremy Christian to
      'True Life': He Should Never Be Released from Prison," https://www
      .oregonlive.com/news/2020/06/live-updates-max-train-murderer-jeremy
      -christian-will-be-sentenced-after-more-victims-testify.html, accessed
      December 2022.

11   D. Perry, "White Supremacists Love Vikings. But They've Got History
      All Wrong," www.washingtonpost.com/posteverything/wp/2017/05/31
      /white-supremacists-love-vikings-but-theyve-got-history-all-wrong/,
      accessed December 2022.

12   L. Keller, "White Supremacist Running Odinist Network from
      Maximum-Security Prison," https://www.splcenter.org/hate
      watch/2009/03/20/white-supremacist-running-odinist-network
      -maximum-security-prison, accessed December 2022.

13   Perry, "White supremacists love Vikings."

14   Perry, "White supremacists love Vikings."

15   R. F. Burley, "Ambiguous Images: 'Vikingness,' North American White
      Nationalism and the Threat of Appropriation," in *Vikings and the Vikings:
      Essays on Television's History Channel Series*, eds. P. Hardwick, K. Lister
      (Jefferson, NC: McFarland, 2019), 211.

16   S. Kamali, *Homegrown Hate: Why White Nationalists and Militant
      Islamists Are Waging War Against the United States* (Berkeley, CA:
      University of California Press, 2022), 162.

17   R. Fahey, "Marauders in the US Capitol: Alt-right Viking Wannabes and
      Weaponized Medievalism," https://sites.nd.edu/manuscript-studies
      /2021/01/15/marauders-in-the-capitol-alt-right-viking-wannabes
      -weaponized-medievalism-in-american-white-nationalism/, accessed
      February 2023.

18   G. McMaster, "White supremacists are misappropriating Norse
      mythology, says expert," www.ualberta.ca/folio/2020/07/white
      -supremacists-are-misappropriating-norse-mythology-says-expert.html,
      accessed January 2023.

19   S. Rose, "Norse Code: Are White Supremacists Reading Too Much into
      The Northman?" www.theguardian.com/film/2022/apr/22/norse-code
      -white-supremacists-reading-the-northman-robert-eggers, accessed
      January 2023.

20   R. Evans, "Shitposting, Inspirational Terrorism and the Christchurch
      Mosque Massacre," Bellingcat, March 15, 2019; G. Macklin, "The
      Christchurch Attacks: Livestream Terror in the Viral Video Age,"
      Combating Terrorism Center at West Point 12, no. 6 (July 2019), ctc.west
      point.edu/christchurch-attacks-livestream-terror-viral-video-age/,
      accessed January 2023.

21   McMaster, "White supremacists are misappropriating Norse mythology,
      says expert."

22   D. Kim, "White Supremacists Have Weaponized an Imaginary Viking Past.
      It's Time to Reclaim the Real History," time.com/5569399/viking
      -history-white-nationalists/, accessed January 2023.

23   Fahey, "Marauders in the US Capitol."

24   Fahey, "Marauders in the US Capitol."

25   Perry, "White supremacists love Vikings."

26   Burley, "Ambiguous Images," 211.

27   E. J. Franks, "White Supremacist Interpretations of Vikings," in
      International Medievalisms: From Nationalism to Activism, ed. M. Boyle
      (Woodbridge, UK: Boydell and Brewer, 2023), 188.

28   "Stormfront," https://www.splcenter.org/fighting-hate/extremist-files/group
      /stormfront, accessed January 2023.

29   Rose, "Norse Code."

30   Kamali, *Homegrown Hate: Why White Nationalists and Militant Islamists
      Are Waging War Against the United States*, 122.

31   McMaster, "White supremacists are misappropriating Norse mythology,
      says expert."

32   K. Fox, "The Northman: Vikings, Nazis, and Historical Accuracy," www
      .pastemagazine.com/movies/the-northman-historical-accuracy-nazis/,
      accessed January 2023.

33   McMaster, "White supremacists are misappropriating Norse mythology,
      says expert."

34   Rose, "Norse Code."

35   H. Gearan, "The Northman Star Responds to Viking Movie's
      White Supremacy Controversy", screenrant.com/northman-movie
      -white-supremacy-controversy-claes-bang-response/, accessed
      January 2023.

36   Fox, "The Northman: Vikings, Nazis, and Historical Accuracy."

37   Franks, "White Supremacist Interpretations of Vikings," 187.

CHAPTER FIFTEEN: MERCHANDISING VIKINGS

1   "The Global Viking Brand," http://www.worldtreeproject.org/exhibits
      /show/viking-branding/globalvikingbrand, accessed January 2023.

2   "Minnesota Vikings Logos History," https://www.sportslogos.net/logos
      /list_by_team/172/minnesota_vikings/, accessed January 2023.

3   M. Arnott, P. B. Sturtevant, "'Viking Tough': How Ads Sell Us Medieval
      Manhood," https://www.publicmedievalist.com/medieval-ads/, accessed
      January 2023.

4   Arnott, Sturtevant, "'Viking Tough.'"

5   Arnott, Sturtevant, "'Viking Tough.'"

6   "Dodge Ram Trucks/Super Bowl Spot/Vikings (2018)," https://www
      .youtube.com/watch?v=rv1qDKmo-ss, accessed January 2023.

7   Arnott, Sturtevant, "'Viking Tough.'"

8   Whittock, Whittock, *The Viking Blitzkrieg*, AD *789–1098*, 199;
      H. O'Brien, *Queen Emma and the Vikings: The Woman Who Shaped the
      Events of 1066* (London: Bloomsbury, 2005), 50.

9   G. Stoller, "Fargo Brewery Brews Craft Beer 'For the Viking In All Of Us,'"
      https://www.forbes.com/sites/garystoller/2020/07/10/fargo-brewery-brews

-craft-beer-for-the-viking-in-all-of-us/?sh=33dd9102305e, accessed January 2023.

10   https://drekkerbrewing.com/about/, accessed January 2023.

11   "The Global Viking Brand."

12   "The Global Viking Brand."

13   J. Clement, "God of War Ragnarök Launch Sales Worldwide 2022," https://www.statista.com/statistics/1347315/god-of-war-ragnaroek-launch-sales/, accessed January 2023.

14   I. Kahloon, "Falling Behind" (published in the online edition as "What's the Matter with Men?"), *The New Yorker* (January 30, 2023).

15   Arnott, Sturtevant, "'Viking Tough.'"

16   T. Birkett, "Introduction," in R. Dale, T. Birkett, *The Vikings Reimagined*, (Boston: De Gruyter, 2020), 12. Also: R. Dale, "From Barbarian to Brand: The Vikings as a Marketing tool," in Dale, Birkett, *The Vikings Reimagined*, 214–31.

17   Birkett, "Introduction," 13. Also: Dale, "From Barbarian to Brand," 214–31.

18   Birkett, "Introduction," 13. Also: Dale, "From Barbarian to Brand," 214–31.

19   E. Dregni, *Vikings in the Attic. In Search of Nordic America* (Minneapolis: University of Minnesota Press, 2011), 44.

20   Birkett, "Introduction," 14. Also: E. R. Barraclough, "The Great Viking Fake-Off: The Cultural Legacy of Norse Voyages to North America," in Dale, Birkett, *The Vikings Reimagined*, 250–66.

AFTERWORD: WHERE NEXT FOR THE AMERICAN VIKINGS?

1   Kolodny, *In Search of First Contact*, 204.

2   M. Strauss, "Discovery Could Rewrite History of Vikings in New World," https://www.nationalgeographic.com/history/article/160331-viking-discovery-north-america-canada-archaeology, accessed January 2023.

3   https://www.age-of-the-sage.org/vikings_north_american/point_rosee_settlement.html, accessed January 2023.

4   The Canadian Press, Toronto Star, https://www.thestar.com/news/canada/2018/05/31/thor-loser-vikings-likely-didnt-live-on-south-coast-of-newfoundland-study-finds.html, accessed January 2023.

5   J. Dalton, "Long-lost North American Viking Settlement Was in Canada, Say Archaeologists," https://www.independent.co.uk/news/world/americas/vikings-canada-settlement-north-america-europeans-birgitta-wallace-archaeologists-discovery-a8247161.html, accessed January 2023.

6   G. Campbell, *Norse America*, 208.

7 For an accessible exploration of different aspects of this Scandinavian cultural presence in the USA over time, see: E. Dregni, *Vikings in the Attic. In Search of Nordic America* (Minneapolis: University of Minnesota Press, 2011).

8 E. Heeb, "Norsk Høstfest: North America's Biggest Viking Party," https://www.canadiantraveller.com/Norsk_Hostfest, accessed January 2023.

9 "About Norsk Høstfest," https://hostfest.com/about/, accessed January 2023.

10 Heeb, "Norsk Høstfest: North America's Biggest Viking Party."

11 https://nordicfest.com/, accessed January 2023.

12 "About Nordic Fest," https://nordicfest.com/about/, accessed January 2023.

13 "About Nordic Fest."

14 J. Brøndal, D. Blanck, "The Concept of Being Scandinavian-American," *American Studies in Scandinavia* 34 (2002), 27, file:///C:/Users/Martin/Downloads/4397-Article%20Text-17029-1-10-20140827.pdf, accessed November 2022.

INDEX

A

Aaron, Jason, 178

Action Comics Issue #1, 175

Adam of Bremen, 20–21, 111–112

Aesir, 15

Ah! My Goddess (*Oh My Goddess!*), 184

Alfred, King, 8

Amazon Prime, 191

Ambudkar, Utkarsh, 190

America First Committee (AFC), 168–171

America Not Discovered by Columbus, 102

American German Federation, 168–170

American Gods, 186–187, 189, 191–195

American Magazine of Useful and Entertaining Knowledge, 136

American Revolution, 86, 93–95

American Vikings
  becoming citizens, 148–149, 160–166
  description of, 2–3, 14–15
  earliest evidence of, 35–36
  future of, 215–220

  history of, 1–11, 18–19, 54–172, 197, 207
  idea of, 159–160, 181–185, 192–193
  legacy of, 2–4, 103–104, 186–187, 201–205, 219–220
  Midwest Vikings, 107–122, 145–149
  New England Vikings, 73, 123–142
  QAnon and, x, 103, 179–180, 195–206
  search for, 2–3, 35–36, 50–173, 197–198, 215–220
  See also Vikings

Amerikadeutscher Bund (American German Federation), 168–170

Anderson, Rasmus Bjørn, 102

Angeli, Jake, 197–201

Anglo-Saxon Chronicle, 24

Anglo-Saxons, 3–6, 20–32, 103, 108–109

Annals of Gottskalk, 57, 59

Annals of the Kings of Iceland (*Annales Islandorum Regii*), 56–58

Antiquitates Americanae, sive Scriptores Septentrionales rerum Ante-Columbianarum (*Antiquities of*

*America, or the Writings of the
Historians of the North about Pre-
Columbian America*), 100, 135
antisemitism, 169–171
archaeology
  archaeological evidence, ix, 21–24,
    30, 52–82, 87–92, 101–159, 166,
    173–174, 208, 216–220
  archaeological sites, x, 2, 10, 21–24,
    30, 46–47, 52–74, 81–82, 87–92,
    101–159, 166, 173–174, 198, 208,
    216–219
  artifacts discovered, 30, 64–71,
    81–82, 88, 91, 101–104, 114–137,
    139–151, 166, 173–174, 208,
    217–219
  carbon dating, 63, 70–72, 130–137
  earliest evidence and, 35–36, 45–47
  searches and, 2–3, 35–36, 52–173,
    197–198, 215–218
  skeletons, 88, 135–136
  tree-ring analysis, 68–71
Arnold, Benedict, 136–137
Aryan supremacy, 160, 169
Asgard, 15, 17, 187, 190
Assassin's Creed Valhalla, 16
Augsburg College, 165
Augustana College, 165
Ave Maria Stone, Minnesota,
  150–152
Avengers, 186–188
Avengers #1, 177
Avengers: Age of Ultron, 188
Avengers: Endgame, 188, 190
Avengers: Infinity War, 188
AVM Stone, 150–152

B
Babcock, Kendric Charles, 167, 172
Badaki, Yetide, 193
Baldr, 15
Bang, Claes, 205
Barnes, Demore, 193

Bath Maritime Museum, 131
Beamish, North Ludlow, 101
beers, x, 1, 10, 210, 216
Belknap, Jeremy, 94
Biden, Joe, 105, 182
Bifrost, 15, 187
Birds of Prey #29, 181
Bishop, Chris, 179
Black Lives Matter, 200
Black Road, 183
Blackmore Museum, 156
Blanchett, Cate, 190
Bloodaxe, Erik, 6, 8
Bluetooth, King Harald, 9
Book of Flatey (Flateyjarbok), 59
Book of Icelanders (Islendingabok),
  36, 91
Book of Settlements (Landnamabok),
  29, 36, 60
Brandeis University, 131, 203
Brave and the Bold #1, The, 175, 181
Braxton Runestone, West Virginia, 155
Breivik, Anders, 202
Brendan the Navigator, x, 75–84,
  88–91, 103
Brendan Voyage, The, 76–82
British Isles, 9, 22–25, 29, 54, 73
British Museum, 156
Brown, Everett C. Jr., 138
Brown, Gary, 183
Brown, Harold, 131
Brown University, 134
Browne, Chris, 182
Browne, Dik, 182
Browning, Emily, 193
*Bund der Freunde des Neuen Deutsch-
land* (Federation of Friends of the
  New Germany), 168–169
Byzantine Empire, 4, 6, 9, 26

C
Cabot, John, x, 45, 93, 98–99
Caboto, Giovanni, 93

Caliphate, 28, 33–34, 114
Canadian Arctic, ix, 124–126, 215
Canadian Historical Association, 204
Caradoc of Llancarfan, 83
carbon dating, 63, 70–72, 130–137
Carl Albert State College, 154
Carlson, Suzanne, 131–132, 138
Catlin, George, 87
CBS, 190
Chansley, Jacob, 197–201
Charlestown State Park, 88
Chicago World's Fair, 96, 120, 148
Christchurch Massacre, 202
Christian, Jeremy, 201–202
Christianity, converting to, 9–11,
    14–18, 21–39, 47–57, 102–105,
    110–114, 183–187, 194–195
Chronicle of the Princes (*Brut y
    Tywysogion*), 83
Chronicle of Wales (*Cronica Walliae*),
    83, 93
Circle of the World (*Heimskringla*), 18
Civil War, 98, 102, 146, 148, 164
Clemens, James W., 156
Clinton, Hillary, 218
Cnut, King, 9
Codex Regius, 18
College of Physicians, 99
Columbian Exposition, 96, 120, 148
Columbus, Christopher, x, 45, 61,
    71, 80–81, 93–105, 110, 120–121,
    140, 145, 148–149, 167–168, 174,
    194, 214
Columbus Day, 94, 96, 105
comic books, ix–x, 1, 9, 13, 16, 173–
    189, 204, 216
Concordia College, 165
conspiracy theories, x, 195–206. *See
    also* QAnon
Coolidge, Calvin, 104, 164
Cortereal, Miguel, 134–135
costumes, x, 10, 105–106, 125, 154,
    162, 197–198, 202, 208–212, 219

culture wars, 105, 186–187, 195–197
Cunniffe, Dee, 184
Curtis, Jenneth, 63
CW Network, 189

D

Dakota War, 104, 117
Danes, 3–4, 6, 8, 31–34, 103, 108,
    146, 161–163, 167
Danforth, John, 133
Daughters of Norway, 162
Daughters of the American Revolu-
    tion, 86
Davey, Shaun, 79
Davis, E. H., 156
DC Comics, 175–177, 181–182
Delabarre, Edmund B., 134–135
Denmark, 3, 9, 22, 25–26, 31–33,
    108, 114, 146
Dicuil, 91
Dighton Rock, Massachusetts, 127,
    133–135
Dighton Rock State Park, 133–135
Discovery of America by the Northmen,
    101
Disney+, 188, 190
Ditko, Steve, 176
DNA, 29, 49, 82, 109, 150, 157, 220
Doctor Strange, 188
Dodge, 209
Drekker, 210
Dubb-gaill (black foreigners), 4
Dudzik, Mark, 151
Durex, 209
Dwight, Timothy, 100

E

Earl of Orkney, 6, 76, 89–90
Edda, 17–18, 22, 24
Eggers, Robert, 205
Egil's Saga, 22
Elder Skalholt Annals, 59
Elliott, Walter J., Jr., 131

emigration, 28–29, 103, 146–147. *See also* immigration

England, 3–9, 20–32, 77, 82–83, 93–94, 108–113, 191, 198

Ennis, Garth, 178

Erik the Red, x, 29–30, 36–50, 54–57, 60, 67–68, 72, 106, 112, 128, 177, 183

Erik the Red's Saga (Eiriks saga rautha), 36–50, 54, 60, 68, 72, 112, 128, 177

Eriksson, Freydis, x, 39, 44, 48–51

Eriksson, Leif, x, 30, 38–52, 72–73, 103–106, 129, 133, 157, 184, 192

Eriksson, Thorstein, x, 38–39, 44

Eriksson, Thorvald, 39, 42–45, 48–49, 141

Essay on the Alphabets of the Unknown Letters That are Found in the Most Ancient Coins and Monuments of Spain, 156–157

Eternal, 184

Ethelred the Unready, 8

ethnic origin myths, 92–107. *See also* origin myths

ethnic theories, 166–173. *See also* racial theories

Evening Telegram, The, 62

Explorations of America Before Columbus, 140

F

Fabry, Glenn, 178

Feder, Ken, 153

Federation of Friends of the New Germany, 168–169

Fenrir, 16–17, 23

festivals, 164, 218–219

films, ix–x, 1, 9, 13, 16, 26, 79, 176, 179–181, 185–206

Finehair, King Harald, 28

Finn-gaill (white foreigners), 4

Fletcher, Richard, 128, 130

Fletcher Stone, 127–130

Focus Features, 205

Ford, Henry, 169, 171

Forster, Johann Reinhold, 89

France, 3–4, 6, 9, 25, 32–33, 77, 109

Franklin, Benjamin, x, 99, 173

Fraser, A. D., 129–130

Fremantle North America, 192

Freya, 175, 180

Freydis, x, 39, 44, 48–51

Freyr, 15–16, 20

"Friends of the New Germany," 168–169

Frigg, 15, 175, 180

Frigga, 175, 180

Fujishima, Kōsuke, 184

Fuller, Bryan, 192

G

Gaiman, Neil, 192, 196

George III, King, 95

German Football Association (DFB), 199

Germany, 3, 25, 146, 160, 167–171, 199

Ghosts, 190

giants, 15–17, 59, 178–180, 187, 199

Gilsson, Bishop Bjorn, 44

Gjerset, Knut, 104

Glover, Crispin, 193

Gnupsson, Bishop Erik, 52, 54–58, 72, 125

God of War Ragnarök, 212

Goddard Site, 139–142

Gordon, Cyrus, 131

Goths, 116, 166–167

Grave Creek Runestone, West Virginia, 155–157

"Great Replacement," 204

Green, Michael, 192

Greenland, 18–19, 27–31, 35–60, 64–68, 71–74, 79, 90, 107, 107–113, 123–132, 139, 147, 152, 191, 215

Greenlanders, 36–50, 54–57, 68, 72,
    111–112, 126–128
Greenman, Dr. Emerson F., 155
Gwynedd, Madoc ap Owain, x,
    75–76, 82–90, 93, 121

H
Hägar the Horrible, 182–183
Hakluyt, Richard, 121
Hako, 128
Halfdan, 4
Hallgren, Gary, 182
Haraldsson, Olaf III, 139, 141
Harris, Kamala, 182
Harris, Llewellyn, 87
Harry Potter series, 16
Harvard University, 131, 133
Haugen, Einar, 131
Head Lopper, 184
Heavener Runestone, Oklahoma,
    153–154
Heavener Runestone State Park,
    153–154
Heg, Hans Christian, 164
Heg Pageant, 164
Hektoen, Ludvig, 104
Hel, 15–16, 180, 190
Helluland (Stone-slab Land), 40–41,
    45, 58–59, 62, 134
Hemsworth, Chris, 187–188
Henry VII, King, 93
Herjolfsson, Bjarni, 38–40
Hermansson, Patrik, 203
Hesthammer, Kleng Pedersen, 147
Hiddleston, Tom, 189
*Historie of Cambria, Now Called
    Wales*, 84–86, 93
History Channel, 191
History of America, 94
*History of the Scandinavians and Suc-
    cessful Scandinavians in the United
    States*, 166, 171–172
Hitler, Adolf, 160, 168, 170

Hod, 15
Holand, Hjalmar, 140–141, 151
holidays, 94–98, 104–106, 194
"Holy Nation of Odin, Inc.,"
    201–202
Hønen Runestone, 114–115
Hop (Tidal Pool), 48–50, 62, 73, 130,
    134, 217
Hopkins, Sir Anthony, 189
Huckleberry Finn, 56

I
Iceland, 9, 13–14, 18–31, 35–41,
    49–50, 54–58, 65–67, 77–81,
    91–92, 107–109, 145–149
Icelanders, 9, 13–14, 18–19, 29,
    36–37, 49, 57, 82, 91, 99, 102, 149,
    199
Icelandic sagas, 19–20, 35–75, 91–92,
    100–101, 111–112, 128, 177
identities
    cultural identities, 1–9, 12–15,
        92–107, 120–121, 136–150, 156–
        157, 159–165, 174–177, 198–205,
        216–220
    national identities, 9–10, 161–162,
        165–166
    regional identities, 162, 211
Image Comics, 184
immigrants, x, 95–104, 115–121,
    145–173, 178, 192–194, 204
immigration, 28–29, 103–104, 117–
    118, 146–147, 178, 204
Indigenous Peoples' Day, 96
Ingstad, Anne Stine, 62
Ingstad, Benedicte, 62
Ingstad, Helge, 62
Inuit, x, 30, 43, 69, 125
Italy, 9, 95–98, 103–105, 109, 149

J
Jaffe, David, 212
Jamestown, Virginia, 45, 97, 214

January 6, 2021, x, 2, 197–199, 219
Jefferson, Thomas, 87
Jesus, 194–195
John of Wallingford, 210
Jones, Reverend Morgan, 85–86
Jormungand, 16–17, 23–24
jotunn, 15–16
Journey into Mystery #83, 176
Journey into Mystery #85, 179–180
Junior Reserve Officer Training
    Corps, 212

K

Kanigher, Robert, 175
Karlsefni, Thorfinn, 44–45, 48, 72,
    128, 134, 183–184, 190–191
Kensington Runestone, Minnesota,
    104, 114–123, 127, 140, 144–151,
    166, 174, 208, 219
Khurdadhbih, Ibn, 28
Kim, Dorothy, 203
King Features Syndicate, 182
Kingittorsuaq Runestone, 130
Kirby, Jack, 176–177
Kirkeberg, O. L., 161
Kolodny, Annette, 216
Kripke, Eric, 189
Kristensen, Todd, 63
Kubert, Joe, 175
Kyrre, King Olaf, 139, 141

L

Labrador, 41, 44–46, 58, 61, 100,
    123, 126, 142
Langley, Bruce, 193
L'Anse aux Meadows, 46–47, 52,
    61–74, 92, 101, 106–112, 121–122,
    127, 139, 157, 173, 217–218
Law Man's Annals (*Logmannsannall*),
    58
Lee, Stan, 176–177, 179
legacies, 2–4, 103–104, 186–187,
    201–205, 219–220

Leif Eriksson Day, 104–106
Leif Eriksson Society, 129
Leif the Lucky, 30, 42–44, 51. *See
    also* Eriksson, Leif
Leif's Camp, 41–42, 46–52, 72
Leifsbuthir (Leif's Camp), 46–47
Lewis, Meriweather, 87
Lewis, Reverend Gordon, 129
Lieber, Larry, 176, 179
Life of Saint Columba (*Vita Sancti
    Columbae*), 76
Lincoln, Abraham, 98
Lindbergh, Charles, 169–171
Lindbergh, Charles Augustus Sr., 170
Lindsay, Ryan K., 184
Lionsgate Television, 192
Llanstephan manuscript, 83
Lloyd, Thomas, 85
Llwyd, Humphrey, 83–84, 93
Loki, 15–16, 20, 175, 178–180,
    188–190
Loki (film), 190
Long, Devan Chandler, 190
Longfellow, Henry Wadsworth,
    135–136
Lord of the Rings, The, 13, 15
Lothbrok, Ragnar, 191
Lothbrok, Ubbe, 191
Luther College, 165
Lyschander, Claus C., 57

M

MacLean, Andrew, 184
Madison Square Garden, 168
Madoc, x, 75–76, 82–90, 93, 121
Maeshowe runes, 114–115. *See also*
    runes
Magnus VII, King, 138
Magnusen, Finn, 134
Magnusson, Sigurd I, 55
Maine Penny, 127, 139–144, 173, 218
Maine State Museum, 130, 140
Manuscript GKS 2087 4°, 56

MAPPA Studio, 184
Markland (Forest Land), 40–41, 45,
    49, 58–59, 62, 134
Martyrology of Tallaght, The, 76
Marvel Cinematic Universe (MCU),
    187–190
Marvel Comics, 9, 13, 16, 175–178,
    180–182
Marvel Entertainment, 176
Marvel Studios, 187–190
Marvel Universe, 175, 180, 187–190
Marvel Worldwide Inc., 176
Massachusetts Historical Society, 94
Mather, Cotton, 133
Mather, Reverend Samuel, 99, 173
MAX Comics, 178
Mayflower Compact, 98
Mayflower Pilgrims, x, 95, 97–99,
    102–104, 116, 148–149, 174, 194,
    214
McIver, Rose, 190
McShane, Ian, 189, 192–193
medieval sagas, ix–x, 17–26, 35–106,
    111–122, 128–135, 166–167, 177–
    184, 190–210, 213–219
*Medievalist Comics and the American
    Century*, 179
Meldgaard, Jørgen, 62
Mellgren, Guy, 139–140, 142
merchandising, ix–x, 176, 207–214,
    216
Middle Ages, 14, 22, 25, 114, 118,
    141, 174, 215
Midgard Serpent, 15–17, 23–24, 168
Midwest Vikings, 107–122, 145–149.
    See also American Vikings
Midwestern Scandinavians, x, 14,
    114–122, 145–149, 165–170,
    213–214
Mighty Thor, The, 180–181
migration, 19, 28–29, 63, 99–100,
    167, 178. *See also* immigration
Minnesota Historical Society, 117, 152

Minnesota State Fair, 104
Minnesota Statewide Archaeological
    Survey, 152
Minnesota Vikings, x, 1, 121, 149,
    208–209
Mitchill, Dr., 99
Mjolnir, 16, 176–178, 198–199. *See
    also* Thor's hammer
monks, 8, 11, 20, 77, 91
mooring stones, 150–152
movies, ix–x, 1, 9, 13, 16, 26, 79, 176,
    179–181, 185–206
Munn, William, 62
mythology
    competing myths, 92–107,
        148–150
    dark side to, 2, 159–172, 195–196,
        200–201
    national myths, 9, 95–96
    Norse mythology, 8, 12–26, 59, 168–
        169, 173–181, 186–196, 198–216
    origin myths, ix–x, 92–107, 113,
        148–150
    Viking mythology, 12–26, 110,
        157–158, 173–174, 189–193, 201
    Welsh mythology, 75–89

N
Naddoddr, 29
Narragansett Runestone, Rhode
    Island, 127, 137–138, 144
National Football League (NFL),
    208–209
National Geographic Fellow, 216
nationalism, 4, 13, 110, 120, 160–169
Native Americans, x, 2, 30, 37–43,
    48–50, 56, 61–63, 69–71, 82–88,
    95–105, 116, 133–141, 144–145,
    151–160, 192, 198, 214–218
Nazis, 13, 168–171, 203
Nelson, O. N., 166–167, 171
New Brunswick, 46, 68–69, 73,
    112–113, 215, 217

New England Antiquities Research Association (NEARA), 131, 138
New England Vikings, 73, 123–142. *See also* American Vikings
New York University, 131
New York Weekly Museum, 99
New York World's Fair, 120
Newfoundland, ix–x, 44–47, 52, 60–74, 79–81, 101, 106–113, 121–123, 127, 130, 134, 139–144, 152, 157, 173, 191, 215–218
Newport Stone Tower, Rhode Island, 127, 135–137
Nickelodeon, 105
Nicolas of Lynn, 121–122
Niord, 15
Nordic Fest, 219
Nordicism, 169–171
Nordmanni (northmen), 3–4
Norse goddesses, 14–16, 20–23, 175, 180, 193
Norse gods, x, 10, 14–17, 20–24, 47, 168, 175–181, 187–193, 198–199, 202
Norse mythology, 8, 12–26, 59, 168–169, 173–181, 186–196, 198–216. *See also* Viking mythology
Norse sagas, ix–x, 19–20, 35–74, 91–92, 100–101, 144–158. *See also* Icelandic sagas; *Vinland* sagas
Norse "Wild West," 107–113. *See also* "Wild West"
Norse-American Centennial, 163–164
Norsk Høstfest, 218
North Africa, 27–28, 109
North America
discovery of, 19, 39–84, 95–107
expeditions to, 1–2, 19–28, 34–115, 153, 191
exploration of, 19–24, 34–115, 123–126, 142–153
North American Indians, 87

North American Vikings, 50–173. *See also* American Vikings
North Atlantic Saga, The, 218
Northlanders, 183
Northman, The, 205
Northmen, 3–4, 6
Norway, 3–5, 9, 18, 22–34, 37–40, 50, 55, 65, 99, 108–109, 114, 120, 126, 132, 139–148, 161–164, 178
Norwegian Lutheran Church, 165
Norwegians, 4, 29–34, 99, 103–104, 108, 116, 146–148, 161–167
Nova Scotia, 46, 69, 89, 127–130, 134, 138, 141–144, 173–174
Numismatic and Antiquarian Society of Philadelphia, 128

O
Obama, Barack, 104
Oddsson, Eindride, 125
Odin, x, 15–16, 20–26, 47, 131, 175, 177, 180, 187–192, 199–205
Odinism, 201–203
Oestreicher, David, 156–157
Öhman, Edward, 115
Öhman, Olof, 115–117, 119–121, 166, 174
Old Stone Mill, 135–137
"Operation Werewolf," 202
origin myths, ix–x, 92–107, 113, 148–150

P
Pacific Lutheran University, 165
paganism, 3, 9–14, 20–25, 28–37, 47, 81, 91, 132, 193–203
Parcak, Sarah, 216
Paris, Matthew, 83
Parks Canada, 63, 71, 217
Paschal II, Pope, 55
Pearl Harbor attack, 169
Peerson, Cleng, 147
Penn, William, 85

Phillips, Henry, Jr., 128–129
Pilgrims, x, 95, 97–99, 102–104, 116, 148–149, 174, 194, 214
pioneers, x, 14, 19, 36–45, 51–61, 68–71, 86–88, 97–108, 144–158, 167
pit houses, 64–65
"Plastic Viking, The," 216
Plymouth, Massachusetts, 45, 97–98, 116
Plymouth Rock, 116
Poetic Edda, 17–18, 22, 24
poetry, 17–24, 47, 88–89, 135–136, 149, 199
Pohl, Frederick J., 140
politics, ix–x, 103, 169–170, 179–180, 194–207, 216, 219
Poteau Stone, Oklahoma, 153–154
Powel, David, 83–86, 93
Powys, Maredudd ap Rhys ferch, 88–89
"Prince Zichmni," 89–90
Proceedings of the American Philosophical Society, 128
"Promised Land for Saints" (*Terra Repromissionis Sanctorum*), 77–78
Prose Edda, 17–18
Putin, Vladimir, 110–111

Q

QAnon, x, 103, 179–180, 195–206
"Q-Shaman," 197–199
Quidnessett Rock, 137–138

R

racial diversity, 160–175, 203–205
racial ideology, 103, 160–175, 203–205
racial theories, 166–173
racism, 100, 103, 167–175, 201–205. *See also* white supremacy
Rafn, Carl Christian, 100–102, 134–136

Ragnarok, 17, 23, 180, 188–190, 194–196, 212
raiding expeditions, 3–10, 27–35, 108–109, 191, 209–210
Regin, 24
Resen, Hans Poulson, 74
Resen Map, 74
Rhode Island Historical Society, 134
Riddles of the Past, 131
Robertson, William, 94
Rogation Day, 125
Roman Empire, 114, 166
Rowling, J. K., 16
runes, 4, 13–14, 22, 25, 114–121, 124–139, 149–157
Runestone Museum, 117
runestones
  Ave Maria Stone, 150–152
  Braxton Runestone, 155
  dating, 130–137
  Dighton Rock, 127, 133–135
  Grave Creek Runestone, 155–157
  Heavener Runestone, 153–154
  Hønen Runestone, 114–115
  Kensington Runestone, 104, 114–123, 127, 140, 144–151, 166, 174, 208, 219
  Kingittorsuaq Runestone, 130
  Maine Penny, 127, 139–144, 173, 218
  mooring stones, 150–152
  Narragansett Runestone, 127, 137–138, 144
  Newport Stone Tower, 127, 135–137
  Poteau Stone, 153–154
  Shawnee Stone, 154
  Spirit Pond Runestones, 127, 130–133
  theories about, 130–135, 151–152
  Wilson Stone, 155
  Yarmouth Rock, 127–130, 138, 144, 173–174

Runestruck, 133
Runge, Ed, 139–140
runic alphabet, 22, 114, 118–119,
    130–134, 137–138, 150–157
runic inscriptions, 4, 14, 22, 25,
    114–121, 127–138, 149–157
Russia, 4, 9, 24–28, 32, 109–113,
    146, 183

S

*Saga of Arrow-Odd (Orvar-Odds
    saga)*, 59
*Saga of Halfdan Brana's-Fosterling
    (Halfdanar saga Bronufostra)*, 60
*Saga of Halfdan Eysteinsson (Half-
    danar saga Eysteinssonar)*, 59
*Saga of the Greenlanders (Graenlend-
    inga saga)*, 36–40, 42–50, 54, 68,
    72, 111–112, 128
Saga of the Volsungs, 19
sagas
    dark side to, 2, 159–172, 195–196,
        200–201
    Icelandic sagas, 19–20, 35–75,
        91–92, 100–101, 111–112, 128,
        177
    medieval sagas, ix–x, 17–26,
        35–106, 111–122, 128–135, 166–
        167, 177–184, 190–210, 213–219
    Norse sagas, ix–x, 19–20, 35–74,
        91–92, 100–101, 144–158
    Viking sagas, 35–74, 91–92
    Vinland sagas, 52, 60, 100–101,
        116–120, 166–168, 178–184,
        190–195, 213–220
Saint Brendan, x, 75–84, 88–91, 103
St. Brice's Day Massacre, 8
St. Olaf, 9
St. Olaf College, 165
Saint Volodymyr, 9, 110
Scandinavia, 1, 3–9, 12–18, 21–34,
    64–68, 102–103, 114–121, 145–
    148, 166–167

*Scandinavian Element in the United
    States, The*, 167, 170, 172
Scandinavians, x, 3–9, 12–18, 21–34,
    43, 54–66, 75, 91–92, 97–108,
    114–121, 124–126, 131, 138–151,
    159–173, 177, 183, 194, 201–204,
    213–220
Schönbäck, Bengt, 63
Second Amendment, x, 204
Seduction of the Innocent, The, 181
settlers, x, 7–11, 14, 18–19, 29–30,
    36–45, 51–61, 65–71, 75–89,
    144–158
Severin, Tim, 79–80, 90
Shawnee Stone, Oklahoma, 154
Sif, 15
Sigurd, 24–25, 55
Sigvatsson, Erling, 125
Simms, William Gilmore, 102
Sinclair, Henry, 76, 89–90
Skaldskaparmal (Language of Poetry),
    199
Skalholt Map, 73–74
Skeleton in Armor, The, 135
skeletons, 88, 135–136
Skull-splitter, Thorfinn, 6
Smith, John, 84
Smithsonian Institution, 156, 218
Snoldelev Stone, 199
Snorra Edda, 18
Snow White and The Seven Dwarfs, 17
"Soldiers of Odin," 203
Sony Pictures, 189
Sony Santa Monica Studio, 212
South Wiltshire Museum, 156
Southern Poverty Law Center
    (SPLC), 201
Spain, 27, 45, 83–85, 93, 109, 157
Speight, Richard Jr., 189
Spicer, Mike, 184
Spirit Pond Runestones, Maine, 127,
    130–133
Stark, John, 136

Starz, 192, 194
Stone Tower, Rhode Island, 127, 135–137
Stone Wind Mill, 137
Stora Hammars I stone, 199
Stormfront, 204
Strandwold, Olaf, 129
Straumfjord (Current-fjord), 46–47, 49, 52, 72–73, 112, 217
Sturluson, Snorri, 18, 48, 89–90, 199
Super Bowl, 209
superheroes/superheroines, 174–187, 204. *See also* comic books
"Superman-DC," 175
Supernatural, 189
Svavarsson, Gartharr, 29
Svenska Cellulosa Aktiebolaget, 199
Sweden, 4, 20–25, 31–32, 58, 108–109, 119, 166, 199
Swedes, 31–34, 103, 115–117, 146–148, 161–167

T
Tales of the Unexpected #16, 177
Tängelgårda stone, 199
Tanner, Väinö, 62
Thanksgiving, 98–99
Thjodhild, 31
Thor, 10, 15–17, 20–24, 47, 168, 175–181, 187–190, 198–199, 202
Thor (film), 187–189
Thor: God of Thunder, 178
Thor: Love and Thunder, 188
Thor: Ragnarok, 180, 188–190
Thor: The Dark World, 188–189
Thor: Vikings, 178
Thorbjorg, 30
Thorbjornsdottir, Gudrid, x, 31, 38–45, 48, 191
Thorgilsson, Ari, 30, 91
Thorir, 42
Thorisson, Sokki, 55

Thor's hammer, 16, 21–24, 176–178, 198–199, 202
Timely Comics, 176
Tolkien, J. R. R., 15–16
Tordsson, Bjarne, 125
Touro Park, 135
Travels in New England and New York, 100
tree-ring analysis, 68–71
Trillin, Calvin, 133
Trivet, Nicholas, 83
"True Americanism," 168
Trump, Donald, 104, 200
TV shows, ix–x, 1, 176, 185–196, 210, 216
Twain, Mark, 56
21st Century Fox, 189

U
Ukraine, 4, 9, 27, 109–110
UNESCO World Heritage Site, 63
"Unite the Right," 202
Universal Pictures International, 205
University Museum, Oslo, 118
University of Alabama, 216
University of Alberta, 204
University of Chicago, 165
University of Michigan, 155
University of Minnesota, 118
University of Western Michigan, 209
University of Wisconsin-Madison, 102
US Capitol, x, 2, 197–200, 219

V
Valhalla, 15–16, 180
valknut, 198–199
Valkyries, 10, 16, 22–23, 50
Van Deusen, Natalie, 204–205
Vanir, 15–16, 180
Varangians, 4
Venus, 179

Vespucci, Amerigo, 94
video games, 16, 176, 187, 204, 212
vik (bay, creek), 5
viking (raiding expedition), 5–6
Viking Age, 7–13, 20–34, 46–54,
  62–65, 70, 101, 108–116, 137–148,
  164–173, 182–183, 198–205, 213,
  217
"Viking brand," 149, 207–216
Viking Brotherhood, 204
Viking Commonwealth, 9
Viking expansion, 32–34
Viking mindset, 12–26
Viking mythology, 12–26, 110,
  157–158, 173–174, 189–193, 201.
  See also Norse mythology
Viking North Americans, 50–173.
  See also American Vikings
Viking Prince, The, 181
Viking sagas, 35–74, 91–92. *See also*
  Norse sagas; *Vinland* sagas
Viking warriors, 6–16, 21–22, 135–
  136, 160, 168–169, 177, 204–214
Viking Wars, 8–10
"Viking Wild West," 19, 42–51,
  107–113
"Viking world," 11, 27–53, 108–109
vikingr (raider), 5–6
Vikings
  cultural attraction of, ix–x, 1–10,
    12–17, 105, 161–163, 173–214
  description of, ix–x, 1–11, 14–15
  discovering North America,
    95–107
  history of, 1–53
  labels for, 3–8
  language of, 4–9
  legacy of, 2–4, 103–104, 186–187,
    201–205, 219–220
  media and, ix–x, 1–9
  mindset of, 12–26
  modern spelling of, 7
  names for, 3–8

religious beliefs of, 14–26
world of, 11, 27–53, 108–109
  See also American Vikings
Vikings (football team), x, 1, 121,
  149, 208–209
Vikings (TV series), 191–192
Vikings on Cape Cod, 140
Vikings: Valhalla, 191–192
vikja (moving), 5
Vilgertharsson, Floki, 29
Vinland (Vine Land/Wine Land),
  ix–x, 24, 31, 35–62, 68–74, 100–
  104, 110–126, 130–134, 140–149,
  166–168, 178–184, 190–195,
  201–206, 213–220
"Vinland Folk Resistance," 201–202
Vinland Map, 74, 140, 149
Vinland Saga, 183–184
Vinland sagas, 52, 60, 100–101, 116–
  120, 166–168, 178–184, 190–195,
  213–220
Vladimir the Great, 9, 110
*Voyage of Saint Brendan the Abbot
  (Navigatio Sancti Brendani Abb-
  atis)*, 76–82

W
Wallace, Birgitta, 63, 217
Walt Disney Company, 17, 176, 188,
  190
warrior ideology, 6–16, 149, 168–169,
  177, 204–214
Washington, George, 94–95, 168
WB Television Network, 189
"Welsh Cronicle," 83
Welsh mythology, 75–89
Welsh settlers, 83–89
Wertham, Fredric, 181
West Virginia Archaeological Society,
  156
West Virginia State Museum, 155
What If . . . Thor Were an Only Child?,
  188

white supremacy, x, 13, 102–103, 111, 145–146, 160–171, 196, 201–205, 213

Whittle, Ricky, 193

"Wild West," 19, 42–51, 107–113

Wilson Stone, West Virginia, 155

Wineland Voyages: Location of Helluland, Markland and Vinland, 62

Wit Studio, 184

"Wolves of Vinland," 202

Wonderful Works of God Commemorated, 133

Wood, Brian, 183

Wood, Robert E., 169

World Heritage Site, 63

World Tree, 15, 184, 198–199

World War I, 146

World War II, 169

World's Columbian Exposition, 96, 120, 148

Wynne, Peter, 85

Y

Yale University, 74

Yarmouth County Museum, 127–128

Yarmouth Historical Society, 130

Yarmouth Leif Eriksson Society, 129

Yarmouth Public Library, 128

Yarmouth Rock, Nova Scotia, 127–130, 138, 144, 173–174

Yggdrasil (World Tree), 15, 184, 198–199

Young, Brigham, 87

Younger Edda, 18

Yukimura, Makoto, 183

Z

Zawadzki, Eric, 184

Zeno, Antonio, 89–90

Zeno, Nicolo, 89–90

Zichmni, Prince, 89–90